The Rise of Persia and the First Greco-Persian Wars

The Rise of Persia and the First Greco-Persian Wars

The Expansion of the Achaemenid Empire and the Battle of Marathon

Manousos E Kambouris

Pen & Sword
MILITARY

First published in Great Britain in 2022 by
Pen & Sword Military
An imprint of
Pen & Sword Books Ltd
Yorkshire – Philadelphia

ISBN 978 1 39909 329 3

A CIP catalogue record for this book is available from the British Library.

Typeset by Mac Style
Printed and bound in India by Replika Press Pvt. Ltd.

MIX
Paper from
responsible sources
FSC
www.fsc.org   FSC® C016779

Pen & Sword Books Limited incorporates the imprints of Atlas, Archaeology, Aviation, Discovery, Family History, Fiction, History, Maritime, Military, Military Classics, Politics, Select, Transport, True Crime, Air World, Frontline Publishing, Leo Cooper, Remember When, Seaforth Publishing, The Praetorian Press, Wharncliffe Local History, Wharncliffe Transport, Wharncliffe True Crime and White Owl.

For a complete list of Pen & Sword titles please contact

PEN & SWORD BOOKS LIMITED
47 Church Street, Barnsley, South Yorkshire, S70 2AS, England
E-mail: enquiries@pen-and-sword.co.uk
Website: www.pen-and-sword.co.uk

Or

PEN AND SWORD BOOKS
1950 Lawrence Rd, Havertown, PA 19083, USA
E-mail: Uspen-and-sword@casematepublishers.com
Website: www.penandswordbooks.com

This book is dedicated:

– to my friend, Professor George P. Patrinos, without whose support it would not have materialized;

– to my uncle Glystras without whose encouragement and help I might have never embarked on any authorship project;

– and to the loving memories of my Mom Dimi, who taught me to speak and write; and of my grannie Pitsa who insisted on studying diligently and doing one's homework although her teaching at the tender age of 4 showed that school has nothing to do with learning and education; it's all about tutoring.

Contents

Introduction:
A True Cultural World War

Revisiting the causes, the infringing and defining past and the conduct of the clash between the Greeks and the Persians in the sixth and fifth century BC – a true world war with participating troops from three continents 2,500 years ago – may be a Herculean task. This is so, especially if attempted with a focus on executive options and decisions at political, strategic, operational and tactical levels. The surprise at Marathon, the guile in Salamis, the valour in Thermopylae and the cold efficiency, drill and skill in Plataea created the picture of the known history of the world as it is, but the details of how and why the events unfolded as they did are hazy and dubious in their interpretation. It was a complicated time in politics, ideology and war-making. Intrinsic facts and motives, hidden, known, understood and misunderstood are intermingled to this day and mar the historical perception of the first clearly ideological struggle between a new world order – promising Light, Justice and Order yet delivering oppression and exploitation – and the ones that simply wanted nothing to do with such heavenly bliss…

It was a prolonged struggle, and the two antagonists thought of it as one, or more, episodes of an older East-West struggle, although this may be a poor choice of words. It was the continuation of previous events, and if they did not believe so, they did pretend it to be so. The concurrent phase of this struggle opened up after the Trojan War, when the Kingdom of Lydia became a world power and subjugated the young colonies of the Greek Nation(s) in Western Asia Minor. The dynasty and the dynast changed, but since then a continuous pressure was to come from the East, up to this day; sometimes repulsed, sometimes exceeding the breaking point and surging across the Aegean. The Greco-Persian Wars of 540–479 were just a phase in this struggle the Greeks had since perhaps the times of the Hittites, well in the 2nd Millenium BC. But this phase was massive and involved new technology, new methods, clearly of a diverging evolutionary course in technology, processes and very different ideologies, making it a dissimilar opponents' game, highly asymmetric in every conceivable way. Previous episodes were symmetric clashes between similar opponents.

No matter the approach followed in trying to elucidate the events, the motives and the ulterior thoughts, the researcher will eventually face a cardinal event: the build-up of the two factions in Greek politics: the Medizing one, siding with the Persian Empire (the Medes for the Ancient Greeks rather than the Persai as is historically correct), and the national-minded one, attempting resistance against the odds. The core issue is to correctly associate and deconvolute the known facts, as there are many missing links and dark spots, and also to interpret them correctly, as there are many vague issues due to a variety of reasons. The past of the two antagonists and other involved parties is helpful, as they both claimed heritage from powers of old. And a comparison with practices and procedures proven during other, better recorded historical times may well dissolve some prejudice and indoctrination of scholar research of times past and present to a better understanding of an era that defined world history as none other.

Part I

Chapter 1

The (Hi)story of the Historian

Our understanding of the Persian wars relies heavily on Herodotus, whose account is full, extensive, relatively complete and chronologically near the main events; a mere two generations from the initial events at most, one generation from the most important ones. There are indeed gaps in the narrative, lacunas and, most importantly, misunderstandings, but Herodotus had access to first-class material, as he saw, transcribed and translated, or had someone translate for him, epigraphic material. He also interviewed persons of authority, possibly protagonists of the events and/or their direct descendants and this material was expanded by personal experience. He had himself visited theatres of the action, and spoke Persian and perhaps some other language(s) of the Levant. He was both a traveller and a national of a city focal to Aegean trade, previously under the Persian yoke. He might have been a merchant himself or the spawn of such a family.

All other historical accounts, such as Diodorus' and Plutarch's, are later by some centuries and secondary, based on now-lost original works. More to the point, Diodorus' is extremely brief; he obviously made a synopsis of his source(s), and Plutarch's shows no cohesion, continuity or completeness. He narrates the events through the biographies of some of the protagonists, and thus outside any operational or even historical context. Some important pieces can be salvaged from other sources, such as: the work of Ktesias, chief physician of the Persian Court some 80 years after the end of the Great Greco-Persian War; rhetoric collections; Art (representative and vocal, the latter exemplified by the tragedy *Persai* of Aeschylus) and, most importantly, from the travel syllabus of Pausanias and the Stratagems of Polyaenus. All these together have no meaning without the full story of Herodotus – and the same is true for some Persian sources.

Judging Herodotus

Herodotus is an honest historian: contrary to the embellished Thucydidian censorship, called 'filtration' or 'critical thought' or 'factuality', Herodotus in most cases transmits his primary information and then argues and presents his own view (VIII.63), allowing the listener or reader to disagree or counter-argue (Her II.20–22 & II.24–6). He respects all sides involved; he considers no community as *a priori* inferior and gets into the shoes of many Barbarians. He underlines his personal thoughts (i.e. Her I.172). His work was narrated, thus he does not support every statement with a citation, but he names his sources as the narration develops. His practices and methods are often questioned, but his intent less so. He is *rather* distant from paid eulogists like Polybius, or contracted character-murderers, like Q Curtius – not to mention present-day examples.

A talented traveller, wanderer and observer, keen listener, with an eye for topography (Grundy 1901) and brilliant skills in ethology and anthropology, he has been dismissed by the much later and narrow-minded, proud Boeotian priest Plutarch. Part of the latter's criticism really holds water, despite his own vices. Herodotus' accounts may indeed be a bit partial, but this, in many cases – though by no means in all – may be attributed to his sources, whom he interviewed many years after the facts. Such interviews produced first-hand or hearsay accounts, but no solid *facts*; his chronology within the narration may be very problematic (Green 1970) but this is something one should expect. He IS the First Historian. Before him, events were recorded, but temporal sequences not that much, not in detail and often only in relative terms, while intentions of the protagonists, individuals or collectivities were a matter of speculation if not of propaganda. Similarly, some of his numbers come from records, but others out of deduction – *not* speculation, educated guesses or hearsay, but definite conclusions based upon data, facts and painstaking deduction and investigation. They may be erroneous, but generally not because of sloppiness.

Military (mis)understandings

Herodotus' work, though, presents some bias: he favours the Egyptians and his native folk, the Carians. He is also well-disposed towards the Athenians and their loyal allies (at the time) the Samians, as he had found refuge in that island. He vehemently hates most Asiatic Ionians, who had always been at loggerheads with the Carians and the Dorians of Asia, despite the fact that the Athenians considered themselves Ionians and were in constant war with most of the mainland Dorians (Aegina, Corinth, Sparta). Herodotus is a fully dorianized Carian who turned Atticizer but *NOT* Ionizer. He is also biased against the Boeotians, who during his time were bitter enemies to the Athenians, possibly more than the Spartans (Thuc V.35–39).

Herodotus may have been a fighter, more or less celebrated during the strife against the tyrant Lygdamis in his native Halicarnassus (EB Herodotus 1911), but he had never been a soldier, so his understanding of military matters is very poor. A minority of scholars (Ferrill 1966) considers him literate in both strategy and tactics but too much focused on epic tradition and aspects to make good use of his sources and literacy. But there are limitations in his sources and recourses. More limitations were imposed onto his work by the discretion necessary due to the fragile trust he had built with current enemies of his overlords, patrons and, wishfully, co-citizens, the Athenians. Still, his descriptions of battles and engagements occasionally show ignorance on the subject. He tries to reproduce and paste accounts of the children or grandchildren of the implicated individuals but fails to fill the gaps. His listeners, with their military background, had little difficulty doing so themselves; we, on the other hand, usually struggle in vain.

An excellent example is the issue of *Pitanates Lochos* (literally translated to English as 'company', but at that era, a Lochos was rather the equivalent of a regiment). This issue is brought up by Thucydides (I.20,3), who belittles Herodotus' account by asserting that there was never such a unit in the Spartan army. True, there is no universe where Thucydides, distrusted with good reason by the Spartans, could have had better intelligence or even information on Spartan issues than Herodotus; he states with some frustration that Spartans do not reveal to him military matters out of distrust (Thuc V.68).

Moreover, the issue of Pitanates Lochos concerned a different Sparta, before the disastrous earthquake of 460s (Thuc I.101,2). This is why Thucydides underlines that such a unit 'had never been' (Thuc I.20,3). The negative declaration, without restoration of the correct pattern, would not have been a problem for a Spartan source to feed to Thucydides without any reservation, as it would increase uncertainty regarding the Spartan system and practices.

Still, Herodotus had interviewed a Spartan aristocrat from Pitana, Archias son of Samius (III.55). The narrative about Pitanates Lochos (IX.53) should be attributed to him. He could have said nothing had it been sensitive, but would not lie. Thus, the only logical solution is that Herodotus had misunderstood something. A believable approach would be to consider the Spartan Archias speaking of his glorious tribe-member, Amompharetus of Pitana, who led his Lochos. Herodotus would have understood this being the Lochos of Pitana, as territorial conscription had been the rule throughout Greece and beyond. If this had not been the system of Sparta, or had Amompharetus commanded a special unit, an excellent misunderstanding would have occurred. And this would have been due to Herodotus, not to his sources.

The Carian connection

A second bias of Herodotus has to do with his origin. His family must have been half-Greek, half-Carian: the names of his brother and his mother are both Greek (Theodorus and Dryo, respectively) but his father's, Lyxis, and that of his celebrated relative, Panyaxis, tell a different tale. Herodotus describes Halicarnassus as thoroughly Hellenized, perhaps in an effort to pass for fully Greek himself, a fact which would increase his credibility and his chances for Athenian citizenship. But he was not. His pro-Carian bias made him magnify any hint of their feats and downplay or delete any 'questionable' events and attitudes, such as their alleged desertion in 496 BC in the midst of the Ionic Revolt. The magnification of the role of Queen Artemisia of Halicarnassus, leading five ships (VII.99) in a royal fleet of 1,207 (VII.89) should be viewed under this light of localism and nationalism (Shepherd 2010). The Persian state was patriarchal; Xerxes had introduced a harem of royal concubines, one for each day of the year. In this climate, even if the Great King had private and personal affections for the p(r)etty she-ruler, it would have been scandalous within the imperial army to grant her any excessive goodwill.

Herodotus says that Halicarnassus was a Dorian city in his days (VII.99), thus the original Carians were intermingled with the Dorians and Hellenized (I.171). But he has not one good word for these Dorians, and it is not a matter of politics: Periclean Athens was close friends with each and every Dorian state which had issues with the Spartans, examples being the Argives (Thuc V.46–7) and the Messenians (Thuc II.9,4 & II.102,1).

The same is the case with the Hoplite shield (*hoplon*), also known as Argive, which he assigns to Carian inventiveness (I.171). But the most important issue is the deep distrust, disregard, disgust or even hatred for the Ionians situated north of the Carian-Dorian zone. His slander could be in part attributed to an effort to bolster Athenian claims and affronts so as to convincingly justify their high-handed or even brutal treatment of their Ionian subjects. But in this case, he goes too far. Such a bleak picture compares unfavourably with other, much more moderate pictures he draws – and that in cases where even outright slander would have been well-received by his intended audience, the Athenians. All the above insinuate he hated bitterly his northern neighbours, with the possible exception of Samos, and makes his account of the Ionian Revolt more unreliable than other parts of his work. This is a real pity, as the ONLY coherent surviving account of these events is his.

Subsidies and Grants: the ultimate handler?

The most important bias is of course connected with patronage. Pedigree and ideology, even personal memories and experiences are important; but patronage is vital, in some cases for both the Art and the Artist. Many of the trips of Herodotus were to areas under Athenian control, as was the Aegean, Egypt between 454 and 450 BC, northern Greece and of course the Euxine. Other places were Athenian trade associates, e.g. the Scythians. In Persia proper he had been well-received and assisted in his research by loyal Persian subjects (Her I.1,1); after all, he himself was one by birth. But the sheer expenses of these travels and the permissions to wander around the Athenian zone of interest(s) imply a sponsorship. Merchant activities could not have coincided so well with his research. Additionally, travelling within the Persian empire, so as to see and to translate inscriptions (Her III.88,3) insinuates satrapal licensing – agreement by a subordinate ruler – after the Peace of Kallias. Thus, to suggest that his research was sustained by direct grants and indirect support may be nearer the truth than any other alternative.

And this is the heart of the problem: Herodotus allegedly appeared in Athens at circa 440 BC, impressed the Athenian audience with lectures and speeches, probably pieces of his later-to-become Histories and got a handsome grant of 10 *Talents* (Plut De Her Mal 26; Hammond 1996). This sum was enough to man a trireme (an ancient galley) for 10 months or a flotilla of 10 triremes for a month; with 6,000 *Drachmae* per Talent and 170 rowers per trireme, paid a *Drachma* each per day (Thuc III.17,3–4; VI.31,3), a sum of 5,100 Drachmae had been the expense of a trireme's crew for one month. The above estimation is not accurate, but intended to make clear the order of magnitude of this grant. It goes without saying that his lectures and speeches were politically correct and the Athenian audience were presented with things interesting, pleasing and with a pinch of objectivity.

The completed work was performed some 20 years later in Olympia, with contradicting accounts of its reception by the audience. Furthermore, nobody *really* knows the place and exact time of Herodotus' death, which may have been Thurii, Athens or Macedon where he could have hoped to cash in the most favourable picture of Argeads and, especially of Alexander I (i.e. Her V.22), the reigning king during Xerxes' invasion. One solid fact is that he mentions the Curse of Talthybius (Her VII.137), which happened in 430 BC (Thuc II.67,2), thus he died *after* 430 BC.

When he received the ten talents, in the mid-440s, he was just 40 years old or less, a wild youth in full democratic fervour, implicated in strife 'overseas', and an admirer of Athens. He had good sources on events past, a gift for telling tales and some travelling experience. It is impossible, at least in terms of time, that he had already concluded the long, impressive travels necessary for his work. The possibility, then, that the magnificent award was granted to enable him to *create* his masterpiece, which he never finished (see Her I.106; VIII.233 and especially VII.213), and not because he had already done so, should not be lost. It would be reminiscent of today's grants for scientific and other projects, including PR pitches.

The fact that Persia was at peace with Athens at the time Herodotus was active (circa 440 BC) thanks to Kallias, the negotiator and friend of Pericles, and thus opened to Greek travellers and commerce, may relate to some legs of his travels. It provides an alternative date for his trip to Egypt, instead of the 454–450 BC, and allows for a most logical continuation to Phoenicia and then to the heart of the Persian Empire. Between the two good neighbours, Athens and Persia, Herodotus had enough time, more than a decade, to visit, ask, cross-reference and finally compile his work.

Of course, subsidised works have some limitations in form and context, which should be added to the issue of the innate objectivity of the author. It is well-substantiated that Athenian theatrical productions were well-attuned to the political situation. Most prominent is the fine to Phrynichus, the author who criticised the desertion of the Athenian task force during the Ionian Revolt by detailing the harsh punishment dealt by the Persians to the hapless Milesians (Her VI.21). Also significant is the extreme debasement of the character of Spartan mythical personalities and heroes – like Menelaus – in tragedies by Sophocles and Euripides (Cilliers 1991). Athenian art had been enrolled to assist the cause and the common goal.

Thus, Herodotus is critical towards the major antagonists of Pericles' family, the famous Miltiades and his son Cimon, the liberator. Their contribution is belittled as much as possible, with the battle of Marathon being briefly described. Any real or sous-real contribution to the common cause of the family of Pericles, the Alcmaeonids, is amplified, and any possible ill-doings refuted. Herodotus takes unto himself to deny their alleged treason during the fight at Marathon in 490 BC (VI.121) and says nothing on yielding Earth and Water to Artaphrenes, Satrap of Sardis in 507 BC to enroll his help against a Spartan onslaught (Her V.73; Sekunda 1989). What is even more untypical for him, he fails to criticise their most impious endeavour, their bribing of the Delphian Oracle (Her V.63), which was the sole reason for the fall of Hippias and the rise of Cleisthenes, of his clan and his supporters, to power.

Herodotus was a vehement Democrat as he actively participated in civil strife when at home against a tyrant, Lygdamis. He was an innovative scholar: he jumpstarted History, a new science, or form of literature, through which he glorified the Athenian deeds and embellished some rather dark events. Since he was also pro-Periclean and pro-Alcmaeonid, as already stated, he had been awarded the massive, 10-talent prize somewhere in the mid- to late-440s for his lectures, possibly parts and drafts of his Histories, which were in the making.

Limited Usefulness

But despite these qualities, Herodotus was not incorporated into the civic body. He had been hand-picked by the staff of Pericles to exonerate Athens and underline its fervour, sacrifice and resilience against the Barbarian at the very time a Peace

Accord was achieved – and fiercely criticised as plain treason. He had applied for Athenian citizenship possibly during the 440s and had been denied. There were some very serious reasons for not considering him eligible for citizenship in Periclean Athens:

- Herodotus was a member of the Pan-Hellenic movement. This was projected as a national goal or, rather, mandate; a concerted action against the barbaric threat, which was 3-pronged: against the Carthaginians, the Etruscans and, the most immediate, the Persians. It was the second time in their history that the Greeks were to potentially form a unified political entity (the first being the Trojan War). This was in stark contrast with the Periclean contemplations of the time, namely to subdue and tax Greece, to keep the Persians neutral and to utterly destroy Sparta. In this panhellenic context, and given the western policies pursued in Athens from Solon to Themistocles, as exemplified by the latter's threat to abandon the alliance and move Athens to Southern Italy before the battle of Salamis (VIII.62), one may suppose that the original plan would have assigned responsibilities. Carthaginians and the Sicilian front would have been left to Syracuse to manage, possibly extending operations to include the whole western Mediterranean. The Persian threat would have been the responsibility of Sparta, at loggerheads with the empire since the latter's first venture to the Aegean by Cyrus the Great (I. 152–3). The assignment of Pausanias, the Victor of Plataea to Byzantium, in the early 470s, who was ejected by the plots of Aristides the Just (Her VIII.3; Plut Vit Arist, 23), supports this assumption. And the Athenians would be assigned to the Italian front, much to the dismay of the ebbing Corinthians – an issue of influence deleterious enough to fuel the brawls of Themistocles and Adeimantos the Corinthian even when facing the ultimate threat (VIII.61–2).
- Herodotus had politically incorrect personal affiliations: most prominent are his sympathies for the Samians, as he had been a refugee, or had been exiled there. The same Samians were massacred by Pericles himself after a rebellion against the Athenian oppression, disguised as the 'Delos Alliance' (Thuc I.117; Plut Vit Per 28; Diod XII.28,3). Perhaps even more 'incorrect' was his contempt for the Milesians, the antagonist of Samos in the limited civil war, which brought about the demise of the former. Herodotus is severely critical if not prejudiced against Ionians and especially Milesians: he considers them voluntary subjects of Cyrus (Her I.169), the first Persian emperor with an interest for the Far West. He accuses them of being the initiators of the Greco-Persian feud due to their revolt (Her V.97) after their disinclination to neutralise Darius in Scythia (Her IV.142) and finds them militarily inept, as amply demonstrated in Ephesus and Caria (Her V.102 and V.119–120 respectively). Such views were not very well-received

by Pericles, whose mistress was the notorious Aspasia of Miletus, the *femme fatale* who caused the destruction of Samos (Plut Vit Per 28) and actually a politician, in addition to being an accomplished *Hetaira*, a type of highly educated consort for hire.

- Herodotus esteemed the Spartans and had established mutual trust with them. The Spartans had been very talkative to Herodotus, except for some military matters. This limitation was well-understood by both parties since the Spartans had been intermittently at war with the Athenians and their subjects, friends and allies at least since mid-450s BC. Despite being all the above and an applicant for Athenian citizenship, Herodotus was well-treated and trusted by the Spartans. Thucydides, on the other hand, admits he was treated with distrust (Thuc V.68); he was an ardent anti-Laconian (Thuc IV.84), a trait never mentioned by scholars but in reality ruining his credibility as a historian.
- Herodotus was a very pious man, a true believer, revering the conventional deities of the Pantheon of Olympus, respectful to any worship and rituals (Her II.49) and well-versed in practices, ceremonies and requirements of religions in general. His approach to alien religions is reverential, with a pious profile and without consideration of distance from the Greek beliefs. A degree of Hellenization and syncretism is evident (i.e in Her I.131), but this is more to normalise information for his audience rather than being an Olympian Pantheon zealot (Her I.214).

This is in stark contrast to the clear-cut atheism projected by the gang of Pericles, with Anaxagoras, himself and later Alcibiades, a trait that ultimately culminated in the institutional murder of Socrates. The latter had been a moral and political personality as anti-Periclean as Lacedaimonians themselves, but has been thrown into the same pit of atheism. It should also be noted that, as underlined by Badian (in his monumental work 'From Plataea to Potidaea'), abject atheism protrudes into the work of Thucydides and saps its value and objectivity, as religiousness had been the order of the day in classical Greece, despite the views of some Athenians. Herodotus' piety enables him to develop empathy, which allows a better understanding of the characters and groups he describes, although his views become less substantiated in some cases.

For all the above reasons, Herodotus was never admitted as a citizen to Athens and had been cleared instead for participation in the panhellenic colony of Thurii; a comfort award for him if not a proper, honourable displacement of all the Panhellenists and enemies of Persia. The new, anti-Spartan Athens of the Pericleans had found an excellent way to get rid of any pro-Laconian and/or anti-Persian elements so as to proceed with its new foreign policy, a way reminiscent of the English colonists aboard the *Mayflower*.

A last and important issue pertaining to the reliability and impartiality of Herodotus is his admiration of Egypt. It is so prominent it does not need citing and referencing, and this holds true especially when Egyptian is compared to Greek. There, almost any measure is lost; a fact harshly criticised as intentional malice by Plutarch (De Her Mal 32).

In reality, he does not believe just anything; he is not persuaded by the Egyptian claims regarding a mixed lineage of none other than Cambyses (Her III.2), which are absurd. Still, he has no reservation about adopting other, just as absurd ones. He *chooses* to do so. Herodotus is sincere and tries to understand causality but this does not mean that he is objective, or that his approach to causality is the best. His lack of moderation is not an issue; moderation, and Occam's razor, may prove slippery roads for the historian.

In this light, Herodotus prefers to adopt his Egyptian sources. Is this because he is impressed by their massive records and thus believes them to be the best-informed and probably most impartial? Is it because he tries to ignite sympathy and to mobilise a Greek intervention anew, after the failed revolt and the half-hearted Athenian support of 450s? This is what a follower of the Panhellenic movement would have done, to offer a better target for the Hoplite spears instead of fellow-Greek throats and thighs.

And who is this Plutarch?

Plutarch was a priest in the Delphic Oracle who lived during the first century AD. He is not, strictly speaking, a historian, but he is a very talented and prolific writer with enormous records at his disposal and with excellent sources on the ancient world – meaning, at his time, classical Greece. He produced a set of biographies that were paired and comparative between Greek and Roman personalities. In these biographies he had the scope, the data and the opportunity to develop much more fully the characters mentioned by Herodotus; the latter was besmirched for dwelling too much on his protagonists, though on a selective basis. Thus, contrary to some scholars who reject Plutarch's reports explicitly because they do not suit their preconceived theories and especially some arbitrary interpretations of Herodotus (Lazenby 1993), he must be taken into account.

In his polemic work, On the Malice of Herodotus (*De Her Mal*), Plutarch strives to discredit Herodotus, to exonerate Thebes for their Medizm (adoption of Persian interests) and in doing so he is much more prejudiced and biased than the man he accuses. The suppositions and extrapolations of Plutarch are virulent and biased and many of his arguments are weak; but the facts he reports and the alternative sources he cites, most of them lost to us, are solid. The reliability of a report may always be questioned, maliciously or not, but the thing is that there *are* reports unknown to, or silenced by, Herodotus and Plutarch uses some of them. It is no accident that his effort to revise the work of Herodotus is centred on the battle of Thermopylae, as it is focal for his aim to exonerate Thebes. But just as focal is the battle of Plataea, and there he revises Herodotus most sparingly and mainly in the life of Aristides. Additionally, he could have edited many things regarding Marathon, the worst part by far, and the least developed, in Herodotus' narrative, but he does not. The editing concerning the Eretrian exploits during the Ionian revolt and the events before and during Thermopylae is focused and selective and thus, must have a strong historical basis. The additions and corrections of Plutarch should be taken into consideration and be used to elucidate many dark spots in the narrative of the Persian Wars by Herodotus instead of being summarily rejected. After all, he had records at his disposal, while Herodotus had informers.

Chapter 2

Geopolitical and Socioeconomic
Status Quo before the Persian Invasion

The prelude: The Trojan War as an instance of the East-West clash

Contemporary scholarship prefers not to acknowledge the historicity of the Trojan War as described in the Iliad, considering it a work of historic fiction, possibly including a nucleus of events, but very distant and corrupt. The ancient Greeks thought otherwise, and so did the Persians, who, although unaffected by these distant events, knew perfectly well how to seize a pretext (Her I.4).

This modern denial leads to underappreciating information embedded in the epic. Cardinal among such is the fact that the Greek world of the time was to a considerable extend facing westwards. In Odyssey travelling from western Greece to Sicily seems a matter of everyday life (Hom Odyss xx.383), and at least two characters originate from Sicily (Hom. Odyss xxiv.210) or further away.

The assembled fleets as described in The Iliad support such thoughts. The House of Pylos mustered 90 ships (Hom Iliad II.591–602), second only to the fleet of the undisputed leader, the Mycenae, with 100 (Hom Iliad II.569–76). With the territories of Pylos at the time being a third of the current district of Messene and much less than the Laconian kingdom of Menelaus, which was covering the same latitude and furnished only 60 ships (Hom Iliad II.581–7), one should wonder how Nestor had been able to maintain so many ships. And the answer is easy; his kingdom was well-poised for Western trade.

One more cardinal issue is the centre of the Greek world. At the time the centre, and also the centre of gravity, must have been the Gulf of Corinth. Heavily populated then and even now, it was instrumental for the communications and commerce among the states of central Greece and those of the northern Peloponnese, with the most important kingdoms lying around it; not around or across the Aegean – yet. This is the reason for the extreme popularity of the Oracle of Delphi, positioned conveniently near the north shore of this 'internal sea'.

The Herodotean account (Her I.94) mentions that the Italian nations originated from Asia and were members of the Trojan alliance/confederacy. After the defeat and fall of Troy, they migrated, bypassing Greece, to Italy. This is clearly a prequel to the Aeniad and it has been considered a fact by the Romans throughout their history. This migration meant that henceforth mainland Greeks would be between hostile landmasses: the emerging Asian waves pushing from the east and the migrated hostile Asian populations pressing from their west, from Italy.

The colonial status within the Mediterranean

The Persian rise coincided with a deep and multi-dimensional crisis in the Hellenic world – an era of interwoven ideological, geoeconomic, national and tribal frictions and international challenges. The Greeks had again become prominent in the Mediterranean and beyond, thanks to a brilliantly set and competently executed colonial plan of some 300 years. Its first eastward phase took place a mere century after the Trojan War and the Mycenaean collapse that ensued and was triggered by the Dorian conquest of southern Greece, especially Peloponnese. Though, this colonial endeavour was the result of the Trojan War (Thuc I.12,2–4), the latter's reality at least accepted, if not believed, by both antagonists of the Persian Wars (Her I.1–4). The Trojan War on the one hand destabilised the Greek mainland but on the other destroyed an aggressive Asian alliance in control of a powerful European constituent (Iliad II.844–50) and thus permitted a Thracian invasion to Asia Minor. The net result was the fragmentation of the interior of Asia Minor, which allowed the Greeks a break from the eastern threats during the ascent of Phrygia in the mainland. Actually, it allowed the Greek mainland states to form or reform, recuperate from the shock of the Mycenaean crash (or meltdown) safely, establish the eastern colonies which became collectively, even if inaccurately, known as Ionia, and colonize the Black Sea.

Some two centuries after the establishment of most of the Ionian colonies, a westward colonial wave developed and a single generation implemented most of it. Thus, within five years a loose Greek colonial empire is set in the Euxine, the Mediterranean and possibly beyond. But the system almost immediately proved unstable, less by overexpansion or overextension and more due to internal, inherent malfunctions. The colonies were official businesses, grafted with the customs, the morals, the lineage and tribal organization of the Metropolis. More importantly perhaps, with the religious worship consisting of ritual, sects, ceremonies, symbols, relics and sacred artifacts or statues/pictures of the home deities and perhaps their clergy and, last but not least, with the form of government. Sending a colony was about relieving the frictions caused by the numerous and impoverished populace in the Metropolis; but it was also about creating trade networks and sources of essential goods. The leaders were chosen amongst the aristocracy, perhaps among the most restless members of it. The colonial project was not coming cheap; the governing aristocracies had the necessary funds and accepted the risk to invest them for expected gains in cash, status, *and* internal peace. Returning colonists of aborted projects were not welcomed (Her IV.156). But the more or less troublesome and ambitious members of the aristocracy who were sent away were enticed with promises concerning *actual* social rise, unattainable in the Metropolis.

On the other hand, the radical throng selected for deportation served as rowers in the 50-oar galleys/pentekonters, which were the vector of the colonization, as fighters upon landing and as a workforce once the land had been secured, so as to build from scratch a new city-state. Understandably, they had not left an intolerable existence back home to face dangers, enemies, uncertainties and hardship only to become the lowly subjects of the disgruntled parts of the home aristocracy across the sea. They had their own hopes and dreams for opportunities and El Dorado.

What ensued was a prelude of the European colonial crisis of the 16th century. Wealth was produced, and in volume, but its distribution left once more many dissatisfied. The combination of the questionable repute of the colonists with the drift of the financial activity from the Metropolis to the colonies brought forth several issues that ignited civil strife in many levels: within cities, metropoleis and colonies alike, among cities, and in some cases between a metropolis and its colony. The net result was a Hellenic World War.

The war for the Lelantine Field (Thuc I.15,3; Her V.99) implicated the whole of metropolitan and colonial Greece and brought the whole Greek world back by one or two centuries; the war between Sybaris and Croton ends with the extermination of the former (Her VI.21). The human casualties are horrific. This development averts the firm establishment of Greek colonies in the western Mediterranean basin. In this way, the probable master-plan of the Greek colonization, that is to turn the whole of the Mediterranean into a Greek lake (similarly to the Roman Mare Nostrum), while achieving the expulsion of the Carthaginians from Sicily and the central Mediterranean, fails (Burn 1962; Grundy 1901; Green 1970).

The failure was not lightly taken, nor uncontested. More colonial waves were sent and would keep coming up to the mid-fifth century, but they were half-hearted, in some cases private efforts and even more riddance-minded than before (Her V.42). The most important is that they were targeting a Mediterranean environment now vigilant and in many respects ready for them.

An issue of prime importance, although unrecognized, is the adoption of the secret of the Greek expansion by their antagonists: the Hoplite kit and methods. The Hoplite is the platform that brought the Greeks to Babylonia, Egypt, Ethiopia, East Euxine and the coastline of SW Spain, Tartessus. Now he is not only Greek, he is also Phoenician/ Carthaginian, Etruscan, Roman, and later Illyrian (Snodgrass 1965; Sekunda & Northwood 1995).

And, most important, the bliss of the colonies saps the fighting prowess of the colonists, especially of the newer generations. The now wealthy colonists were not eager for aggressive undertakings likely to disrupt business and cost them their own lives. They preferred strife, so as to collect something from their fellow citizens. Contrarily, the impoverishment of the Metropolis reinstates, or at least maintains, its martial prowess, while its inhabitants and citizens are also engaged in strife.

The radical brew in the Greek world

The constitutional struggle was fierce: the colonization was an opportune by-product of aristocracies getting rid of rivals and anyone deemed unwanted, and thus the colonies were aristocratic in constitutions. But once a middle class was firmly established, tyrants were selected to overthrow the aristocrats; and they did so in a tidal wave sweeping both the western colonies and the mainland (Nilsson 1929), except for Sparta. The peculiar constitution of the latter firmly established a residual, constitutional monarchy, or rather diarchy, with two royal families each providing a ruling king. This royal duo was coupled to an oligarchy providing a senate, and a body of all-powerful but once-in-a-lifetime representatives of the People (this means The Peers), the *Ephorate*, the latest but most influential power in Spartan politics. It was five-strong, possibly representing the five original villages which formed the Spartan state.

In the mainland, the city-states able to recuperate and profit from the 'global' commercial network formed by the colonies took the constitutional changes a step further: during the fifth century, they made their move towards more egalitarian formats, which brought about, as a final result, the radical democracy. This sequence occurred in Athens. The lore projected in the Periclean era suggested that it was their *second* time; the first time was with their arch-hero, Theseus, whence the process was allegedly initiated and completed within a generation.

Things were different in Ionia, as the primitive equalitarian regimes developed there were trampled by the conquering Persians before evolving to Democracy. The tyrants known by the narration of Herodotus in Ionia during the late sixth century were a step backwards, not the focus of the public struggle against the aristocrats, but the once-upon-a-time ruling aristocrat(s) who struggled to return to power. In this struggle, different breeds of Enemies of State are recruited by the Aristocrats, whatever the occasional definition of 'enemy' may have been, to help them to power, or to keep them in power. A standard case was a tyrant becoming a wilful subordinate to an alien overlord, preferably of feudalistic background so as to favour appointed rulers over elected magistrates. The tyrant, appointed or recruited by the alien despot, was supported and preserved by the latter; he mostly kept the public order and collected tribute. He did not *rule* but only *administered* (with some leeway for corruption, of course) as *the* intermediary between the overlord and his hapless subjects, as exemplified by Histiaeus of Miletus, Koes of Mytilene and the would-be Hippias of Athens (Her IV.137 & V.96 & V.11).

The Dorian ebb

At the same time, the predominantly Dorian western commerce and colonial expansion ebbed. The western expansion was, to a great extent, a Dorian project in terms of mainland Greece geopolitics. Not only Aegina and Corinth had been the two most sophisticated colonial and trade powers (both of Dorian demographics) but the co-ordinator was the Oracle of Delphi, a shrine very near to Doris, the cradle of the Dorians, where Apollo, the prime Dorian deity, was introduced and worshipped.

But by the mid-sixth century the Dorian championship changes from Argos to Sparta (Her I.70 & I.82), both major states in times Mycenean, but currently occupied and colonized by the Dorians since circa 1000 BC, with their old inhabitants enslaved, integrated or expelled (Paus III.1,5 & III.2,5–7). Sparta in particular, a typical Dorian meta-Mycenean state, with the usual quarrelling, strife, industry and trade instincts and interests, suddenly, somewhere in the sixth century changed course radically (Thuc I.18,1). By an apparent withdrawal from the international trade map and a deep alteration in government, law and politics, it became a peculiar state, but definitely the most prominent war machine: the exemplary military, though not militaristic, state and of unsurpassed power and prestige within the wider context of the Greek Metropolis (Dickins 1912; Hodkinson 2006). Sparta, as the new champion of the Dorians, was the official protector of the Oracle, but was not interested in colonization, nor in international trade any further. Sparta did not share the vision for a westward Greece.

The Return of the Phoenicians

The Hellenic crisis allows a Carthaginian counter-attack (Burn 1962), assisted by the emerging Italian power, the Etruscans (Her I.166). Raised through commerce with Greek profiteers and merchants and kick-started by a powerful immigrant group of artisans, soldiers and politicians who followed the expelled Damaratos of Corinth, circa 660 BC (Polyb VI.11a, 7; Dion Ha Ant Rom III.46,3–5; Strab VIII.6,20 & V.2,2; Livy I.34,2), the Etruscan power stems from their early and proper adoption of the Hoplite Phalanx and especially their weaponry (Diod XXIII.2). Expelled with all his retinue and supporters, Damaratos, the ruling aristocrat of the Bacchiad dynasty had been overthrown by the ascending tyrant Cypselus. Fleeing from home, he lands in Etruria and with some persuasion and more brazen arguments, he hellenizes the Etruscans with Hoplites and pottery. The Hellenization did nothing to mend Etruscan morals and beliefs: they remained forever a feudalist state, like most Italians of the era, and somewhat monstrous and cruel in worship and distraction (Tzetz Chiliad VIII. 882–8). Human sacrifice and institutional manslaughter, in the form of gladiatorial games, continued and were immortalized in masterpieces of painting and sculpture, while part of their aggressiveness turned to, and was expressed through, trade. It would be tempting to suppose that during the fierce struggles of the sixth century, some Greek states took the side of the Etruscans and other Italians, as happened later, with the Athenian expedition in Sicily in 415–3 BC, where the Athenians recruited Segesta and other non-Greek states against the Sicilian Greeks/*Sikeliots* (Thuc VI.17,6).

In any case, within 30 years, the Carthaginians checked the Greek advance in Sicily (Her V.42; Burn 1962) after having, in alliance with the Etruscans, intercepted the Greek expansion to Corsica, attempted by Phocaeans fleeing the first wave of the Persian conquest under Cyrus' general Harpagus (Her I.164–6). The battle of Alalia cost the two allies dearly, but caused the withdrawal of the Greeks (Her I.166) and thus had been a decisive strategic success.

It was so decisive that the Greeks in the first years of the fifth century were considering a mass migration to Sardinia, which was closer, by the full manpower available from a massive flight from Ionia in the face of the Persian punitive campaigns against the rebels. This was refuted by Hecataeus the Milesian (Her V.124–5) who had – or was to acquire – precise knowledge on Persian matters; too accurate to exclude some unknown agenda. He was to become a cardinal source for Herodotus.

This behaviour reminds us of the case of the most ardent of the Phocaeans who had migrated when facing the lieutenants of Cyrus (Her I.164) and were to re-emerge in the initial, ill-omened counsel of the Delphic oracle to the Athenians to migrate to the west, allegedly in early 480 BC (Her VII.140), which most probably suggested as their destination the site of the deserted city-state of Siris. Such counsel was incorporated into the argumental toolkit of Themistocles before the battle of Salamis (Her VIII.62).

With the gift of hindsight, this could have been the salvation of Ancient Greece: the transplantation of the state of the Athenian Democracy to Italy would have reinvigorated the expansion there to reach and tame the Roman blitz before maturation, while still nascent. And, most importantly, a troublemaker would have been evicted from mainland Greece, thus easing the whole Ionian-Dorian rivalry. This rivalry was obsolete at the mainland, but was rekindled by the Athenians so as to muster mainland supporters against the Spartans in the years of Herodotus. The bitterness between the two Greek tribes had already been fiery in Italy, but a national cause might have eased it much more easily than in the ancestral lands, while the division between Greater Hellas and Greater Peloponnese (the former in Italy, the latter in Sicily) provided one more barrier.

The Athenian candidacy

In this vacuum, Themistocles of Athens, an ardent supporter, instigator and champion of the masses and one of the three paramount visionaries of that unimportant state, reset his own and the state's sights on the west. Consequentially, he must have become a privileged mediator for the Oracle. In times past he would have been dismissed as an antagonist of the Dorians. Their metropolitan commerce was facing competent antagonism from Athens for quite some time; both Solon and Peisistratus shifted the export focus to the west since the east, a privileged market due to the close relationship of Athens and Ionia, was practically closed by the fact that the Athenians had sided with the losers of the Lelantine War. And, not to a small extent, by the later rise of the Persians. By choice and by luck, when a silver vein was discovered in Athens, a new acolyte could be based there to proceed with the faltering westward plans of Delphi. This understanding with the Oracle allowed the Athenian entrepreneur and later politician to call, in his time of need in 480 BC, upon the Oracle's 'understanding'.

The westward thrust of Athens peaked under Themistocles and was supported by the Oracle of Delphi. With Sparta's attitude, especially under the infamous Cleomenes I who was prone to disengage Sparta from the spiritual leadership of the Oracle, or to manipulate it, if things were not going his way (Her VI.66), Themistocles might have been posing as the answer to the prayers of the priesthood of Delphi. Once the championship of the Dorian stock, which formed the main body of believers for the oracle, was seized by the new-model Spartans from the Argives, the Oracle needed a vigorous state to reinvigorate the western expansion and colonization policy. The new Spartan state, with its differentiation of priorities and absence from the arena of exporting commerce, was a good and steadfast champion of the Oracle in Greece, neutral to trade antagonisms and very pious, but very reluctant to enforce expansionist and commercialist policies (Her V.42–43 & 46; Dickins 1912). This was especially so once the clouds were gathering to the East, a fact not missed, forgotten or forgiven by the Syracusan Greeks (Her VII.158) who were bearing the brunt of Carthaginian aggression. Indeed, the Persian pressure on Ionia is transduced almost instantly to the mainland in a way the Lydian one had never been. Thus, the westward expansion takes lower priority, and few new operations are planned, while reinforcements in manpower are scant.

Despite these facts, the Greek colonies of southern Italy, or at least some amongst them – with Cumae being the epicentre, or rather the fulcrum – were able to crush the Etruscan power and aggression at the point of its becoming an existential threat. And they did so twice in two successive generations: in 524 BC (Dion Ha VII.3) and 478 BC (Pindar, 1st Pythian Ode). Ultimately though, they fail to capitalize on their success as they are too busy brawling with each other (i.e Her VI.23). Petty local bitterness simply makes the feud between Ionians and Dorians more complicated and lethal, as other races (such as the Achaeans) take part but not always on a consistent side, as will be discussed later.

Thus the western Greeks were unable to tame the successors of the Etruscans, i.e. the Leucanians, Oscans, Brutians and Romans, early enough, so as to contain an Italian deluge southwards. As the western expeditions of Spartan kings (Archidamus III of Sparta) and pro-Macedonian Hepeirote champions (Alexander the Molossian, Pyrrhus) ultimately failed (Strab VI.3,4), Magna Grecia will eventually succumb within two centuries to the Italians and ultimately to Rome – the same Rome whose allies were saved by Cumae in the nick of time from another Etruscan project of murderous punishment for a republican coup against their local petty Etruscan dynasty (Lib II.14,6–7).

With Carthage, the Greeks fared even more poorly: they were never able to utterly neutralize it as a threat and/or to uproot its Sicilian bridgeheads, as a continuous flow of African and West European mercenaries was periodically fed to the island.

The Time Of The Persian

In this timeline, more or less, in the mid-sixth century, the Persians in Central Asia present their own military and much less political revolution under Cyrus II the Great and conquer vast areas within a formidable generation. The Persians under Cyrus II the Great are a rather poor but definitely competent and a hardy nation. Delbruck (1920), in 19th century Imperial Germany is well-poised to notice a knightly disposition in the Persian army, which probably was the case, at least under Cyrus II and his son(s) and definitely in the fourth century. This miraculous horde makes contact with the Greek world in Ionia, and the latter expresses mixed feelings.

The Persians at the time of Darius I, or even of Cyrus II, had passed through a consolidation phase that led their many tribes and communities, with local governance through chieftains, to an empire (Waters 2014a). As Herodotus has it, they considered the more – or rather less – equalitarian forms of governance of similar Greek communities not as retarded but as backstepping, because this diffusion of authority was inhibiting the natural consolidation of power. Indeed, it took the Greeks another two centuries to reach – or fall into – a monarchical model under Alexander and his successors; and even then the adoption of that model was far from total. Although this distancing from consolidating power was exactly what most Greeks wanted, the Persians thought of it as inability and incompetence which, by divine right, they had to address through their King-of-Kings and his blessed authority – a concept remarkably similar to Chinese ones referring to the Heavenly Mandate for the ruler.

The Ionians, or rather the Greek colonials in Asia, were reluctant to fight even against Croesus of Lydia, let alone against the ascending Cyrus II of the Persians. Some of them were happy to see Croesus fall, delighted by the crumbling of the Lydian dynasty, the first destroyer of their freedom (Her I.6 & I.26–8), but were frustrated by the prospect of delivering their autonomy and dignity to the Persians (Her I.164 &168). More of them were rather happy to be integrated in a global empire, run by feudalists with little respect for commerce, money, tribute and similar debasing issues, but very prone to protect such endeavours among its subjects so as to profit by taxation and dues and keep them occupied instead of contemplating revolts. An empire provided a secure investor environment and access to a huge market, from the Aegean to Bactria in Central Asia. Commerce would be conducted under the active protection of the conquerors, with a most reasonable tribute (Her III.89). Such Greeks were the Milesians, who had just lost their business associates in the West, the Sybarites, literally exterminated after their defeat by Croton (Her VI.21).

Others, with profitable dealings with the Lydians, are truly bitter, especially considering an imminent trade embargo with India and the Far East by the new key-master of Asia. Both areas are sources of luxury items and known and appreciated enough to have been included in the lore of the god Dionysus (Benaissa 2018). But the religious tolerance, the political moderation and the administrative flair of Cyrus are recognized by everyone, even if actually nothing extraordinary (van der Spek 2014). And thus many Ionians will assist the Egyptian campaign of his son, Cambyses, spontaneously (Her III.44,1 & 19,3 & 139,1).

Still, the hard facts were that the successful colonization of western Asia Minor had created a buffer zone, a protective barrier which was shielding the Greek mainland from eastern invaders and this was no more. Although Ionia was subject to the Lydians, a *modus vivendi* was developed more or less and the latter were sucked into the Hellenic world, presenting no existential threat. The Persians showed no such signs. Greece had been for the first time (but by no means the last) squeezed in macro-geopolitical pliers **(Map 2.1)**. Persians pressed from the east and Carthaginians and Italians – spearheaded by the Etruscans – from the west (Strauss 2017; Deligiannis 2014). As long as the Persians, mainlanders *par excellence* commanded no fleets, the Hellenic World was almost safe and, more important, poised to do business with the vast East once more as they did with Croesus. A degree of bribery and flattery might have been necessary and unpleasant, but it was all that was needed.

Things change with Darius I; as soon as the empire is firmly established, a centralized, religious despotism ensues (DB 55, 63, 72, 73). The knightly, feudalistic character (Delbruck 1920), implied by Herodotus' references to Persian (I.125) and Median (I.101) tribes, if applicable at the time, is more form than function, with the possible exception of some areas of special interest, as the backward Bactria and even Persia proper, where Xenophon partially corroborates Herodotus (Cyrop I.2,5). Now all resolutions lie upon the Throne – a principle indicating anything but a really powerful aristocracy. With Darius I, all three tiers of the Persian society, slaves (*mariaka*), retainers/bondsmen (*bandaka*) – who are free – and aristocracy (*azata*) are *bandaka* of the King, who does as he pleases with absolute, god-given power (Sekunda & Chew 1992). Possibly the class of mariaka are the ones unable to graduate to the public training system due to lack of means (Xen Cyrop I.2,15).

The spontaneous surrender of the Phoenicians shortly before Darius, during the reign of Cambyses (Her III.19,3), brought a most unwelcome trade and naval competitor within the empire and its huge internal market. Their fleet allowed both the conquest of Egypt and the ultimate fall of Cambyses and the rise of Darius to the throne by their flat insubordination to a campaign against Carthage (Her III.19). It was no mystery that they enjoyed the support, patronage and preference of the newly established King of Kings. As a result, the Greek commerce, flourishing under Cambyses and Cyrus, declined sharply; the Phoenicians were now the trusted merchants uniting the empire with the west through Carthage, their colony.

Furthermore, the hillbilly-knights of Cyrus practically despised money, resulting in a tolerable taxation; their notion of wealth was land, livestock, subjects. But Darius I really loved money: greedy and efficient, he was proud of in his taxation and revenue system, the best-organized feature of his empire, possibly with the help of the bankers of Babylon after its final submission. The whole administration was centralized, in a totalitarian manner, with himself receiving divine blessing and status so as to legitimize his dubious rise and to discourage possible rivals and imitators (DB 55 & 63). And now, taxation is really heavy, and not dependent on taxpayers' revenue. With a set taxation and evaporated trade, as the empire is not on the best of terms with overseas Ionian trade associates, the Ionians face bankruptcy and starvation.

Thus, with Darius, the international Greek commerce with the East plummeted and this holds true for both conquered and free Greek city-states; the latter are simply embargoed from the empire. A demonstrably hostile superpower emerged in striking distance from the mainland of the Greek world, not buffered any more by the eastern colonies as it was for some three centuries. The two main sources of wheat imports were effectively blocked: within a generation, Egypt falls to Cambyses and Darius conquers Thrace, but, most importantly, he also occupies the Straits to the Euxine, thus cutting the commerce with the Black Sea colonies and the natives which were providing a considerable portion of the necessary wheat. The only available source of cereals now lies to the West – Sicily, allegedly home to Demeter and sacred to her, the matron-goddess of agriculture. Even this sole but considerable source is insecure. It is threatened by Carthaginian progress and disposition. The Delphic Oracle has been extremely accurate in its predictions and priorities. The Persian menace manifoldly increases its prestige, despite limiting its international influence by removing from power the most affluent and firm late believer, the Lydian King (Her I.13–14).

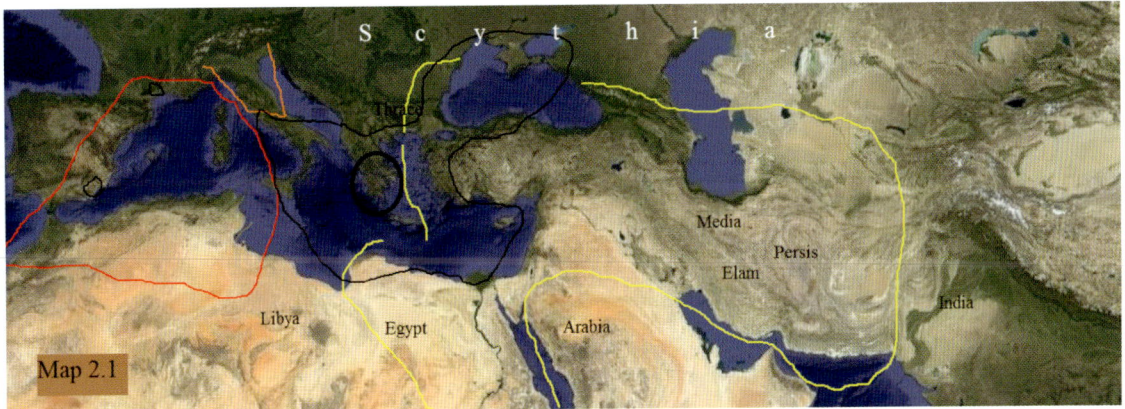

Map 2.1. The Achaemenid Empire (yellow lines) with its three nuclear geopolitical entities (Persis, Media, Elam) threatens the Greek World (black line) from the east and south, as the western Phoenicians (red line) and the Italians (orange line) press from the West.

Chapter 3

The Military Balance in the Era of the Persian Expansion

The Persian military system was decimal (Lazenby 1993; Fields 2007), with the ten-man file (Dathabam) being the basic unit, the century (Satabam) being the technical unit, the thousand (Hazarabam) being the tactical unit and the myriad (Baivarabam) the operational unit (Sekunda 1989 & 1992; Fields 2007). Half-commands, based on the number 5, that is of 5, 50, 500 etc. troops (Xen Cyrop II.1,22–6), and possibly of vessels as well, must have been divisions of a unit rather than separate echelons. Consequently, the second-in-command was able to readily assume the command of half the force for a tactically or administratively differentiated mission (Sekunda & Chew 1992).

The oriental innovation

The Persian expansion was based on a novel spin-off of the standard Middle Eastern mode of warfare. By combining missile warfare with the mobility of cavalry and the protection, massiveness and steadfastness of infantry, albeit not in the tactical level, the Persians fielded a veritable power multiplier. Our reconstitution of their military establishment of the early 5th century provides for cavalry/*Asabari* (Fields 2007) organized in units used for independent action, flanking attacks and assault with missile weapons. These latter were mainly javelins (Her IX.18 & IX.49), which reminds the *palta* of the time of Xenophon (Xen Hell III.4,14; Anab I.8,2) but bows were used as well (Her IX.49). Peculiar metal helmets (Her VII.84) and perhaps a panoply, a complete suit of armour, under the clothes was used, as insinuated by the scale armour of one of the high commanders, Masistius (Her IX.22). Thus, either the full cavalry force or a part of it (Delbruck 1920) may have been already armoured, as might be deduced from the obscure reference to cuirassiers (Her VIII.113), regardless of conventional scholarship, which considers the 4th-century armoured Persian horse a development due to the unpleasant contact with the mainland Greek Hoplite heavy infantryman (Sekunda 1989; Sekunda & Chew 1992).

Still, their armour in the 4th century is more prominent (Xen Anab I.8,6), and during the 5th century, the Persian cavalry supposedly charged only broken, frontally engaged, numerically insignificant, out of formation or fleeing enemy infantry units and implemented raiding warfare and hot pursuit autonomously (Hammond 1968). It is more than possible that the Persian Asabara was, in the day, armed with both javelins and bows, plus sidearms. After all, this was the Scythian standard and, actually, the Byzantine and Sassanid standard of a later day. Similarly to Sparabara infantry, this approach effectively doubled, in functional terms, the available manpower and was far from marring the focus of the knightly warriors, who had time and means aplenty for this dual training. This format was very important given that cavalry was supposed to fight isolated and with a numerical disadvantage. It is supported by Herodotus' statement that 'The Persian cavalry were armed like their infantry' (Her VII.61,1), implying directly both spear, or perhaps shafted weapons in general, and bow (Her VII.84). This is corroborated by the royal self-introduction of Darius (DNb 2), repeated verbatim by Xerxes (Xnb): 'I am a good archer on horseback and on foot, I am a good spearman on horseback and on foot' (Llewellyn-Jones 2012) and also by a list of the kit of the Persian cavalryman during the last quarter of the fifth century, where javelins, shield and quiver were included in the kit of the mounted warrior along with sidearms (Fields 2007).

The lore that limits the education of the Persian scions to riding, archery and candour (Her I.136) refers obviously to *azata* nobility and directly implies the ability of *all* cavalry, not of a portion, to shoot the bow. The insightful analysis of Matthew (2013a) which concludes that the Persian shafted weapon was not only shorter but also thinner and flimsier than the Greek *dory*, with a very limited reach as it was balanced at the middle so as to be suitable for casting, too, most probably refers to the cavalry weapon (*palton*/javelin) and explains a certain reluctance of the Persian nobles to come to grips with Hoplites, in stark contrast to knightly forces of Medieval Europe armed with the long stout lance, held underarm.

Persian cavalry did not shirk from close engagement (**Photo 3.1**): adequately protected and suitably armed, with the advantage of the mass of their mounts, the imperial Asabari cavalrymen would close in with enemy infantry, even unbroken, to trample and slaughter (Sears & Willekes 2016). The first is attested for Artybius' horse, which reared and trampled enemy troops (Her V.111,1); the latter by Xenophon, when a Greek trooper is mentioned as holding his entrails with his hands (Xen Anab II.5,33); a secure indication of a slashing blow by sabre, not a piercing thrust by shafted weapon or arrow. But smashing onto a phalanx front were *dory* spears which were inclined densely and in successive lines, wielded by armoured infantrymen, partly impervious to initial missile barrage during the charge, that was another thing altogether.

Photo 3.1. Persian *asabara* cavalryman, with helmet (A), *akinaka* dirk (B), horse armour (C) and downward thrusting shafted weapon (D).

The decimal organization of the cavalry and its assignment by units to infantry armies indicate a highly organized and disciplined force, standardized and thus organized centrally and consequently not suffering from a number of limitations and drawbacks inherent in knightly armies. As the governance of Darius was very centralized, the carefree European knight might be an unsuitable paradigm for his and Xerxes' cavalry. But there were no combined arms. In many descriptions of battles, even before the invasion of Xerxes, the cavalry is missing from the accounts, and it is never reported to have taken positions at the two flanks of the infantry line. It is always in one body, not divided between wings or any other tactical entities; this is implied in Malene (Her VI.29,1) and explicitly stated at Plataea, (Her IX.32,2). The Achaemenid cavalry operates independently at Plataea in 479 BC (Her IX.14; 17,3; 20,1;40; 49,1) and before, at Eretria in 490 BC (Her VI.101,1) and when pursuing the Paeonian fugitives in 499 BC (Her V.98,4).

The size of the Persian mounts, coming from the Nyssean Fields in Media, was astonishing (Her IX.20; VII.196) and a factor contributing to the success of such cavalry. Additional momentum when charging or casting javelins, higher seat for downward crushing and cutting blows, higher speed and the endurance to carry weaponry and additional armour; all this contributed to the legend and mystique of a force actually much smaller than indicated by its lore. The usual proportion was supposedly less than 1:10 cavalry to infantry (Sarantis 1975; Ray 2009), the latter being the *Greek* optimum (Plut Vit Aris 21). In Marathon, a force of at least 18,000 and probably 24,000 infantry was probably supported by *one* hazarabam of cavalry (Lazenby 1993).

There is a theory suggesting the opposite: that an imperial army corps under Xerxes was composed of five infantry and one cavalry baivaraba, making a 1:5 cavalry-to-infantry ratio (Munro 1902). Solid facts are that some Persian subjects, such as the Sagartians, were fully mounted (Her VII.85); that the classical Greek doctrine favoured already a 1:10 ratio (Her VII.158; Plut Vit Arist 21), which Alexander improved to 1:7.5 when invading Asia (Diod XVII.17,4), to be increased by Arrian to 1:4 (Arr Tact 10,8 & 18,1).

The infantry (*pasti*), on the other hand, was the main branch of the Persian military at the time (Fields 2007); the line infantry were the famous Persian archers, allegedly combined so effectively with the cavalry to create a combination of manoeuvre and firepower which catches the imagination of modern scholars. In fact, the combination was operational, not tactical. These two arms in the Achaemenid army had neither the training, nor the doctrine to fight in a combined and integrated fashion (Hammond 1968). They were fighting together occasionally, but still separately – not unlike today's air and land campaigns, which overlap to a degree, but are not fully integrated.

Infantry-wise, the Persians had recast the already ancient fighting *duo* of shield-bearer and archer, seen in Mesopotamian illustrations and occasionally mentioned in the Iliad (VIII.266–72), so as to maximize the firepower. The Persian version included one shield-bearer (similar to the *pavisarii* of the Middle Ages) followed by nine archers, in a single file, which provided a deep landing zone for the arrows (Sekunda 1989). This depth accommodated for errors in aiming and was also excellent for assaulting in depth an enemy deployment, destroying its cohesion. It also insinuates that the archery duels were fought with arrows flying at relatively low angles, in direct shooting; else the *spara* shield would offer but little protection to the rear ranks. The high angle used by the English archers during the Hundred Years' War may not be an accurate paradigm. Xenophon, having fought both against and alongside Persians, mentions high-angle shooting by Cretan archers as an oddity due to the lack of proper ammunition (Xen Anab III.4,17) and, while corroborating Herodotus on the large size of the Persian bows (Xen Anab III.4,17 and Her VII.61,1) he makes clear that their range was less than the range of the Rhodian slingers (Xen Anab III.4,16), implying direct shooting.

Moreover, all archers were armed with spear and sidearm (sabre, dirk, as well as the '*akinaka*' or axe and the Scythian '*sagaris*') as was the shield-bearer; thus they could all engage in hand-to-hand combat (Raaflaub 2013); again the reader of the Iliad feels at home (Il XV.466–75). Once the arrows caused casualties and disruption, a violent charge disintegrated the enemy, and this onslaught was performed by all the field troops, increasing both impact power and killing efficiency.

This was the Persian line infantry, called *Sparabara* due to the *Spara*, the long, rectangular leather-and-wicker-made shield of the file leaders; very different and lighter than the (mainly) plank-constructed pavises of the Middle Ages. Other nations of the area, like the Medes, used it or a version of it and, in any case, adopted it under the Persian sovereigns. It is possible that their use of such kit pre-dated that of the Persians, but this cannot be surmised. In his seventh book, Herodotus describes at least three more national contingents outfitted similarly to the Persians (Her VII.62).

The *spara* was rectangular and flat, thus providing a standard coverage without any seams and openings, especially when in contact with the other spara of the rank. It was easy to set on the ground, to create a seamless barrier or rather field fortification from where to shoot in relative safety, without burdening the wielders' hands and interrupting his firing sequence. It was very light, which allowed the wielder high mobility, such as forced marches, violent charges, manoeuvring at a jog and pursuing fast and hot. Its beauty though was that it was not issued to all troops, but only to file leaders.

It is unclear whether *all* troops of such a combined formation were called Sparabara; this issue relates, most probably, to the existence or not of shields for the nine archers-spearmen. The reliefs of Persepolis show Persian archers in ceremonial dress, with conventional quivers or combined '*gorytos*' quivers/bow cases, carrying spears and occasionally straight dirks (*akinaka*). What is a bit more confusing is that Greek pottery shows sabres, or rather cleavers, but the Persian reliefs and Herodotus refer to *akinakes* dirks (Her VII.61). The cuirass might have been issued selectively (Charles 2012). The obvious choice is to the dathapata file leaders of the sparabara who would bear the brunt of close-quarter combat and perhaps missile barrages; such armour must be identified with the Egyptian-style mentioned in Herodotus (Her I.135) and seen in Greek art (**Photo 3.2**). Additionally, the other type of cuirass, the iron-scale type (Her VII.61) was issued to or otherwise used by cavalry, at the very least by noble cavalrymen (Her IX.22,2) if not by the entire mounted host of Persian stock, and/or by the elusive cuirassiers (Her VIII.113,2), should they have been an infantry unit (Charles 2012).

It is also unclear whether the spara-bearing file leader (**Photo 3.2**), portrayed with cuirass or jerkin (obviously the Egyptian-style mentioned in Her I.135 made of stuffed linen) in Greek pottery, had been an archer as well. The spara could be solidly planted on the ground, as seen in the pottery, so both hands were free, but only a portion of the above mentioned representations show the bow (not quiver), for spara-related troopers. Herodotus (VII.61) endows all Persian national infantry with a full kit of wicker shield of unstated shape and size, short spear, longbow hanging from the shoulder (from where it could be brought to notch position with just one move within the left palm), with one quiver at the back (for fast drawing of the reed arrows), with iron scale-armour and with a dirk hanging from the belt to the right side. And here lies a problem: there is not one image of a Persian with so full a kit, making the description of Herodotus reading like the inventory of the infantry unit, not the standard-issue kit of the infantryman.

The spara was quite a feat of manufacturing, despite the mundane materials; and of sizeable footprint. The size and form of the spara (**Photo 3.2C**) allowed

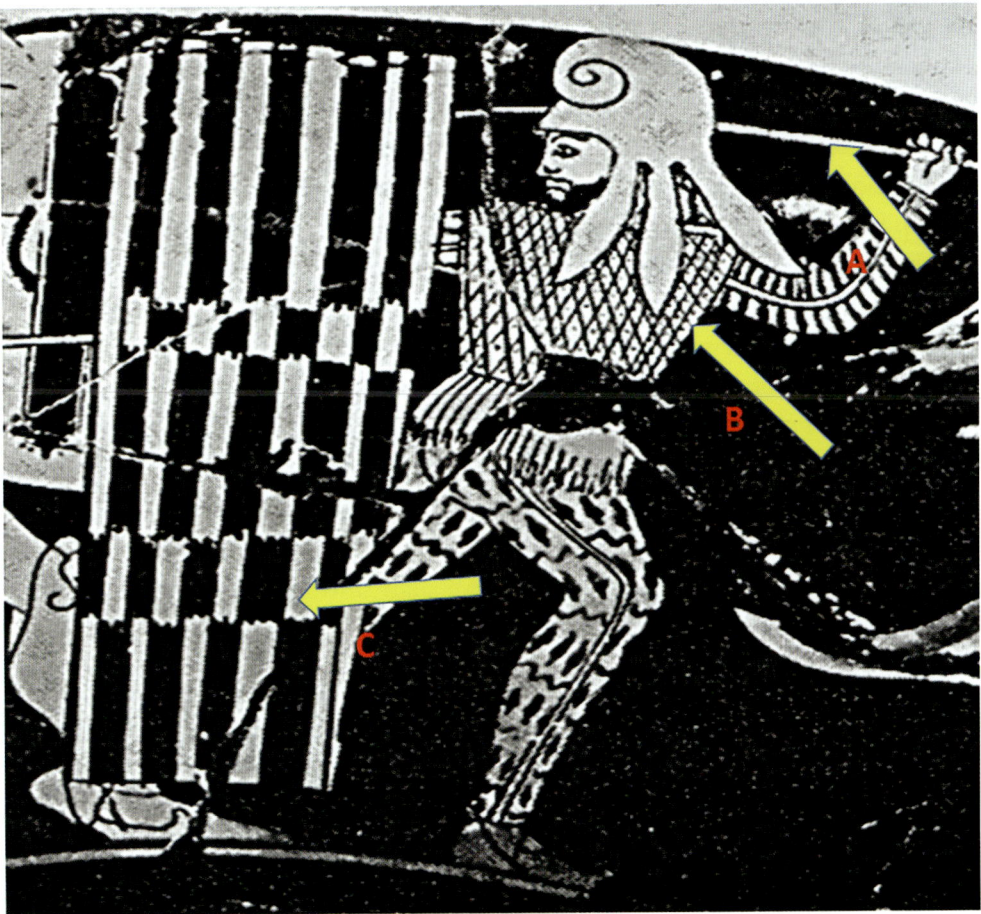

Photo 3.2. *Sparabara*, equipped with (A) spear, (B) jerkin/corselet, ostensibly of Egyptian style (Her I.135) and probably made of stuffed linen and (C) the rectangular, leather-and-wicker, big *spara* shield.

the formation of a veritable shield wall, as mentoned above, with the file leaders planting their spara one next to the other to create a portable and movable linear field fortification, from which they were entrusted to repulse by spear-thrusts any enemy resilient enough to cross the hail of arrows and assault their shield wall. It should be noted, though, that – contrary to some views – there can be little possibility of more than one spara-bearers per *datha* (10-man file). Even less so for an adjustable number of spear-bearers according to the tactical situation (Ray 2009). The idea that an array of weapons was available to all soldiers and the selection was done before deployment is impractical in anything but pitched battle, as it denies the ability to deploy promptly after a forced march or in battles by encounter.

Thus the Persian armies had multiplied their firepower, as almost all of the line infantry shot bows and then doubled as shock troops (Raaflaub 2013). The Persians had practically doubled the effective sizes of their armies, and by fielding quite large ones they were really able to cloud the sky with their arrows (Her VII.226). An ethnic Persian boy was taught from the age of 5 until 20 to ride, shoot the bow and speak the truth (Her I.136), and then he was serving his tour of four years as a conscript private (Strabo XV.3,18), followed by either a military career or a release to the civilian life as a reservist (Strabo XV.3,18; Ray p31–32). There is a slight problem, though: the infantry was by far the decisive Persian arm; Xenophon (Cyrop I.2,15) estimates the Persians, obviously the conscription-liable, to 120,000. The bondsmen/ *bandaka* were the intermediate social stratum, between the slaves/ *mariaka* and the Aristocrats/ *azata* (Sekunda & Chew 1992) and accounted for the equivalent of the free citizenry, who obviously were the bulk of the manpower. These could not own a horse and had no war use for it. So how, and, most importantly, why should they have to 'learn to ride since childhood'? Most probably, the renowned motto referred to the scions of the Persian nobility, similarly to the – slightly more expansive and diversified – syllabus of Homeric heroes and medieval knights. Or this kind of training was provided to all enfranchised Persian youths who could afford the public training (i.e. azata and bandaka) since the acquisition of a horse could happen during manhood due to gains or promotion, training in their early years should have anticipated such a case.

The long Persian bow, firing a long, hollow arrow shaft (Her VII.61) had quite a range (Xen Anab III.3,15). The massive firepower practically reduced any need for defensive weaponry, which brought down the cost and increased the flexibility, speed and endurance of the troops. Although Persian troops are regularly mentioned as unarmoured (Her IX.62,3), Herodotus mentions iron-scale cuirasses for the Persian national infantry, possibly implying the first-rank sparabara (Her VII.61). Such armour was a quantum leap compared to the bronze-scale panoplies of centuries past. Moreover, quilted jerkins and equivalents to Greek *linothorax* models are shown in pottery for imperial troops – basically archers and/or sparabara. By any account, the protection afforded by the Persian shield and armour was optimized against arrows, as they were the only actual threat to the Persian war machine, and secondarily against the chance slashing blow in the melee. Still, this picture of both literary and representational evidence is very far from the picture of 'naked', fully unarmoured troops explicitly referring to the Persian line infantry and considered a focal reason for their defeat in Plataea (Her IX.62,3).

The short spear with the apple-like (or spherical, *sensu lato*) counterweight (Her VII.41) was more important than usually acknowledged. Short in length, it was handy in congested conditions, such as the melee after a storm of arrows. Its spherical counterweight and short length made its use safer for the rest of the ranks, contrary to the constant danger for the following ranks represented by the butt-spike of the Greek spear. This, usually disregarded, spherical counterweight allowed holding the shaft far towards the back end, which permitted maximization of the useful length and reach within a handy total length with minimal projection backwards – a feature further enhancing the collective safety and reducing the cumbersomeness of such a weapon. It must be noted that the Greeks had difficulty in spearing in congested conditions and preferred spear-fights at a distance in set-piece battles and/or on open ground.

The Persian spearman, due to his more nimble weapon, could be more mobile in the open and more dexterous in congested conditions, although at the cost of a somewhat reduced reach. Some projections assign central grip at an overhead position as the sole technique of using the Persian infantry spear, resulting in limited reach, 1.4m. Both this conclusion and the notion of fragility due to smaller diameter (Matthew 2013a) might be due to a misunderstanding that confuses the dual-use *palton* of the cavalry with the counterweighted infantry spear attested by Herodotus (VII.41,3) and shown in various reliefs. The counterweight allowed, as mentioned before, a very asymmetrical hold, near the rear tip, and also both high and low positions, with the latter offering longer reach and being reminiscent of the *Iklwe* of the Zulus under Shaka; the former was the only suitable grasp for use from behind a fully developed spara wall, where spearing over the upper edge of the spara was mandatory.

Moreover, the counterweight allowed a police function, as a less-than-lethal club for riot control, and an alternative military function: as a lethal club to strike at heads and to break inflexible shields and armour, thus giving the user a dual-use weapon: a battle club with quite a reach paired to the conventional spear. This is by itself a noteworthy innovation compared to the armament of the Assyrians in the Army of Xerxes, which included lance, club and dagger (Her VII.63).

Furthermore, it is as yet unresolved what the Persian spearman-archer was doing with his spear when shooting arrows: leaving it lying on the ground would make picking it up rather difficult; the possibility that the sphere allowed it to balance upright should be taken into consideration and tested, at different types of ground. Without the butt-spike of the Greek weapons (see **Photo 3.4**) it might have been planted on the ground head-on (Ray 2009), which would expose its point to damage and rust; but also infest it with soil microbes, adding a septic dimension to any wound.

After all, the sparabara may have not been intended for the defensive pinning and bleeding of the enemy, as is commonly projected (Ray 2009). Their purpose must have been the decimation and stunning of the enemy. This would allow them to tilt sideways or retract by any other means the few and light spara, thus enabling the massive exit of the spearmen-archers. The latter would deliver a violent charge with close contact weapons to disintegrate the enemy by eroding his unity and dissolving his line, very much like the practice of the Roman legionaries some centuries later. Without this in mind, one cannot explain the use of spears hardly reaching a target positioned two ranks ahead by all the ten ranks. Practically the fighting style of the Persian infantry was very Roman-like, perhaps lacking the body armour in kind or, at the very least, in type and using the bow instead of the javelin as a missile and the short spear instead of the *gladius*-type sword for close-quarter melee.

The practice of enumeration of the Persian host of Xerxes reported by Herodotus (VII.60), whence 10,000 men were standing and a fence was built around them to promptly enumerate the army, was rather a measure to divide the army to baivaraba; then, each *baivarapatis* would segregate and delegate hazaraba to his hazarapata, who would then delegate sataba to the satapata designated by baivarapatis and so on to the dathabam.

The file of ten men was both operational and administrative. It was the administrative unit, but also the standard file of one shield-bearer who led and commanded the file (Dathapatis) and nine probably unshielded archers. All ten men were armed with spear and sidearm. Thus, the standard file depth of a Persian unit was ten, and to increase depth for better defensive function or adaptation in confined spaces, the successive deployment of units in successive lines was probably the standard procedure. If a higher echelon was depleted or undermanned, the personnel were reassigned and restructured to create full units. For example, a Persian century (Satabam) may be understrength, chiefly because some dathaba are taken for other – guard/outpost – duties; thus less than ten dathaba were present. In mobilization, such detachments would return to bring it up to strength for expeditionary duty. Still, low manning and casualties are also reasons for understrength dathaba. Consequently, a Satabam, if left with 70 men, would cut

3 Dathaba and use the manpower to fill 7 Dathaba to full strength (Ray 2009; Sekunda & Chew 1992). The net result was that understrength units may cover smaller fronts but always had a steady, 10-man deep landing zone for their arrows, assaulting at depth the enemy.

The infantry baivarabam was probably escorted by 1,000 cavalry, a hazarabam, but this is speculative as the 1:10 cavalry to infantry ratio is a Greek standard (Plut Vit Aris 21). Still, if more than one baivaraba took the field, as in Marathon, it is not clear whether a single cavalry hazarabam would be attached, being considered the cavalry arm of an expeditionary force, or the ratio – had it been thus – remained steady with additional cavalry hazaraba being dispatched. The use of the cavalry was to control space in width and depth (Her VIII.23), to provide awareness, and to take independent action (Her IV.20) similar to the Confederate cavalry of Johnson under Lee in the American Civil War. It did support the actual fighting and in cases was proven decisive, as in the battle of Malene (Her VI.29). This supposition provides two possible, complementary conclusions: that the optimal heavy infantry/cavalry ratio of the Greek military experts, 10:1, might have been based on the Persian system, but it also might not; and that extended or total absence of either the infantry or cavalry from a battlefield (as happened in Marathon, 490 BC) was not unusual under the Persian doctrine. No cavalry is mentioned in Mycale, 479 BC and in the early 4th century, Greek invasion forces regularly clash with cavalry forces deprived of infantry, with mixed results (Xen Hell IV.1,19; III.4,14 & III.4,22–4).

This independent, poorly integrated mode of action is occasionally noticed and remarked (Hammond 1968) and had been adopted by the Athenian cavalry under Pericles (Thuc II.22,2). In truth, it does not exclude a combined-arms approach but makes the limits of the latter more obvious. Additionally, the explicit notion of Herodotus that the imperial cavalry had been arrayed by itself in Plataea (Her IX.32,2) parallels the dispositions reported by Xenophon above. Thus, the notion of Persian cavalry stationed at the wings, in *Parataxis*, for example in Marathon (Sekunda 2002) is not convincing; whenever the imperial cavalry was deployed for pitched battle to support an infantry force, a *Protaxis* in one body, in front of the infantry line, or *Epitaxis* in one body *behind* the infantry line, is more plausible.

It is an issue of debate whether the rank and file of the Persian dathabam had smaller, elliptical and/or crescent-like shields for personal defence in close-quarters combat. This issue lies at the heart of a more complicated issue. Were the sparabara (*sensu lato*) the only type of Persian infantry? Because sparabara were archers and not all Persian infantry were archers, after all. There is pottery showing Persians with the (small) shield and spear, lacking bows. Additionally, in the battle of Issus archer units were specifically mentioned (Arr Anab Alex III.13,1), implying that the

Persian line infantrymen were not such. These observations can be explained by the successive transformations of the branch, but they do call for some further research.

The personal defence shields of the Persians of the ranks behind the dathapatis might be the relatively large double-scalloped shields, which are seen in Persepolis reliefs arming spearmen with no archer attire (**Photo 3.3** middle; then there is a crescent-like shield similar to the Thracian peltast (**Photo 3.11C**), and a single-scalloped circular shield (**Photo 3.6D**) used by Persian spearmen in Greek pottery. One cannot be sure whether such shields were used by the rank and file of the dathabam of sparabara or by different troop types, such as the *Arstibara* and the *Takabara*.

The sparabara was line infantry. For many other functions, from amphibious operations and naval engagements to assaulting fortifications and patrolling extended areas they were not ideal; capable perhaps, but not ideal. Line troopers may build, or acquire an empire, but they cannot sustain it. A lesser, more persistent and cheaper troop type is needed for such tasks; usually medium or light infantry. The Greeks reached the same conclusion despite their sentimental and ideological reliance on the Hoplite – and then the Romans likewise. Once imperial expansion started, at any rate and scale, medium troops were necessary. The Greeks had the *Psiloi* and afterwards the Peltasts (**Photo 3.11C**). The Persians probably developed the takabara (Sekunda 1989; Sekunda & Chew 1992), medium infantry armed with shield and spear and possibly with a sidearm (**Photo 3.5D**), although their emergence is disputed in temporal terms. A very late appearance some decades later is proposed by some scholars, based on Greek art (Sekunda & Chew 1992). After all, sparabara were light enough, definitely by Greek standards, but objectively as well; Alexander's Phalangites were in some cases used as light troops and were considered such (Arr Anab Alex III.23,3), although by default they were troops of the line and heavily armed (Arr Anab Alex I.28,7).

Though there is no reason for buying into this argument for the late takabara emergence; had they been another arm of the infantry branch, they could be used as flank-guards for the sparabara or as the main troop type of an expeditionary force. It is uncertain whether they were in the field during the Persian Wars or had been a later development of future decades, as mentioned. Their shield, the *taka*, was reminiscent of the Greek-mentioned *pelte* (**Photo 3.11C**), but its identification with the three aforementioned types is unclear; the double-scalloped shield (**Photo 3.3**) most probably does *not* qualify. The scalloped-off circular shield (seen in Greek pottery for shield-and-spear Persian infantry) is a better candidate; as is the crescent semi-circular one and, apart from the possibility of a problem of artistic fidelity, there is also the distinct possibility that they *both* were taka; simply different models. The latter would imply spin-offs of the same item due to evolution or different local lines of manufacture.

Takabara presence is conceivable at Marathon. Herodotus (VI.112) narrates that the Persians thought the Greeks were frenzied to attack them at a run without the support of archery (NOT archers) and cavalry, which means they were perfectly familiar with charges as long as they were properly supported. This report should have ended any argument for a defensive Persian infantry function centuries ago and outlines how a *Persian* charge was meant to develop; with archery and cavalry support. But there is no mention of anything reminiscent of a spara wall, and the hand-to-hand contest leading the Persians to push back by quite a distance an unyielding Hoplite Phalanx fits poorly in the Sparabara context, with the unwieldy spara-shield. The above may, of course, have been due to Herodotus' comparatively inept description of Marathon. Still, Sparabara are explicitly mentioned in Plataea and Mycale in 479 BC, but not in the first two days at Thermopylae – an action allegedly ideal for the takabara. If the imperial troops in Marathon were takabara (**Photo 3.6**), which is a sounder choice for an invasion fleet and amphibious actions, separate units of archers should be understood. After all, a charge *supported* by archers means that it was not *conducted* by the archers.

Another reported troop type, the *Arstibara*-spearman (Sekunda & Chew 1992) comes to complicate things even further. Darius must have been one, as Herodotus, who evidently speaks Persian, refers to him as spear-bearer and not guardsman or anything similar. The Persian war court had a Master of the Bow (*Vacabara*), a Master of the Horse and a Master of the Spear (*Arstibara*), who is believed to be a Chamberlain rather than the director of line infantry (Sekunda & Chew 1992); but this might have been an additional, administrative office for his title. As the line infantry used bow and spear, one can assume that the spearmen had nothing to do with the double-role line infantry. Indeed, reliefs show spearmen without shield or bow. Even if the court names and ceremony reflected a previous era, with separate archer and spearman units, before the advent of double-role Sparabara, there are issues to tackle. If (some categories of) spearmen were called Arstibara, were they shieldless? If *not*, could the term include the takabara and the dathapatis of the Sparabara and been descriptive and generic? This would have been the case, if the rank and file of the Sparabara were spearless, as Greek pottery implies; still, the context of such scenes is usually missing. In an army of different (combined or not) arms, everything is possible; simply, we lack sufficient clues to reach a conclusion. Herodotus' testimony, for what it is, does not corroborate. In the cases where sparabari are implied, the Corps of the Immortals in the Parade of Xerxes' army and in the Battle of Plataea, spears are mentioned for all the troops in the former case and are implied in the latter.

But the actual function of Arstibara seems to have been different. They most probably were bodyguards of the king and the viceroys/satraps (Kuhrt 2001), possibly to the number of 1,000 per commission (Her III.127,1; VII.41); not field troop types, not a generic description of field troops' kit and function, a praetorian guard of sorts, similar to the Bodyguard of Alexander the Great (Kambouris & Bakas 2017; Kambouris et al 2019), and responsible for the protection and security of top officials (Sekunda 2002), not field duty – except if necessary. They would guard the palace and, when on campaign, the tent of the King/Karana, and his selected position, either within the army, as Darius III, who took the field in person at Issus (Arr Anab II.8,11), or at a remote observatory-headquarters-command platform, as Xerxes did at Salamis (Her VIII.90,4) and Thermopylae (Her VII.212,1). This guard function did not require a shield; both hands had to be available to allow prompt and successful intervention if need be. It was an excellent opportunity for royalty and aristocracy who wished to become 'networked' to fulfill their military obligations. Thus, spearmen without shields and bows in Persian representations must have been the *Arstibara* guards, probably corresponding to the *aichmiforoi-doryphoroi* (spear-bearers) of Herodotus (Her III.127,1 & 139,2). When and if deployed for battle, as most probably at Plataea, they *might* have been issued with shields, perhaps the double-scalloped ones also seen in reliefs arming spearmen without bows (**Photo 3.3** cente). Still, the scalloped shields may be characteristic of *one specific* guard unit, as Herodotus mentions *two* guard units (1,000-strong each), but only one may be the King's Arstibara. This view is supported by the fact that shielded and shieldless spearmen appear together (**Photo 3.3** right), which means a mixed guarding pattern. Contrarily, the Immortals, an elite corps but actually a field unit, *not* guards (Charles 2011), are depicted with both spear and bow, as proper sparabara (**Photo 3.3** left).

The actual novelty which troubled the Greeks was the massive archery combined, in space and time, by cavalry manoeuvre and infantry onslaught. Although, as mentioned earlier, Persians did not use combined arms in any modern sense (Hammond 1968), the mainland Greeks did not know that and had to prepare for such an unfortunate eventuality, especially once details of the battle of Malene (Her VI.29) became available but remained foggy. It was the last battle before the Persian invasion and the only one decided by the cavalry – and possibly the only one in Ionia where the imperial cavalry had played any role. More armour for the Hoplite was not the solution to this problem and was discarded in the 6th century either as a failed experiment against massive archery or as the ultimate evolution of the Hoplite kit for more individualistic and initiative-intensive missions, i.e. within a colonial context. The reason for the rejection of this solution may have been due to cost, or technical considerations. Evidently, up to that day, the Greeks had not found any definite answer to the eastern challenge and were still experimenting: drill, tactics, technique and

Photo 3.3. Elite achaemenid troops, in ceremonial Persian, or rather Elamite, court dress. Left: with bow, quiver and spear and retracted headgear an Immortal elite infantryman. Right: two different guardsmen (spear-bearers) with headgear erected. One of them is shielded, indicating members of (the two) different guard units.

weaponry were all taken into consideration. The intellectual efficiency was to decide the struggle. For 230 years Greeks and Persians were trying to learn from everywhere and to adapt to each other. Greeks showed a marked superiority in terms of military intellect during the Third Persian War and were able to adhere to it despite many setbacks, until they delivered the *coup de grace* by the hand of Alexander the Great, in 330 BC.

The Greeks

For the Greeks, the thing is quite different. Most of the Greek mainland, that is east of the Pindus mountain range, operates the Hoplite heavy infantryman (**Photo 3.4**), fully armoured and excellently protected. His frontal aspect was that of invulnerability, presenting, when at the ready, minimal exposure: with the shield in position and adopting a striding stance; an oblique stance angled at the line of the front (Luginbill 1994) with the upper body leaning slightly forward, left projected, right denied, there were virtually no naked spots. This hoplitic preponderance was true though for the *civilized* societies, the city-states.

More backward states/areas, like Aetolia, were content with javelineers and slingers, a common choice throughout Eurasia at the time. They lacked the material, intellectual and social means and the mentality to field Hoplites, and perhaps the need to do so. At the time, in mainland Greece, the Dorians ruled supreme, along with relatives – more or less distant – and friends; consequently, their method and style were the commonest. They fielded the most numerous and most efficient Hoplite armies and imposed the accepted tradition. Missile warfare was allegedly despised among almost all civilized Greek states, especially the bow and that, mostly, among the Dorians, with the notable exception of the Cretans. Similarly, the Dorians had little intimacy with the horse, perhaps due to their hilly/mountainous origin. Other Greek tribes were more broad-minded and appreciative of archery, especially against non-Greeks, and of cavalry as well.

Greeks of that era were not unfamiliar with combined arms concepts, largely – though not exclusively – due to the Mycenaean tradition. Still, the reality check found them poised to face the innovative land threat of the Persians while they themselves were based on the Hoplite, which was a standard troop type of extremely wide distribution. He had literally conquered the Mediterranean and created lore and mystique, but had fared poorly against the Persians, at least in Egypt and in Asia Minor, if not in Mesopotamia as well. Still, only in Asia Minor were the Hoplites fighting in defence of their own country and communities and under their own officers throughout the chain of command. The change from contempt to utter terror between 500 and 490 BC, evident in Herodotus, shows that previous clashes had not instilled any doubt regarding the ability of the Hoplite to tackle the Orientals.

Glory of times past: the Hoplite

It is a common mistake to consider the Persian Wars as the defining moment of the Greek fighting model to prominence. In part, Herodotus is to blame, trying to assign more laurels to these generations than their true share and demeaning previous Greek military achievements. His motivation might have been to read

Photo 3.4. The Hoplite at attention. The warhead of this model of *dory* spear is wide to reduce penetration so as to facilitate extraction and increase the width – and the resulting bleeding – when thrust in soft tissue. The *sauroter* butt-spike allows firm fixing on the ground without compromising the warhead. The large *hoplon* shield, which named the troop type, is prominent and perhaps the reason the Persians referred to Greeks as *Yauna Takabara*: shield-bearing Ionians (Greeks), despite the administrative context of the reference (DNa 29) which focuses on their status as subjects and thus shows them disarmed. The helmet here is the fully enclosed Corinthian model, but crestless. (*Copyrights: Association of Historical Studies "KORYVANTES" - koryvantes.org*)

or sound more pleasant to his Athenian democratic audience while keeping an otherwise balanced and reasonably objective account.

At that time, the Hoplite was a long-established troop type. Armed and armoured to tackle multiple attacks from all directions in individual combat, he was even better and more effective in collective action (Raaflaub 2013): the phalanx formation was sweeping its opponents from the battlefield (Nilsson 1929) and fending off clouds of missiles by the overlap of the concave, large Argive shields, preferably, but not necessarily, coupled by full panoply (Plut Apoph XXVIII). Although a sword was important for hand-to-hand combat, the main weapon was the spear, long so as to reach over the shields of a tight phalanx and bring down a horseman before the latter could use a slashing sidearm delivering downward thrusts and blows (Snodgrass 1967).

The Hoplite made possible the first and, more importantly, the second waves of the Greek colonial expansion, enabling small numbers of colonists to stand against multitudes of locals (Krentz 1985). The style and attire were exported, copied and imitated. Fugitives from Peloponnese, the retinue of Demaratos of Corinth (Polyb VI.11a, 7; Dion Ha Ant Rom III.46,3–5; Strab VIII.6,20 & V.2,2; Livy I.34,2) taught it to the Etruscans, instigating their ascendance, and – directly or indirectly – to other Italian peoples, amongst whom were the Romans.

As already mentioned, the Hoplite reigned supreme for at least a century, conquering the central and western basins of the Mediterranean. Corinthian pottery illustrating Hoplite battle may well represent, in some part, the clash between Greek colonists and barbarians having adopted the same gear, as were the Etruscans, the Romans etc. (Snodgrass 1967). In such clashes, better familiarization would offer the Greeks an advantage, but this was not always so, nor had it been always decisive as quantity always mattered between technological equals.

In the east, the Hoplite gear was adopted by populations of distant Greek origin or intermingled with Greeks, such as the Lycians, Carians, Cypriots etc. and even the Phoenicians might be added to the list, at least partially, as they adapted the Hoplite kit (Her VII.89). Moreover, the Hoplites had established presence in the Middle East as celebrated mercenaries in Babylonian service (Alc *fr* 350) and, of course, in Egypt (Her III.11). If Diodorus is to be believed (in this particular case an anachronism is possible) even during Xerxes' reign, mercenaries, Greek in form and origin, were used for internal security missions (Diod XI.6,2). Indeed, during Herodotus' time, this was the case. The policy might have been introduced earlier, though, due to the excellent record of Hoplite mercenary service in terms of reliability and effectiveness.

Origin and evolution

The Hoplite was the main type of warrior of many different states and this supremacy lasted for quite some centuries. His birthday is unknown, but what IS known is that he showed considerable adaptability. When his armour emerged, it was expensive (Nilsson 1929); one might add quite expensive as it elaborated on previous Mycenean armour, which means it required considerable quantities of metal, while mere novelty is always a reason for inflated prices, even for cheaply fabricated goods. But it DID constitute a quantum leap in protection and user-friendliness. Thus, its acquisition being a sign of status, it remained expensive on purpose and an upper-class privilege. So, the 6th-century Hoplites are citizens of means, aristocrats and bourgeois alike, thanks to the expansion of commerce and the wealth it created. The considerable investment represented by the Hoplite kit could be used to earn a living as a mercenary, as was the case with Antimenidas, the brother of the poet Alcaeus (Alc *fr* 350), or to secure privileges at home – especially if the investment of an aristocrat was expanded to arm any trustworthy clients, as might be the case with the above mentioned poet Alcaeus himself (Alc *fr* 357). This context would have been the standing social format for the Etruscans and, to a considerable extent, for the Romans before the advent of the maniple (Snodgrass 1965 & 1967; Nilsson 1929). Such social mechanics inform *against* a rigid phalanx formation (Anderson 1991), which demands discipline and belongs to later evolutionary stages.

A well-armed and trained Hoplite could wreak havoc to opponents less well-kitted, similar to the effects of fully-armed heroes of the Homeric tradition (Iliad V.600–6) who might have used less ergonomic and closely-fit armour. The Hoplite armour provided, in its fullest form, full and all-round protection, obviously meant for open-order melee (Anderson 1991). The Argive shield, the definition of the fighter, was a technical feat, as with its double-grip system it allowed better handling, more secure holding, a better distribution of the weight among wrist (handgrip-*antilabe*), lower arm (armband-*porpax*), and shoulder (outward rim-*stephane*) and a steady protection footprint irrespective of turning (Anderson 1991; Hanson 1991; Snodgrass 1967; Sekunda 2000; Krentz 1985; Luginbill 1994; Goldsworthy 1997). If its distance and tilt were kept steady, turning it around its axis during combat did not open any windows of vulnerability, while the convex shape deflected blows and allowed offensive use, especially shoving. The aristocrats must have been very reluctant to allow the arming of non-aristocrats with such a marvel (Snodgrass 1965; Anderson 1991; Hanson 1991).

Still, it was a matter of cost, and between armies of aristocrats, the one with the most Hoplites was winning. To field more Hoplites, an issue of vital importance in early Greece, both in the colonial quest and in the mainland strife where whole communities were wiped out after a defeat in the field (as in Her IV.1), *bourgeois* started buying into *Hoplitikon*, the body of Hoplites. This evolution demanded concessions in government and privileges, giving rise to oligarchies, and resulted in more Hoplites but of lesser quality. The bourgeois had other things to do, especially the merchants and the farmers, and thus were unavailable for the long training of an Aristocrat. Still, the Hoplite kit as a whole system had a secondary function – a safety mode, requiring less training should massive acquisition be required for the entire force. If masses of Hoplites simply took a close position so as not to allow infiltration of enemies and provide mutual cover frontally and laterally, they could sweep off the field a less numerous, even if better trained, force of opponents if they held together. After all, the Hoplite kit was by design modular, and some parts could be discarded, if not due to weight, definitely due to cost. The rest, and especially the Argive shield, allowed a tight formation with extreme cohesion in two dimensions – an innovation never before attempted in such extremes. The troops interacted in a coordinated manner not only by ranks, but also by files, bringing the weight of a whole file of men onto one shield, to shove the opponent. *This* was the Hoplite phalanx.

Enter the phalanx

Once collective action became important, cohesion was the most important factor, as it afforded a good measure of passive and active defence of the individual. In a wide Hoplite body, some normalization was also needed. Formal training to learn basic skills and scheduled calls-to-arms to refresh the drill were only one side of the coin. Skills were instilled individually through dance and athletics (Krentz 1985; Anderson 1991) and such engagements, reasonably pleasurable, probably constituted the other, more sustainable part of the training syllabus of the Hoplites throughout Greece. This syllabus was not as formalized and differentiated as the Athenian 'Ephebeia' of the 4th century (Arist Ath Pol 42,4–5; Recaldin 2011; Ridley 1979), but it should have done the trick.

And the trick was that the phalanx setting demands steadiness most of all, which is the combined result of strength, endurance, resilience, determination and courage. The decision of the clash is usually swift (Adcock 1957; Sekunda 2002), a fact that lightens the requirements in stamina. Nimbleness, agility, dexterity, speed, ambition, bravado, aggressiveness, all basic factors for the heroic fighter, are secondary – or worse; they may become counterproductive if sapping the solidity. Even pure strength is of little importance. Thus, senior citizens can be used effectively, if not within the first ranks, definitely bringing up the rear, as the experience, cool head, cold blood and sheer persistence make them invaluable to the stability and coherence of a phalanx body, while increasing its numbers. The latter are expanded thanks to technology and innovation: the *linothorax*, with or without metal scales (**Photos 3.11B & 3.12A**), is cheaper, lighter, more ergonomic and less burdensome to wear in terms of chafing, heating and scratching or bruising the wearer.

This private soldier provides his own rations, addresses his specific needs, his weaponry and his motivation AND decides where, when and whom to fight (Hanson 1989 & 1991 & 1999). He is strictly individualist but a concerted team-player, self-supported, life-long amateur (Rey 2011) who distrusts mercenaries (Hanson 1983 & 1989 & 1999). He has come a long way from his ancestor, made renowned as a spear-for-hire and, to a lesser degree, as a single combatant belonging within a warrior elite (Anderson 1991). It is he who will emerge triumphant from the Persian Wars. The State saves huge sums by not investing in extended campaigns, deep magazines and collected and stored provisions (Hanson 1989 & 1991 & 1999), in elaborate fortifications and long-standing troops for garrison duties. It simply supervises the correct fulfillment of civic duty in terms of training, mobilization and, to a less extent, outfitting.

When the Persian Wars erupted, the Hoplite, as a warrior and a socioeconomic entity had undergone quite some evolution, as mentioned above, and operated mostly within the phalanx. In conceptual and technological terms even more so. His panoply had evolved in all three main parts (helmet, cuirass, greaves) and most of the secondary parts, such as thigh and arm guards and lower-belly guard (**Photo 3.11A**) had been discarded to reduce weight and cost; that is in the mainland, as in the West the need for enhanced protection in fluid battlefields resulted in retaining them for some time. The *dory* spear, after some evolution (as is the pair of single-pointed, cast-and-thrust weapons of the 6th century), had been standardized to a single, thrust-only weapon. It was powerful enough to negotiate armour and long enough to counter cavalry and protrude out of the front of the phalanx in order to intercept the foe before a physical impact onto the shields of the first rank (Anderson 1991; Snodgrass 1967; Matthew 2013a). It was outfitted with a leather strap or rope thong (visible in art and misidentified regularly for the launch thong of javelins) attached to a similar handle to secure the grip even when sweat, blood and fatigue make the shaft slippery. And there was a butt-spike (*sauroter*) to allow solid fixing in the ground, without corroding the warhead (**Photo 3.4**). The *sauroter* could be used in an emergency as a warhead, i.e. in cases of shaft breakage due to hacking or shattering, and offered a counterweight that made a hind grip possible, to capitalize on the length of the shaft in terms of reach (Matthew 2012).

The Hoplite spear was used in low (**Photos 3.6C & 3.12B**), underarm (**Photo 3.6B**) or overhead (**Photos 3.5C, F & 3.12A**) grips, with the scholarly debate on the subject still raging. There was also the reverse overhead (Matthew 2012), with the spear positioned as in overhead but the arm and hand oriented as in low (**Photo 3.5B**).

Photo 3.5. Different iterations and types of Greek infantry (details in text). (*Photo from the "Marathon 2011" International Reenacting Event. Copyrights: Association of Historical Studies "KORYVANTES" - koryvantes.org*)

Photo 3.6. Hoplites against takabara. (*Photo from the "Marathon 2011" International Reenacting Event. Copyrights: Association of Historical Studies "KORYVANTES" - koryvantes.org*)

The low and underarm grips, preferably with the shaft at a high angle, so as not to cause injuries to the troops that followed (**Photo 3.6A**), could be used at a run, as they permitted free movement of the torso and lower body, accurate aiming and transfer of the kinetic energy of the body to the spear-point for a lethal penetrating effect through armour. Both low and underarm grips were adequate to spar with an enemy (**Photo 3.12**) and repel cavalry; the latter suggested a semi-kneeling position

(**Photos 3.6C and 3.7**). But with closely packed phalanx, in *synaspismos* mode with interlocked shields, the overhead grip (**Photo 3.8**) was the best choice, similarly to sparabara practice.

The interlocked shields could not open for a thrust: re-enactment has shown that the right part of an Argive shield must be placed *behind* the left part of the shield of the trooper to the *right* to produce a line withstanding the shock delivered by enemy troops crashing on the shield wall, and not the opposite as is usually assumed (**Figure 3.1** upper and lower rows, respectively).

In such cases, low or overhead grips are possible, but not underarm. Contrary to some views (Matthew 2013a; Matthew 2012) the overhead grip was immensely

Photo 3.7. Hoplite in semi-kneeling position extending to thrust from an underarm grip against higher positioned enemy, as was cavalry. (*Copyrights: Association of Historical Studies "KORYVANTES" - koryvantes.org*)

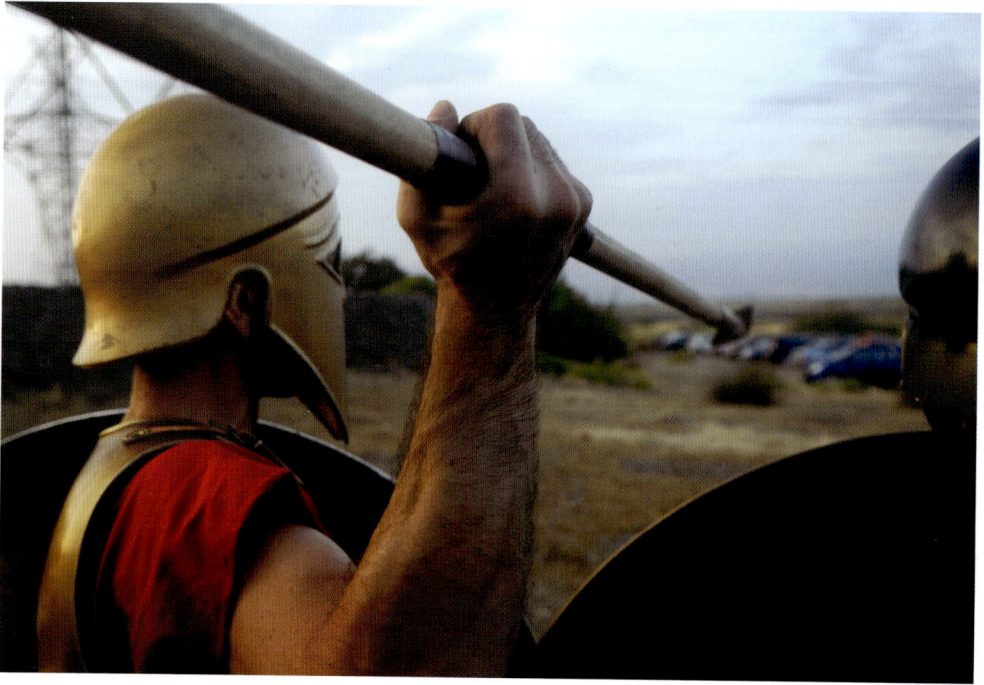

Photo 3.8. The overhead grip is the only one allowing powerful thrusts in close-packed phalanx formats, especially *synaspismos*. (*Copyrights: Association of Historical Studies "KORYVANTES" - koryvantes.org*)

practical and is well attested in art, although *some* confusion with javelin casting did occur (Matthew 2012). The overhead grip produced shorter reach indeed, but when used from a standstill, as in a phalanx confrontation, it was putting a much higher proportion of the body weight onto the thrust, thus achieving better penetration. Additionally, the downward thrust was taking the blow *behind* the

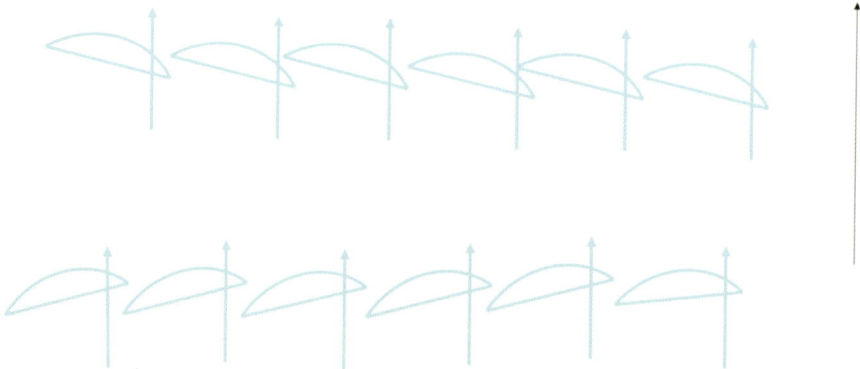

Sliding the right part of the shield behind the left part of the hoplite at the right gives maximal rigidity to the shield wall (upper line). The opposite, which is the usual assumption (lower line, does not properly support the left part of the shield which tends to give way under pressure.

Fig. 3.1.

shield of the enemy (**Photo 3.12A**) and between the latter's shield and helmet, to either unarmoured or less armoured areas. Such were the vicinity of the lower part of the face and the lower neck, at the upper side of the ribcage, especially when *linothorax* jerkins were used instead of full metal cuirass (**Photo 3.12A**). The spearhead of the *dory* at the time of the Persian Wars must have been narrower than it had originally been, that is during the sixth century, in order to achieve better penetration, whereas the very wide base of earlier models (i.e. **Photo 3.4**) was intended to maximize wound width and bleeding and *restrict* the depth of the penetration so as to facilitate extraction of the weapon.

The *hoplon* shield – another term for the Argive shield and the origin of the name of the Hoplites – had been improved in terms of ergonomics and manufacture; its bowl was deeper and bronze-faced and so more resistant to tear from slashing weapons. Additionally, it was handier against contacting enemies, allowing the wielder actually to wear it and put his weight *in* it, to shove off opponents and also support friendlies within the phalanx when at a shove. Its carriage, especially the peculiar central armband, the *porpax*, improved it in terms of technology and handiness as well, as did the complete suspension subsystem, with the long-haul cords and bands (**Photo 3.5D**) which made the shield an expeditionary sack for utensils and supplies when on campaign, wearable as a backpack.

A leaf-bladed straight, cut-and-thrust sword replaced the longer, straight or triangular one of the geometric era as slash-and-thrust sidearm (**Photo 3.9B, C** respectively). A concave curved sabre, the *Kopis* ('cleaver') possibly came into fashion at roughly the same time (Snodgrass 1967; Anderson 1991). The *kopis* could be mass produced and was intended for slashing blows with less dexterity and skill, especially in a vertical or diagonal direction against enemies bereft of heavy headgear. In its most advanced, forward-curved version (**Photo 3.9A**) it allowed a thrusting blow by skirting the upper face and rim of the Hoplite shield, thus targeting the face of the enemy with minimal warning. It also could be driven behind the shield by a diagonal thrust up and forward, piercing either the neck or the upper torso (Kambouris 2000).

The Hoplite phalanx which emerged triumphant in Thermopylae and Plataea was more than an assembly of Hoplites. Collectivity and co-ordination are quintessential for a phalanx, outputting much more than the sum of the parts – a real synergy. Such collective action demanded a very high degree of familiarization among troops, as seen in contemporary re-enactment experiments, drills and exercises. Thus, the phalanx was not a well-dressed assembly of troops, but a precisely (*sensu lato*) positioned entity, the precision all the more important in case of shoving or manoeuvring. The Hoplite had to know, feel and create empathy with the troops surrounding him, and thus the positions were set within a phalanx and

Photo 3.9. Different eras and models of Hoplite swords (B, C) and sabre (A). (*Left: Copyrights: Association of Historical Studies "KORYVANTES" - koryvantes.org; Right: Courtesy of Association of Historical Studies "KORYVANTES". Photo: A.Haimantas*)

altered only during drill and transformations. A century later Xenophon declares that Spartan peers were the only Hoplites trained to fight in phalanx next to any of their peers (Xen Lac Pol 11.7) and that they could manoeuvre in combat, changing front, depth and density in a way simply impossible for other Hoplite forces.

The above mentioned drill changes the relative positions of individual Hoplites within a phalanx and is practical only with warriors able to fight effectively in the vicinity of any of their peers, or at the very least of a rather large selection of their peers. The argument that follows predicts that a phalanx of a certain city or community may become with training and drill a rock-solid formation, or even a nimble and somewhat flexible, still solid, formation. But a phalanx of different states fighting next to each other is another thing altogether. This might have been a valid reason for numerous Hoplite defeats: especially in the years of the Ionic Revolt, posting Hoplites of different contingents, which had never trained together and perhaps each group were using different tactics (depth and density, mode of advance) might have invited defeat.

Accordingly, it should be noted that three out of four successful major engagements of Hoplites during the Persian Wars were accomplished by homogenous, single-state phalanxes. In Marathon, it was the Athenian phalanx, with just 10 per cent Plataeans at the far left (Her VI.111; Just II.9; Nepos Milt V). In Thermopylae, Leonidas was rotating city contingents in a very narrow front (Her VII.212), allowing them to fight each by themselves. And the massive battle of Plataea was decided by two separate actions: the Athenian phalanx tackling the Medizing Greeks and the Spartan taking on the Orientals; the small Tegean contingent was accustomed to fighting by the Spartans, while at the same time it was tiny and set, it too, at the extreme left of the Spartan line (Her IX.28).

Then why field Hoplite armies of multiple contingents? For numbers. A Greek phalanx may carry all before it and win the day promptly by shock: either by massive spearing or by the collision of its first line with the opponent's. If neither happens or neither proves decisive, the orthodox approach is the concerted shoving action of the whole phalanx, which concentrates the weight of the whole of the file onto the shield of the file leader. It is the shove (*othismos*), which performs miracles, but needs some time to take effect and also needs the greatest possible density and depth. To achieve this, a finite number of troops will present a rather short phalanx. In such a case the opposing formation may envelop the wings and launch flank or even rear attacks, destroying the phalanx before the greater depth can be brought to tell. This fact puts great importance on the size of a phalanx, especially in symmetrical clashes; the sales-pitch for the phalanx, that it was a formation where few could overcome many, applied mainly to asymmetrical engagements, against non-Hoplite assemblies and troops. Then it was another story: a phalanx was needed to counter a phalanx.

Mobility supreme

The new, better, closely fitting and more protective greaves (**Photo 3.10A**) increased the mobility in rough terrain and the protection from missiles when the formation advanced, compared to the shorter previous models (**Photo 3.10B**). The new, semi-open helmets like the Chalcidian model (**Photos 3.10C** and **3.5A**) increased awareness, which seems a no-need in the confines of a phalanx, but becomes a must whenever concerted, co-ordinated action is at a premium. Combined with the linothorax, which was occasionally stiffened with metal additions such as scales (**Photo 3.11**), the sum allowed more flexibility, manoeuvrability and mobility in general, which translate into capability for mobile tactics, at least for a portion of the troops.

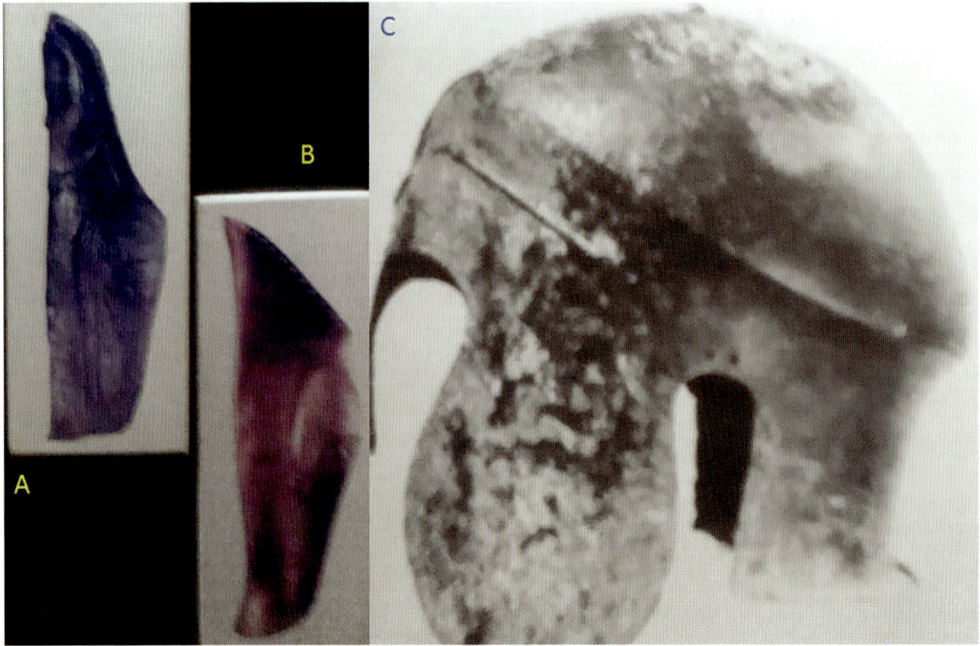

Photo 3.10. Greaves (A,B) and helmet (C) from the Athens War Museum. (*Photo courtesy: Maj General HA-Ret Papathanasiou B.*)

Thus, the standardization recedes. Young troops are trained for extreme mobility, to rush to the charge so as to shirk aimed volleys of arrows by marring the distance estimation in both direct and indirect shooting and to deny the enemy time for more volleys. They are the *Ekdromoi*, which will become renowned in the 4th century by Xenophon, but must have started their drill as early as the late 6th century. The Ekdromoi are the younger Hoplites, usually 20–30 years of age, (Xen Hell V.4,40 & IV.5,15; Sekunda 1986), able to charge at a run, as the one attested in Marathon and practised in the guise of *Hoplitodromos* since 520 BC at the Olympic Games and other Panhellenic festivities and sports events (Sekunda 2000 & 2002; Sage 1996; Sweet 1987). They may have adopted lighter body armour, such as *linothorax* (**Photo 3.12A**), jerkins (**Photo 3.5E**) or no body armour at all (**Photo 3.5G**) to gain additional mobility. As the evolved, lightened kit, exemplified by linothorax, is represented since the mid-6th century on pottery, one may doubt the causality of the changes; the new fashion was much cheaper, easy to store and much more comfortable. Still, the Persian danger at least accelerated ongoing developments towards more mobile tactics.

Photo 3.11. Two Hoplites (A, B) with transverse-crested helmets indicating Lacedaimonian high-rank officers; metal cuirass (A), *linothorax* with copper scales (B) and a Thracian peltast javelineer (C). (*Copyrights: Association of Historical Studies "KORYVANTES" – koryvantes.org*)

The Specialists return

The phalanx is an offensive and a defensive formation, the competent use of which requires excellent commanders and decently trained men. Still, a conquering phalanx does little more than disrupt the enemy formation. To increase the loss exchange, the winner will ultimately engage in close-quarters combat with the vanquished (Plato Laches 5), but from an advantageous position. This close-quarters battle, reminiscent of the highly dexterous heroes of the past, is a personal matter – at least in Athens. The *Hoplomachoi* (literary 'Weapons-fighter') are the Close-Quarter-Battle instructors (Sekunda 2000 & 1998; Anderson 1991; Krentz 1985) who teach, for a handsome fee, the proper use of shield, sword and spear, their combinations, proper moves with and without them, evasions, parries and so many more intricacies (**Photo 3.12**).

The catch is that men trained adequately in such combat may prove unwilling to remain within the phalanx where success and failure – which means death –

Photo 3.12. Hoplites sparring. (*Copyrights: Association of Historical Studies "KORYVANTES" - koryvantes.org*)

are out of their control as they depend on sheer luck and on concerted action. It is a return of the Hero and thus Plato vehemently opposes and discourages such practices with the doubtful argument that the Spartans do not allow such ilk to teach to Lacedaimon; nor even to enter the borders (Plato Laches 6). This is a rather misguided conclusion: during the Persian Wars the late phases of all land actions and of some sea actions degenerated into confined CQB fighting and not sustained solid-phalanx engagements. In these conditions the Greek Hoplites had better weapons, training and skills and engaged with an advantage; after all, the Athenians introduced the skill topic into the syllabus of the reshuffled Ephebeia in 337 BC (Recaldin 2011). The Spartans had introduced, at the end of the 5th century, the Laconian blade, an extra-short sword (practically a dirk) requiring close proximity and utmost dexterity in its use (Plut Apoph VI & LXIX). This begs the assumption that they drove CQB gurus away because they did not *need* them as they were already masters of such skills themselves (Krentz 198); and because they were fearful of their expert prying eyes.

Professional, mercenary Hoplites were the last phase of the Hoplite Epos, closing full circle. Starting with the voluntary military service of the 4th century for imperial campaigns by both Athens and Sparta, the expertise in the new set of skills became once more the property of the few; civic bodies of full-time soldiers, the Elites or Picked ones (*Epilektoi*) appear once more after 418 BC at the very latest (Thuc V.72,3). Actually, even at the heyday of the Citizen-Hoplite, in the Persian Wars, mercenaries were available in mainland Greece, and some went to seek employment by Xerxes (Her VIII.26). It is the dislike of the era for such practices and the lack of cash that prohibited wider use of such services from the Greek side; still, one can doubt whether the political correctness of some narrators would have allowed the transmission of such stories of mercenary virtue. After all, Herodotus clearly states that the Cretans sent no help to the imperiled mainlanders (Her VII.171), but this obviously refers to allied troops dispatched under state sponsorship. It by no means extends to mercenary or even volunteer contingents which could well fit with the testimony of Ktesias (FgrHist688F13.146–8) for Cretan archers fighting for the Greek Alliance in Salamis.

The Hoplite could take on any troop type in a field action. He was at his best if supported by cavalry and missile troops, but was often used exclusively. This ability, to face any opponent, defeated the purpose of using them with other troop types. He was the quintessence of standardization and equality; and the ability to afford the attire provided civic rights and defined the constitutional status of the states raising and fielding him and with different results in different cases (Hanson 1983 & 1999).

All told, the Hoplite was a thing of the past, established and well-known. The Persian Sparabara was a novelty, bringing a new operational context, the really massive archery (Snodgrass 1967). But after the first encounters in the mid-6th century, the Hoplites evolved rapidly to cope with the Persian threat. As stated above, the main changes were:

(1) The development of new skills and tactics, such as the running charge, which was made possible by the introduction of *hoplitodromos*, a feature of athletic festivities since the late 6th century and
(2) The modification of the Hoplite kit, especially shield, helmet, sword and cuirass, for more mobile tactics.

Beyond the phalanx

All the above does not mean that the Hoplite was preferably deployed alone, especially in major actions. True, mercenary Hoplites (the original form) were contracted alone, without support elements and arms; this remained so for 200 years or more. Additionally, seldom, if ever, other troop types of mainland Greece are known to have served as mercenaries abroad. But this had been so because their employers usually operated adequate light infantry, missile troops and cavalry of their own, or were hiring them from other sources. The mercenary market for the Hoplites was always the same: a need for heavy, shock infantry to support or spearhead other, more mobile but less protected and steadfast troop types. This does not mean that there were no other troop types at home; it does mean though that the Hoplite reigned supreme.

Before the Persian Wars the Greek cavalry made it into legend and excellent scholarship tackled the issue adequately (Gaebel 2004; Spence 1993; Bugh 1988). There are areas in Asia Minor, in Italy and in Sicily where Greek colonies had been credited with excellence in mounted warfare. Both *Magna Grecia* and Sicily had adopted the Hoplite as the main warrior type and still operated effective and massive cavalry arms; the example being Syracuse, with its cavalry winning the day at the battle of Himera, 480 BC (Diod XI.25,1 & XI.21,2 & XI.22,1). There is no conceivable reason to deny the same for mainland Greece whenever and wherever the conditions had been favourable. Actually, the Thessalians and the Boeotians (both Aeolians by race) had decent cavalry arms and a campaign was launched by the Allies to fend off Thessaly from the Persian invasion and thus recruit a considerable cavalry arm (Her VII.173). Despite such intentions, the Persian diplomacy prevented the alignment of both areas with the Greek Alliance, thus writing off any prospect for a worthwhile cavalry arm. The remainder of the Alliance fielded only token cavalry formations, as were the 100 Athenian cavalry, led by Cimon, son of Miltiades, who boarded the triremes first, after offering to Athena the reins of his horse and taking an Argive shield to fight as a marine (Plut Vit Cim V.2). As a result, the only viable option for the defence of Greece on land was dismounted, infantry warfare; in that function, there were available superb Hoplites and a collection of mediocre light troops (mostly javelineers), who were definitely inferior in numbers, if not also in quality when compared with the vast arrays of javelineers available to – and employed by – the Empire

The notion of a one-dimensional way of warfare for the Greeks is due to some extent to Herodotus. While he never states so, he has Mardonius delivering a notorious speech criticizing both the Greek propensity for bloody outbursts of strife and border conflict and the semi-formalized form of warfare that decides issues quickly but with considerable bloodshed (Her VII.9). Starting from this, the Athenian-centric scholarship maintains that this semi-formalized, practically ritualistic kind of Hoplite warfare was the norm. This bloody ritual involved Hoplite phalanxes operating under strict knightly rules – a prequel of medieval warfare amongst knights, minus the concept of the Lance and the presence of the Sergeant. The essence of Greek warfare remained unaltered until a revolution in military affairs during the Great Peloponnesian War. This line of thought (Sekunda 1986) places the introduction of hit-and-run peltast warfare to the Greeks as late as the mid-5th century, during the Athenian expansion in the Macedonian-Thracian region, exemplified by the defeat at Drabescus (Thuc I.100,3) and a second contact during the Archidamian War, in 430 BC at Spartolus (Thuc II.79,4–5). Such concepts were integrated into the Athenian war machine by 425 BC in Sphacteria (Thuc IV.32,2–3) and evolved to their highest with Iphicrates (Xen Hell IV.5,13 & IV.8,34 & 37) in 390 BC.

This had never been so. The ritual mentioned was similar to modern international laws of war, not to the rules of a game of football. They were meant to contain atrocities, although with limited success – not unlike modern efforts along the same lines. The ritualistic clash never happened, but by convention – not unlike the mutual abstaining from the use of chemical weapons during the Second World War. Herodotus' account is full of stratagems and ruses, where the Spartans excel (Her VI.77–8), but others also make do. The example of Phoceans against the Thessalians (Her VIII.27–8) is quite enlightening. Additionally, Thucydides refers to Chalcidian peltasts off Spartolus, in 430 BC and the local peltasts in Amphipolis, in 422 BC (Thuc II.79,4–5 and V.10,9 respectively) who dealt heavy blows to the Athenians. But the Theban peltasts did so in Delium in 424 BC (IV.93,3) and Thebes at the time had nothing to do with Macedon or Thrace. Athenian light infantry in Sphacteria, one year before, was not Thracian-type peltasts (**Photo 3.11C**), nor were the Aetolians who smashed an Athenian expedition in 427 BC.

Furthermore, there is nothing in Herodotus' account to dismiss the existence of Greek light infantry, nor to indicate doctrinal or ideological disinclination to employ it, or lack of operational know-how. On the contrary, the reference that Spartan Helots were the only light troops adequately armed for proper operational use (Her IX.29,1) indicates intentional, planned and not *ad hoc* deployment of a massive light infantry arm, understanding of the peculiarities of such troops and adequacy of armament. The latter implies proper *kopis* sabres of fine Spartan steel as sidearms instead of agricultural tools (i.e. axes, cleavers) and fighting javelins instead of hunting ones. Furthermore, even the sub-standard armament of the light troops of other city-states, which are explicitly earmarked for combat despite their deficiencies, shows clearly a universal understanding of light infantry operations and their integration in an expeditionary doctrine by all the Greek states. Be their role actual fighting, skirmishing or simply plundering, reducing and devastating the enemy territory, the Call to Arms was, for every Greek male, a functional combat, not a mere support slot (provisioning, engineering, repairs, MedEvac).

Modern warfare instead of rituals

The campaign of 479 BC to expel the Persians from the mainland, with its moves, countermoves and manoeuvres, with the arguments and intentions, shows a mature concept of warfare where battles are instrumental but not necessary events. Similarly, despite some obvious failures as in Thermopylae, the campaigns of 480 BC are exemplary regarding the conduct of flexible positional/territorial warfare, which was the only possible solution due to the vast imbalance of power and strategic mobility. These remarks can be integrated into the fragmental accounts of Herodotus on the third Messenian war that erupted in 464 BC (Her IX.64). So, a picture emerges, that of continuous employment of the principles of modern territorial warfare all the way to the start of the Great Peloponnesian war; a picture alien to ritualistic clashes of phalanxes. After all, it is probable that Herodotus projects his own thoughts about the prevalence of Hoplite warfare instead of territorial warfare as the most suitable way for the armed settling of differences between Greeks, by narrating alleged Mardonius' arguments to Xerxes (Her VII.9). This shows a clear grasp of the principles, requirements, advantages and disadvantages of territorial warfare by both the historian and his audience and may constitute an insinuation for the operations developing at his time. It is either irony or poetic justice that the campaign of Xerxes, and that of Mardonius, suffered greatly due to the imaginative application of territorial warfare practices.

The latter are not a myth, nor a retro-projection (Lazenby 1993). They did occur, possibly – but not certainly – in a way similar to what we reconstruct in retrospect, but this conformity might not have been the norm. As we observe today, operations within the same theatre of war may not develop identically and may take different forms, not just the most modern or the most current or common; we should extend the concept to times past. The occasional clash would have developed as a function of the level of technology, society and intellect, but also of the personal, political or ideological affections and preferences of the main players involved (leaders or civic bodies).

Heavy infantry was decisive. Its clash determined the victor in a set-piece battle and all other events and results were confirmed or nullified by the result of the phalanx clash. The verdict of a Hoplite clash was final, but this was also an ideal outcome. There have been battles where the verdict of the heavy infantry was overruled by other arms, although mostly at a later date. And of course, not all battles were set-piece. Carian Hoplites exterminated a Persian contingent during the Ionic Revolt by a brilliant night ambush (Her V.121) and so did the Phocians against a Thessalian onslaught some generations back (Her VIII.28).

In short, heavy infantry and cavalry (if available) cost much and caught the public eye in parades, public speech and argumentation much more than more humble arms. Catching the lights of publicity and being a symbol of power and martial virtue has always been a factor in developing an arm/branch, according to vogue and technology. Tanks and jets are the most trendy weapon systems today, but that does not mean that other ones are berated or of limited importance. This was the case during the Persian Wars as well.

Box 3.1

Xenophon offers a possible and plausible explanation for the takabara, that has not been adequately explored previously. The fictious character of *Cyropaedeia* makes his assertions debatable, especially as they sound very much like projections of Sparta. Still, he provides some interesting details: at his time the Persian nation was made up of 120,000 Persians (Xen Cyrop I.2,15), although whether this incudes only full citizens (*mariaka* being excluded) and what age-classes is not clear. These are divided into twelve tribes (Cyrop I.2,5), although Herodotus (I.125) enumerates only nine. Each tribe was further divided horizontally in four age-classes: boys, youths, adults, elders. (Cyrop I.2,4).

There is also a division in social classes, although Xenophon does not elaborate on the latter and implies just two classes, enfranchised and disenfranchised Persian nationals (Cyrop I.2,15). The criterion was family income adequate for a boy to follow the public schooling. Graduation was prerequisite for enlisting the youths so as to be eligible for full citizenship (ibid). Becoming a youth at age 16–17 (Cyrop I.2,8) meant a ten-year military service as standing army, and expeditionary forces and garrisons were routinely manned by such youths (Cyrop I.2,9) who were archers/spearmen (i.e. sparabari), but also learned the Persian *palton* double-use javelin (Cyrop I.2,9), so as to serve as cavalry, obviously if they could afford a mount or get subsidized. Their deployment is at a 50 per cent of their total force in a rotational basis (Cyrop I.2,9). Once the ten-year tour of duty was over they were full Persian adults/citizens, liable for mobilization for 25 years (Cyrop I.2,13), following which they entered the Elders (Cyrop I.2,13).

The Adults, when mobilized, for home or expeditionary duty, were not archers (Cyrop I.2,13). Xenophon mentions they were close-combat fighters, using sabre, shield and being endowed with cuirass (ibid). It is explicitly stated that their shield is as depicted in contemporary art (ibid), which rather settles the issue for the identity of the takabara as depicted in Greek art. Additionally, the mention of cuirasses (ibid) allows a plausible identification of the takabara with the Persian cuirassiers (Her VIII.113,2). Xenophon does not mention spears, but does not exclude them, as he does with bows and javelins (Cyrop I.2,13). Thus, spears may be within the arsenal of the takabara, as they are a prestigious weapon among the Achaemenids, since it is used by the Guards of the King and his representatives, the satraps. Under this light, the possibility that the spear is artistic license by the Greek pottery-makers is unwarranted.

Still, other troop types WERE berated at the time. This had much to do with politics, especially in oligarchies. The aristocracy, and later the middle class as well, probably did frown upon the lower classes in social and martial terms. The same held true with the medieval knights and their contempt for the infantry; still, the medieval battle cell, the *Lance*, included infantrymen and entrusted them with vital duties and responsibilities. The conclusion is that both the alleged unavailability of and contempt for non-Hoplite infantry by the Greek communities of the time may have been current or historical projection and misunderstanding; or a social reality, perhaps due to prejudice among classes and parties. It may have been a retrospective interpretation of events and attitudes due to the realities and realizations catalyzed by the Great Peloponnesian War which were developing while Herodotus and others were creating their works. But it also may have not been so after all, or, at least, not so much so.

Chapter 4

The Geopolitical Frustration of Darius I

The main enemy of the Greek independence had been the Persian monarch Darius I, third or rather fourth monarch of the Persian imperial throne and first of his name. He was a pure eastern despot, cruel, efficient, capable, greedy and insatiable, who changed thoroughly the character of the empire he acquired and initiated the renowned dynasty of Achaemenids (Burn 1962). 'Acquisition' is the term to cover the double event of inheriting and usurping the throne, while 'initiation' implies that the Dynasty, contrary to Darius' allegations, had not been the same before him.

The Persian past

Briefly, the empire was founded by Cyrus II, born a petty noble, son of a Persian aristocrat, probably named Cambyses and possibly a vassal king to the Median emperor; and of the daughter of the Median Emperor Astyages (Her I.107 & 113). The Median kingdom, in tandem with the (neo)Babylonian one, emerged from the cinders of the Assyrian Empire (Her I.106) and had been weakened by a Scythian invasion (Her J.104). Thus Cyrus, leading a persistent rebellion campaign beset with reverses (Polyaen VII.6,1 & 9), finally overthrew the ruling emperor – his grandfather Astyages – and inverted the tribal social *status quo*, making the Median Empire Persian (Her I.127 &130 & 210). This might have been a bit more complicated. Unobserved by Herodotus, there was another, third ethnicity in the hard nucleus of the Persian Empire. It was the ancient Elam, in Greek usually called Cissia or Susiana, which was only one half of it. Its importance is obvious, in context, by the fact that one of the three imperial capitals under Darius and his successors, Susa, was here. The others were Ecbatana in Media, and Persepolis in Persis.

Elam's two main areas were divided by the Zagros range; Anshan east of Zagros, an area roughly surrounding the city Anshan; and Susiana (Shushan) west, around the city of Susa (Potts 2005; Waters 2011). The western part was in close contact with Babylon and was fairly recently crushed by Assur-banipal, Emperor of Assyria. This allowed the Persians, an Aryan race who were quietly living further east from the Zagros as vassals or rather subjects of different distant overlords, such as Assyria, to eventually veer to independence after the destruction and division of Assyria between Media and Babylon. Subsequently, with Babylon ruling – or suppressing – Susiana, the Persians assimilated the eastern Elam, the Anshan, by infiltration and intermingling and aryanized it. Cyrus II, the Great, had an Elamite name, from his father an Anshanite (Potts 2005; Waters 2004) and the first royal robe was used to signify his rule over the Persian Empire was the old elamite robe of days past (Sekunda & Chew 1992). By a velvet assimilation, the Persian-Elamite factor, which was vassal to the Medes after the fall of Assyria, eventually rebelled and defeated the Medes and then incorporated them (Llewellyn-Jones 2012; Henkelman 2011a), but never quite assimilated them. The lack of evidence regarding the religious beliefs of Cyrus II implies either a milder Mithraistic (Soudavar 2012) or a non-Zoroastrian, Elamite set of religious beliefs (Farahmand 2015; Henkelman 2011a), in stark contrast with Darius' vehement Mazdaic Zoroastrianism (Soudavar 2012).

Subsequently, Cyrus furthered his acquisitions and not only met head-on the invasion of his western neighbour, Croesus of Lydia, who ruled central and western Asia Minor and stopped him cold, (Her I.76) but with a brilliant out-of-season campaign invaded the Lydian territory (Her I.79), defeated the limited number of Home Troops Croesus was able to muster on the spot (ibid) and occupied the Lydian Capital, Sardis (Her I.84). Subsequently, he also conquered the subjects to the Lydian throne, the Greek cities of Asia Minor, while some of the nearby islands, which were not subjects of the Lydians, succumbed voluntarily, without suffering any assault, utterly terrified (Her I.161 & 169).

Cyrus then turned his attention to the other powerful state of the area: Babylon. The Median alliance with Babylon and the bad blood between Mesopotamia and Elam made the clash between Cyrus and Babylon a geopolitical necessity if observed in retrospect. Babylon succumbed after a relatively brief campaign (Her I.191), proving more vulnerable from within (Lazenby 1993) than Lydia, possibly due to the Jewish community allegedly assimilated by the Babylonians due to the Babylonian Exile. This aspect of the conquest, important though not unique for the success of the Persians, may be substantiated by the extreme generosity, seemingly unwarranted, of Cyrus to the Jews (Holland 2005; Lazenby 1993), who pronounced him Chosen and Marked by Jehovah (Isaiah 45,1). This interaction brought about the massive Jewish return to Palestine (Ezra 4,1–2). The issue was to have several new episodes; the term *Marked* is the one translated to Greek as *Christos*–Christ, while the pompous statements that Jehovah would open the gates of enemy cities for Cyrus to enter and level everything before him (Isaiah 45,2–3) read rather as a reminder than as a promise. In the cruel and real world, emperors do not grant wishes to their subjects for the *expectation* of their assistance (in person, by proxy, through influence or by their deities). The emperors simply grant *rewards* for solid accomplishments in their name. It is no surprise that this debt was finally settled by Darius I, an emperor advertising rewards to be expected for good services (DB 63), who saw the task of the Jewish repatriation fulfilled (Ezra 4,24) despite his open enmity to Cyrus II (Soudavar 2012); this may imply a repeat performance of service to the throne, possibly for the recapture of the city.

After Babylon, Cyrus was to engage the third and final hostile empire, the Egyptians. But first, he turned to the east, either to expand or to stabilize his rule in Bactria and Sogdiana, along with other areas of central Asia (Her I.153). There, despite his success, death struck him down while fighting against the indomitable Scythians (Her I.214). His son and heir Cambyses, after a viceroyal sojourn and actual training in administrative tasks in Babylon, turned his head west. Under his rule the Persians for the first time delivered submission by conquest (not by convention) across the sea, sacking the Greek island of Samos (Her III.139). A result of the initiative and greed of the local Satrap of Sardis, the rather mutinous Oreites (Her III.125 & 126) and of the brewing internal strife within the island (Her III.140 & 143), it was no small feat.

Samos, under the autocrat Polycrates, was a wealthy and prosperous pirate state (Her III.39) ruling the waves, excelling in eastern trade and Aegean commerce and achieving some illustrious feats of engineering: such as the magnificent aqueduct of Eupalinus, the temple of Hera (Her III.60) and the great breakwater; all leading to a school of exceptional engineers, one of whom was to build the bridges over the Bosporus for Darius' invasion to Scythia (Her IV.87) in mid-510s BC.

This island had at the time a sizable and ultra-modern navy (Her III.39 & 44), following an established tradition in matters concerning naval innovation (Thuc I.13,3). Moreover, a massive archer corps (for Greek standards) of 1,000, recruited among Samians themselves (Her III.45) was available to enforce the sovereign's will at home and assist in war, topping the massive mercenary contingents (Her III.45). The powerful island had spectacularly endured a Spartan-led siege (Her III.56), possibly undertaken to tear off a maritime vassal from the grasp of the Persian throne. Sparta had opened an account with the latter during Cyrus' reign. Incidentally, this endeavour – and intention – was falling in line with Sparta's attempts to expel tyrants (Thuc I.18,1); at least the ones prone to incubate problems in the future, especially if combined with Persian imperialism or interventionism. Still, with the head of state removed in Cambyses' time, Samos fell to the Persians and a bloody fall it was (Her III.147). It was also swift and final, taking place during the early reign of Darius I (Her III.140), with strife claiming a role (Her III.142–144) and a toll (Her III.143).

But Cambyses' sights were set S-SW. The Phoenician states submitted willingly, providing him with a fleet, followed by Cyprus (Her III.19), which seceded from the brief Egyptian rule (Her II.182) and turned happily against the previous master. After striking a pact with the Arabs to the S-SE of Phoenicia (Her III.4 & III.7), Cambyses was able to invade Egypt and occupy it with less difficulty than expected (Her III.11–13). Making Memphis his base of operations (Her III.25), he ventured westwards and southwards.

His westward expeditionary force was eliminated, swallowed by the desert while trying to reach and raze Siwa (Her III.26). Still, he accepted the capitulation of Libya and Cyrene (Her III.13 & IV.165) making of them vassals by convention. There, his westward progress stopped. His voluntary Phoenician subjects flatly declined to campaign against Carthage; and, despite his terrible temper, Cambyses accepted such gross insubordination, to the point of mutiny, and delivered no punishment whatsoever (Her III.19).

In here lies a little problem: the Phoenician squadrons were by no means the only fleet of Cambyses, even with the addition of the Cypriot ones. Herodotus knows it and scolds the balance of the imperial navy as incapable of serious endeavours (Her III.19). This might not be so. Cambyses had the whole of Asia Minor under his command and fleets from the Hellespont and the whole Mediterranean coast up to and including Cilicia could have been mustered. It is true that the main Ionian and Aeolian fleets were coming from the islands and less so from the east shore of the Aegean, but this was a later development (Her IV.97 & IV.138 & VI.8). And this did not apply to Lycians, Pamphylians, Cilicians, nor to Carians and Hellespontines (Her VII.91–2 &95). Moreover, the islanders, either under a pact with Cambyses or still under the provisions of the Convention with Cyrus, *did* furnish ships: Polycrates' contribution of 40 triremes (a staggering 8,000 citizens) was an example of the former, and the massacred Lesbian messenger ship at Memphis an example of the latter (Her III.44 &14 respectively). Under Xerxes, the Phoenician and Egyptian squadrons were less than half the fleet; with Cypriot squadrons added, they were just over half, 650 out of 1207 ships of the line (Her VII.89–90). Thus Cambyses should have had considerable naval resources without the Phoenicians. It must have been their *wrath*, touching on some leverage unknown to us, not their *essentiality*, that made him abort the campaign against Carthage without extracting vengeance.

Whatever the reasons for aborting the campaign against Carthage, Cambyses himself pushed south towards Ethiopia with a substantial part of his army, but met with a bloody failure (Her III.25). Or that is what Herodotus says. Persian sources imply a limited but important Nubian conquest with the Cushites (Cush being the Nubia of the Greeks) mentioned as a subject people and an outpost established at Elephantine (Klotz 2015; Holland 2005). More importantly, Herodotus' account of the host of Xerxes clearly includes the Nubian Ethiopians (Her VII.69) and assigning their conquest to Xerxes' campaign of 484 BC to quell the Egyptian rebellion (Her VII.7) is a bit far-fetched. Finally, and most importantly, the annual tribute to Darius as described by Herodotus himself (III.97) mentions the tax quota of Nubian *Ethiopians* (tax payable in kind) and obviously refers to their subjugation by Cambyses.

The failure story, an Egyptian view no doubt, but accepted as a lore by Darius I, records a disaster a little after covering the 20–25 per cent of the distance from Thebes to Ethiopia (Her III.25). Thus, the correct reading is of a bloody failure in terms of objectives but with considerable territorial gains southward, gains expensive in troops, morale and treasure.

And at this point, things all started going wrong for Cambyses. Herodotus states that he misunderstood a religious festival in Egypt as jubilation for his defeat and commited atrocities against the population (III.27–30). But Cambyses' ill-fame obviously came through the Persian aristocracy down to the days of Herodotus, and may have something to do with his social programme of forswearing taxation throughout the empire, possibly – or rather probably – extended to include the recently occupied Egypt (Klotz 2015), or, less probably, starting from there. This was a fatal blow to the Egyptian clergy and Theocracy, definitively strongly contested by them and possibly harshly imposed by Cambyses, who wished to sap and disprove them (Her III.37). Violent measures might have been taken indeed, but to a lesser extent, and in a targeted manner against the clergy. As Holland (2005) points out, some sources disprove the popular story about his patent lack of respect for the *Apis* bull, while he admittedly paid all due respect to Neith, (the Egyptian Goddess related to Greek Athena), patron of the city of Sais and of the last native dynasty emerging (Klotz 2015).

It was not a matter of romanticism; Cambyses had fewer quarrels with the Egyptian religion than anticipated; one indication is that he had taken to heart an oracle by such source (Her III.64). His quarrel had been with the clergy that guided the population spiritually and politically and was capable of instigating resistance or rebellion; it was also absorbing vast state resources, and so could cause popular dissent against the ruler with the proper manipulation. The worst: the clergy paid no taxes to the throne, but collected dues from the population and possibly demanded donations from the sovereign as well. If the clergy could be disproved, taxes from its vast resources would be collected without dissension from the populace, which would breathe and pay its own, much lowered, taxes to the Persian throne without too much fuss. The balance would be excellent for both Egyptian people and Cambyses; not for the Egyptian clergy, which took on the holy mission of tainting his memory for all eternity (Klotz 2015).

The Persian aristocracy who served in the army of the Egyptian campaign and beyond was already dissatisfied due to failure, absence and casualties and must have been furious, since taxation was the basis of their income as overlords; the same applied to the Egyptian clergy, for the same reasons. On top of that, the lore of Cambyses killing without reason or trial high-class Persians (Her III.35), or killing them *to* confiscate their fortunes, sounds suspicious. It is a repetitive motto in historiography, whenever taxes are levied from higher classes that attempt with all their might (and might they usually have) to shirk paying. Among tax evasion, corruption and high treason, such attitudes are harshly dealt with, as an example to others. The story of Robin Hood, the story of a disenchanted aristocrat persecuted by a tax-imposing, control-minded sovereign, should be brought to mind. Cambyses might have had a double policy of taxing the Persian aristocracy – incidentally, Darius, the ultimate tax-hunter, exempted Persia proper from taxation (Her III.97) – and of relaxing taxation and recruitment of subject peoples. Had he implemented it, he would have preceded Alexander the Great in provisioning for his subjects. He did precede him in suffering from slander and probably in suffering attempts against his life. The Persian aristocracy, by default speaking for the Persian nation not necessarily with the latter's sanctioning, did not like this concept at all (Malye 2007).

Cambyses was away from home for too long and decided to return as omens were not very favourable. If a social reshuffle was attempted in Egypt, it was his idea and making. If another was intended for the empire, it *might* have been his idea. It is a bit difficult to locate the site of all the atrocities cited by Herodotus (III.30–5). When in Memphis, with brewing resistance and some failed campaigns, did he have time to spare, not just to commit murders of noblemen – that might have been so – but to indulge in marital dramas (Her III.31–2)? Had he carried through the desert his wife and household in Egypt? Where did he have the Persian nobles executed? In Memphis? Herodotus never states it; we are left to our own devices and *suppose* so. Our argument for Memphis is that he had no chance to see his capital(s) again, according to Herodotus; Ktesias, though, has him dying in Babylon (Ktesias 14).

On his way home, in Syria, under mysterious conditions the monarch was wounded; a self-inflicted wound due to a spontaneous failure of the sheath of his dirk, which festered and became fatal, reeking pus and, most of all, conspiracy: a clean, accidental wound by a sheathed weapon (Her III.64) had no real reason to fester. There is no mention of an official second-in-command, nor of anyone stepping up to lead the decapitated army home. But a second-rate aristocrat and guardsman emerged: Darius, son of a certain Hystaspes (DB 2; Her I.209 & III.70), a somewhat important nobleman (Hyland 2018), probably of a priestly family (Soudavar 2012) and without any claim to the throne of Cyrus himself. He was the spawn of another, distant branch of the royal family, ruling the Parsa province of the Persian kingdom (Cyrus' branch had been lording over Anshan). Darius somehow was found to command the support of the expeditionary force of the Egyptian campaign (Holland 2005). An innovative interpretation of the Iranian sources explains the facts by actually adopting Darius' claims and interpreting the dynastic orthodoxy among the Persians as being basically Achaemenid, with Cyrus II being a digression (Soudavar 2012) and Darius achieving a re-alignment. This explains well the devotion of the conscripted nobles of the army, whose factual support is never mentioned, nor ever recited, but becomes evident in the eradication of the massive wave of nine rebellions which followed Darius' coronation. It took 19 battles fought victoriously either in person or by proxies in just two years (DB 52; Sekunda 1989).

Herodotus' storyline has Darius and the army vanish for some months after the demise of Cambyses; the former went home and after some months, for no special reason, left Persia, the seat of his father (Her III.70), and reached Susa in western Elam (Sushan). Smerdis, or Bardiya by DB 10, or Tanyoxarces as by Ktesias (Photius Bibl LXXII), the younger brother of Cambyses, had been declared king by succession and was enforcing the programme of easing taxation and forfeiting recruitment for three years (Her III.67). As already said, that may have been his brother's idea, or his own. Darius found some other partisans, Persian aristocrats (Her III.70, DB 68), of course, of the highest order. He tempted them, possibly by the triple motive of foregoing the taxation imposed on their class by (Pseudo) Smerdis (DB 14); of participating in a greater conspiracy organized by their class to get rid of the two kingly siblings, a conspiracy brewed within the army in Egypt; and of following someone who had either a mandate from that very army, or a hand in the death of Cambyses, or, most probably, both, *plus* a certain claim to the throne (Soudavar 2012).

The notional number Seven is a religious choice (i.e. number of days in a week) and the actual number of conspirators would have been managed to satisfy it and provide a sense of divine providence to the coup retrospectively. As *Ahura mazda* had six divine sparks /archangels, the *Amesha Spenta*, to fight the Darkness (Boyce 1983) so did his human representative. Darius had six lieutenants (DB 68) – not comrades, the distinction is very crucial – to help him conquer the Darkness of the imposter and fulfill his divine mission (DB 5). It might be of some significance that in his all-out effort to subjugate Greece and purge the daemons nesting in there (Holland 2005), Xerxes was commander-in-chief (*Karana*) over a panel of six marshals (Her VII.82).

Regarding the Seven Conspirators, whom Herodotus' names, i.e. Otanes, Intaphrenes, Gobryas, Megabyzus, Aspathines, Hydarnes (Her III.70) are very similar to the ones inscribed by Darius' order at the cliffs of the passage of Behistun, the Gate of Zagros: Otanes [Utâna], son of Thukhra [Thuxra]; Intaphrenes [Vidafarnâ], son of Vayâspâra; Gobryas [Gaubaruva], son of Mardonius [Marduniya]; Megabyzus [Bagabuxša], son of Dâtuvahya; Ardumaniš, son of Vakauka; Hydarnes [Vidarna], son of Bagâbigna (DB 68). There are only two obvious anomalies: the name of only one of the conspirators is not easily identifiable, Aspathines in Her III.70 and Ardumaniš in DB 68. Moreover, the name of the father of Otanes is given as Pharnaspes (Her III.70), and as Thukhra (DB 68). Contrary to this, the account of Ktesias (16) which names Onophas, Idernes, Norondabates, Mardonius, Barisses, Artaphernes, and Darius has only two names directly attributable, Idernes (Hydarnes) and Artaphrenes (Idaphrenes) plus one with a temporal error of a generation: Ktesias mentions Mardonius instead of his son Gobryas.

These details hide an important fact: the father of Otanes as declared by Herodotus (Her III.68,1) is the same as the father-in-law of Cyrus II the Great (Her II.1,1) making Otanes uncle of Cambyses. Furthermore, Otanes subsequently became Cambyses' father-in-law (Her III.68,3). Additionally, it was Otanes who exposed the usurper (Her III.69), and assembled the other conspirators (Her III.70 & III.84,1), which made him the natural leader of the coup and probably justified his aspiration to kingship. Darius was the last to join, and in Herodotus, he brushes Otanes aside in two key instances: the timing of the attack (Her III.71,2 & III.76,1) – practically meaning the whole operational planning – and the decision on the Persian constitution and statesmanship (Her III.83). As a result, Otanes resigned from any claim to the throne, in exchange for a less heavy yoke than the one prepared for the bandaka/subjects of the future King (Her III.83,2). The Behistun version was designed to cover up all such details and launch the official Darius story: the Chosen One of Ahura Mazda with his lieutenants killed the usurper and brought order and justice.

The group of conspirators, amounting to seven (Her III.70; BD 68), attempted a most daring and formidable coup. Herodotus does not mention where the conspirators intercepted the King's Court because his sources were not that explicit. He understands a royal residence, but the security described in both his own (Her III.76–8) and Ktesias' (Ktesias 16) accounts of the murder is lax at the very least. Thus, residence in a formal capital is not very plausible. Darius himself declares it was in a stronghold called Sikayauvatis, in Nisaia of Media (DB 13). One cannot conclude whether the King had been there to keep clear of his disgruntled Persian noblemen, or because the fortress was a station along the itinerary of his seasonal travel (Holland 2005), from Ecbatana to Persia (Parsagadae, most probably) or Babylon; Susa was not a royal capital yet and Persepolis had not even been planned.

The conspirators seized the moment by deciding among themselves for the next form of government, ensuring that it would be, forever, a proprietary issue between the seven through exclusive intermarriages. After some fuss, Darius became king as Darius I, introducing the dynasty of Achaemenids. Although his father's name was Hystaspes (Her I.209; DB I) and should have been used for the dynasty, Achaemenes was the ancestral link with the line of Cyrus and provided legitimacy (DB 2–4), although other, religious aspects have been proposed to explain the issue (Soudavar 2012).

Further legitimacy was provided by a fabulous story about overthrowing not the brother of Cambyses, named Smerdis, but a usurper Magus pretending to be Smerdis and of the same name. The latter was assisted by his brother Patizeithes, who was the substitute left by Cambyses in his stead (Her III.63)! The propaganda line heaped upon Cambyses the early murder of his true brother, thus besmirching his memory even more and exonerating the conspirators of regicide. The person of the King was sanctified after enthroning, *but* Magus had not been enthroned properly as he projected a fake and stolen identity. Consequently, in this case, there was no regicide….

Herodotus' account is one of many, the primary being the inscription at Behistun. It is no simple inscription, as it was carved in stone, read in the presence of Darius I (who obviously had been illiterate), copied in parchment and sent (to be proclaimed) throughout the empire (DB 70). The different accounts, with Herodotus' being in many details irreconcilable to the later account of Ktesias, the physician of the Persian court and thus with much better access to archives, say a lot about a fabricated story. The conspirators could not decide on the number and name of the alleged usurpers; Behistun mentions one, Gaumata (DB 11), Herodotus mentions two, Smerdis and his brother Patizeithes (Her III.61) and Ktesias gives the name Sphendadates. Nor on their own numbers, roles and names: the brother of Darius, Artaphrenes, later to play a most significant role in dealings with the Greeks, is omitted by Herodotus who names Darius as the killer (III.78). Herodotus' account is bolstered by the Behistun inscription (DB 13). But Artaphrenes is mentioned by other sources, and considered moreover the one who delivered the *coup de grace* to the alleged usurper (Aesch Persai 776), thus keeping Darius unblemished from any notion of regicide.

The whole thing has an Egyptian aftertaste, reminiscent of the struggle of Akenaton, a legitimate but rebellious Pharaoh, who came to blows with the then established clergies, especially that of Ammun, as he had changed his name from Ammun-hotep IV to Akenaton (EB Akhenaton 2018). Similarly, Darius' own clergy, the Aryan fire priests of Zoroaster, of whom he might have been a member (Soudavar 2012) must have come off the deepest Bactrian valleys to supplant the established guild of Magi (*Magu*). The latter practised a Mithraistic dualism and were obviously pro-Median, as they were the official clergy of the Median empire, but were also one of the six tribes of the Medes (Her I.101). This detail of the double character of the Magi, priests and tribesmen, is reminiscent of the issue of Levites, the priestly tribe of Moses' Israelites.

There was a clandestine note on Cambyses. Cyrus was the Father of the Persians, but he was half a Mede, and of royal stock at that. Moreover, his claim to Persia was as the son of the ruler of Anshan, not of Parsa. Anshan had been conquered from Elam by one Persian ancestor of Cyrus a century earlier and given to one of his two sons to rule – the other took Parsa, which is Persia proper (Holland 2005). The alternative is a *Median* infiltration in Anshan, which would explain the Herodotean account and the conspicuous lack of any mention of Anshan in Greek historic literature. It also fits well with the picture drawn by the Greek historians: Cyrus' realm was a vassal of the Median emperor, not at any point subjugated or conquered by the Medians (Soudavar 2012). Under this light, Cyrus continued to use and honour Median officials, the new *status quo* being rather a dynastic change than anything else. Cambyses might have acted, felt or been more Mede than Persian. Herodotus reveals, mostly haphazardly, at least two indications, and Diodorus adds a third.

Firstly, according to Herodotus, Cambyses, just before passing away, recited a nefarious omen he received when in Egypt. His death was foretold to occur at Ecbatana, and he erroneously understood death by old age at Ecbatana, Media. The story has problems concerning Cambyses' whereabouts at that point, but reveals that as an emperor, son of Cyrus II, he was settled in Media, not Persia nor Elam. True, Cyrus removed the Median treasure from Ecbatana and took it to Anshan, without specifics as to the city of destination. The only one fitting the puzzle is Parsagadae. This city must have been founded by Cyrus (Soudavar 2012) and there Cyrus was taking refuge from his reverses (Polyaen XII.6,9). Alexander III found the treasure there (Arr Anab III.18,10) and Cyrus' tomb was located nearby (Arr Anab VI.29,4).

The second indication is the story of Herodotus, reciting that Cambyses became aware of the coup committed by the two Magi and the Medes behind them; the pretext of the usurpation is not clear, as he was alive and kicking and with an army on the way home. When he was disabled by the accident with his dirk, he cursed the Persians should they not reclaim the supremacy and lordship. The disbelief and suspicion attested by the nobles (Her III.73) amply shows not only the strained relations between king and aristocrats, a good substrate for conspiracy and usurpation, but the likelihood of *actual* foul play by the nobles, so as to justify vindictiveness by the dying monarch. This prerogative, privy to a close circle of

Persian nobles of the army, including the spear-bearer Darius, was a constitutional blank cheque and a notion that even Cambyses declared against the Median component of the state *and* the respective 'church'/clergy, the Magi. Given the affiliations of Cambyses, as already mentioned, this story actually implies that he did not.

The indication hidden in Diodorus (XI.6,3) lies in his statement that in Thermopylae Xerxes sent as a first wave the Medes, so as to have them slaughtered and thus punished; this possibly referred to the Revolt of Phraortes, suppressed by Hydarnes and Darius (DB 24, 25, 31, 32). Additionally, a good Spartan beating would humiliate and neutralize them as a potential future threat, since the House of Darius, contrary to Cyrus, had no affiliation with Media. The suicidal order to take the Greeks alive, mentioned by Herodotus (VII.210), fits nicely; according to Herodotus (*ibid*), the Susians (Cissians) were part of this assault wave. Not accidentally, they had been amongst the first to rebel against Darius' coronation, refused Ahura Mazda as their deity and lord (DB 72, 75) and were smitten by the new Persian acolytes, who expected earthly but also after-death rewards (DB 73, 76) during a holy war against the infidels.

Thus, a Median background cannot be ruled out when considering the regime of Smerdis, fake Smerdis or true Smerdis, who might have succeeded Cambyses on his throne upon his demise or usurped him while still alive. The Median tribe of Magi (Her I, 101) were the main clergy among Persians and Medes (Her I 132 & 140). They were NOT Zoroastrians (Farahmand 2015; Soudavar 2012) and were considered the Interpreters of Truth (Her VII.19). Their latter prerogative was very dangerous for a flight of conspirators and regicides and thus they were slated for termination. As the first usurpers of the throne of Cambyses were conveniently declared Magi, they instantly became enemies of the Persian people. In a pogrom making the Sicilian Vesper sound like a brawl among chaps, they were slaughtered, changing the map of the religion of the empire as the Magi were the most prominent clergy. To safeguard the outcome, Darius declared himself the Owner of Truth (DB 55–57) and Judge of it (DB 56–64), a delegate of Ahura Mazda (DB 5). A Persian theocracy had been established to cover up a possible double regicide and usurpation, similarly to later changes of state doctrine according to political necessities and dynastic whims. A theocracy based on Bactrian and Parthian hard-core Zoroastrism and the religious prerogatives of the House of Achaemenes (Soudavar 2012); after all, Zoroaster allegedly was from Bactria (Garcia-Sanchez 2014).

Resolving and deconvolution

According to the above, a more coherent version might be that Smerdis/Bardiya/ Tanyoxarces had been appointed Satrap of conquered Bactria and other provinces, namely Chorasmia, Parthia, and Carmania, without paying tribute to the central government, headed by his father Cyrus (Ktesias 8). This means he was rather a viceroy, a member of the Trinity, along with Cambyses who was viceroy in Babylon and not a Satrap. Cyrus presided over all, seated either at Ecbatana or at Parsagadae. Much more important, Smerdis was the overlord of Parthia, which is explicitly mentioned by Darius as the satrapy of his father Hystaspes (DB 35), along with Hyrcania, which was usually considered a part of Parthia.

Cambyses was probably slain, perhaps in Babylon (Ktesias 14) but definitely out of the Medo-Persian plateau, before entering it through Behistun, by the hand of conspirators among the nobility of the army of the Egyptian campaign, who were both terrified by his gimmicks and furious over the bloodbaths of the westward and southward campaigns in Africa. Cambyses' demise happened either before or after Smerdis/Bardiya/Tanyoxarces was declared king.

This 'before or after' makes a vast difference: if Smerdis moved to kingship *before* his brother had died, he would have been an imposter. Most probably the conspiring nobles had not made their move against Cambyses before Smerdis' declaration, either due to inadequacy or to avoid being charged with regicide. When Smerdis declared, they were in a grey area; Smerdis was no king, he was usurper plain and simple. But once Cambyses had been taken care of, all was nice and set and the succession confirmed, even if in a most unorthodox way. Smerdis was officially enthroned *after* Cambyses died and thus the succession was legitimized.

Had Cambyses passed away first, as would have been the plot of any normal conspiracy, and Smerdis succeeded him, the implicated nobles were regicides and Smerdis totally legitimate. It is most probable that there was an agreement for the latter but the conspirators did not follow the plan, so as to remain unblemished. Still, Smerdis would be impostor for as long as Cambyses lived, a loose end that was now taken care of promptly *without* the nobles being regicides. Since a new king was already declared, the nobles simply took sides. The inscription of Darius in Behistun, that 'Cambyses died his own death' (DB 11) should be understood as 'died, was not killed' and although rather hazy as a narration of the past, it is perfectly compatible with both Herodotus and Ktesias, who report an accident with a short blade, possibly an *akinaka*: Herodotus mentions his side weapon as he leapt on his horse in Syria (Her III.64,3), Ktesias mentions an accident as he was carving a piece of wood in Babylon (Ktesias 14). Both these sources report a self-inflicted wound by accident with his own blade before he could cross to Iran.

After enthronement, Smerdis initiated the tax exemption to the conquered nations, making himself extremely disagreeable to the Persian nobility. This estrangement may have been caused by his declining to receive them in audience, which of course might have been a precautionary measure to avoid any accidents with sharp objects of his own, similar to what had happened to his brother; or due to his displeasure for their belated purging of the throne.

This estrangement and hostility would catalyze another conspiracy. Darius, according to Herodotus a royal spear-bearer (*Arstibara*/Guardsman) but possibly having risen to the rank of the Master of Spear in Cambyses' court, commanded respect with the army of the Egyptian campaign. The other Persian nobles were probably positioned throughout the realm. Although Herodotus has Darius coming from Persia, the satrapy of Hystaspes, his father (probably a mistake as Hystaspes was governing Parthia), it is conceivable to imagine him with the veteran army from Egypt camped south of Zagros, meeting with the other conspirators somewhere safe. The latter brought vital information on the whereabouts of Smerdis, as Holland (2005) believes. After all, contrary to Herodotus' hazy narration of Cambyses' death, Ktesias exclusively says he passed away in Babylon, his former seat as viceroy.

Thus the conspirators intercepted the royal retinue at a station/stronghold on the road of Khorasan (Chorasmia of Ancient Greeks), called Sikayauvatiš (DB 13), a story perfectly matching the Herodotean account where a city and royal dwelling are mentioned but a name is never provided and the court format seems most informal and, perhaps, residual. With some of the court members so friendly, as to confirm the story of the severed head of the alleged usurper (Her III.79,1) and possibly to have been actively implicated so as to facilitate the infiltration (Ktesias 16), the conspirators had their way in terms of events and narrative.

The role of Darius had been cardinal and indispensable; thus kingship must have been his prize for his involvement which was decisive in planning, determination, execution and support. The only reason for a different official narrative, passing to Herodotus and to the realm, was to safeguard Darius from any blame of regicide, before he himself took the holiness of the king's person to new heights.

In this, of course, the realm who loved Smerdis (and Cambyses) revolted (Malye, 2007). Darius was able to count on the army (Ktesias 15; Holland 2005; Malye 2007), of Parthia, the satrapy of his father, where rebellion was speedily quelled (DB 35, 36) and possibly on Bactria (Garcia-Sanchez 2014) and generally eastern Iran (Waters 2004). He had either embraced beforehand, or at this very instance, radical Zoroastrianism (Farahmand 2015), to promote it to be the official dogma of the new empire. This case is closely reminiscent of the ascendance of Christianity under Constantine the Great. Interestingly, Bactria never revolted against Darius, despite being the seat of a well-liked Smerdis/Bardiya who, unfortunately, might have not been a devoted Zoroastrian, being a true son of Cyrus II (Farahmand 2015).

Darius I the Achaemenid

Hystaspes, the father of Darius, must have been the ruler of Parsa (Kuhrt 2001) who resigned from his throne in favour of Cyrus; the latter, when he united the nation and overruled the Median overlordship, took his seat and perhaps granted him something to rule over in due course (Holland, 2005). This is the only plausible explanation for Darius' very own storyline where his bloodline were kings (DB 4) until he himself became emperor, on one hand, and on the other his reference to his father Hystaspes as ruler of Parthia (DB 35). Herodotus, who reports that he had conversed with Persian scholars (Her I.1,1) and probably reads Persian (he definitely speaks it), was well-informed on the high seat of Hystaspes (Her III.70,3) in Parsa, which he confuses with Persia, the successor state of both Parsa and Anshan created by Cyrus II. But his knowledge does not include the understanding of Hystaspes with Cyrus II and the assignment of he former to Parthia.

In Herodotus' version Darius met the fellow-conspirators at Susa, himself coming from his residence (Her III.71,3); if this is understood to be his father's seat, which was Parthia (DB 35) and not Persia, one may conclude that after his return from Egypt he had travelled suspiciously close to Bactria, the cradle of Zoroastrianism, to ask guidance, possibly leading to his strict authoritarian rule, and to strike deals, possibly for overthrowing the established Mithraic dogma and promoting radical Zoroastrianism. This religious mantle and support combined with a bloodline from one of the two regal houses of the Persian people and possibly an inherited religious office (Soudavar 2012). Added to these, the networking within the army of the Egyptian expedition, which in its years of absence had developed a remarkablee *esprit de corps* and a special identity, made him not only useful or even indispensable for the other conspirators, but also their eventual leader who brushed Otanes aside (Holland 2005) and, ultimately, became Emperor (Her III.71 & 83).

Darius I has been projected to this day (Grundy 1901; Burn 1962; Fields 2007) as a tolerant if not benevolent ruler, and the example has always been Egypt and the local religion there in sharp contrast to Cambyses and Xerxes (Her VII.7). In plain Persian, this meant that the privileges of the Egyptian clergy in taxing the populace had been restored, along with the solemn acceptance if not enforcement of the native religion to the locals (Klotz 2015). It was a nice, profitable exchange. Possible help in getting rid of Cambyses must not be ruled out, in the form of toxins, poisons or lack of medical care. Darius employed Egyptian doctors when he was emperor (Her III.129), which means he had proof of their value and dependability. When they failed him he almost had them beheaded. Since Democides, a Greek doctor, succeeded (Her III.130), Darius might have thought that the Egyptians were repeating on him the play staged for Cambyses – that they were unable to help the patient.

Thus, Egypt was instrumental in bolstering the fame and authority of Darius, in matters cultural, religious and of infrastructures. The digging of a canal to allow shipping from the Nile around the Arabian peninsula to the Persian Gulf allowed massive deportation of Egyptian workers for the building of Susa, the revamped imperial capital situated at Sushan, Elam (Klotz 2015). This was as good a reason as any to instigate rebellion later on. Herodotus casually refers to the execution of Aryandes, the Satrap appointed by Cambyses in Egypt (Her IV.166,1), under the pretext of revolting but in reality due to his regal appearances, including minting an excellent silver coin (Her IV.166). Satraps were by decree of Cyrus little kings under the King of Kings (Xen Cyrop VIII.6,10); many minted silver coins (Bodzek 2014), thus this particular crime of Darius I should be attributed to any or all of the following: the brewing of a genuine sedition, which resulted in one revolt during his first regnal years (DB21) and the revolt of 486 BC (Klotz 2015); following an erroneous or unsuccessful policy of conquest and expansion (implied in Her IV.165 & 167 & 200–4) without proper sanctioning; and/or a continuous loyalty to the memory of Cambyses, perhaps demonstrated by said campaigns.

Darius declared the forfeit of taxes void, and of course, a widespread rebellion ensued throughout the realm, including Susa and Babylon. Babylon was the home field of Cambyses, appointed by Cyrus to rule under him as viceroy, before stepping up to the throne. Herodotus does not report the name; he still criticizes the administration which allowed a rebellion to foster, while fully escaping any notice. And this surely is a Persian source besmirching Cambyses. It is worthy of our attention that Xerxes was also Satrap of Babylon before inheriting the throne (Green 1970) and Herodotus' account of the host of Bactria during the campaign of 480 BC names as its commanding officer (CO) Hystaspes, son of Darius I and brother of Xerxes (Her VII.64), while the Satrap of Bactria was another brother, Masistes, who was appointed marshal (Her VII.82 & IX 113). His name must have been substituted by his title, as *Mathista* means 'Successor' (Garcia-Sanchez 2014).

One is tempted to presume a connection between Babylon and the heir-apparent, similar to the princedom of Wales in the English succession. Furthermore, there are signs of a Persian ruling trinity (Garcia-Sanchez 2014; Sekunda & Chew 1992) formed by the emperor and two most powerful provincial governors, one in Babylon and the other, obviously, in Bactria. This was an analogue of the Holy Trinity; *Ahura mazda, Mithra, Anahita* at the times of Artaxerxes (Plut Vit Artax), but the original, during the times of Cyrus and Darius, might have included another third pillar, *Apam Napat,* instead of *Anahita* (Llewellyn-Jones 2012; Soudavar 2012) or, more probably, Varuna (Heliopoulos 2020). The royal trinity is traceable during the reign of Cyrus, with Cambyses and Tanyoxarces/Smerdis in Babylon and Bactria, respectively. With Darius, the trinity included Xerxes and Masistes in Babylon and Bactra respectively. And in a much more subtle way, there are similar traces in the reign of Darius III. When the latter retreated from his last refuge, Ecbatana, it was Bessus, his relative and Satrap of Bactria who usurped the kingship with the military vote and was proclaimed king (Arr Anab III.21,4); no other satrap or general. Thus the two most important cities OUT of the Iranian nucleus, Babylon and Bactra, were under viceroys while the three capitals, one in each of the three nuclear nations, were visited within the year by the Emperor and his court who resided there; imperial quarters were situated to other provincial capitals as well, especially royal cities of subjugated nations, such as Memphis, where Cambyses spent most of his regnal years, and Sardis, where both Darius and Xerxes resided for quite some time.

Among other things, Cambyses must have nullified the directive of Cyrus which allowed a Jewish return. The biblical text of the Book of Ezra is inconsistent but speaks for an official from a province usually associated with Babylonia (Ezra 5) who seems to have been responsible for the area. The latter agrees with the concept of a hostile Cambyses when he was appointed Satrap, or viceroy of Babylon. In any case, under Darius the return was completed; possibly as one more action of spite against Cambyses or as gratitude for the second fall of Babylon, after its insurrection. A kindred religiousness, between an ardent monotheism and a semi-monotheistic ideal, must not be rejected as a contact point between Darius and his mazdaic clergy and the Judean establishment in Babylon. After all, the much more vehement Zoroastrian, Xerxes, selected Jews to post as guards in southern Egypt (Gertoux 2016; Stein 2014; Waugh 1995), meant as a trusted occupation force in a troublesome province. It must be noted, however, that the Book of Esther obviously takes place *after* such events and insinuates a strong Jewish presence, if not influence as well, in Babylon *after* the return to Palestine and the reinstatement of the Temple in Jerusalem.

It took Darius I, his supporters and his relatives two years of bitter fighting to pacify the realm (DB 52), with utmost brutality. It is obvious that the only army a self-proclaimed monarch, imposed by conspirators, would be able to count on, was an army known to him and cohesive beforehand. It was the army of the Egyptian campaign. In this endeavour, the ardent Bactrian Zoroastrianism helped him impose his rule, truth and divinity (DB 5 & 9), while Bactrian troops advanced his cause with great fervour. It was the original version of the events leading Constantine I to the Roman throne and Christianity to prominence.

Under Darius the previous Persian national religion, Mithraism, possibly incorporating beliefs from Media and Elam (Henkelman 2011; Waters 2004), seems to have been overthrown for the more radical Mazdaism (Henkelman 2011; Kuhrt 2007). Not a tolerant religion *per se*, as Ahura Mazda *had* to be worshipped, or, at the very least, denial of his stipulations invited retribution (DB 72–3). And this must be acknowledged, despite the efforts of some scholars to assign religious intolerance to practicalities within administrative and political framework (Kuhrt 2007). This quintessential change is evident by the discovery of the grave of Cyrus II in Parsagadae by Alexander III in 330 BC (Arr Anab VI.29,4–6), and by the funeral performed to the body of Mardonius (Her IX.84), in stark contrast to the funerary rites of Zoroastrianism (Her I.140). Possibly the mass murder of the sect of the Magi (Her III.77) corresponds to the massive slaughter recounted in the Bible, in the Book of Esther (Gertoux 2016). The ardent character of the ascended new sect of the religion deified the throne, making Darius the human representative of Ahura Mazda on earth (DB 9 & 63), similar to a Pharaoh. It was a divine monarchy, with the king protected by constitution and religion.

Thus, the absolute, if occasionally casual rule of the Median and Persian kings all the way to Cambyses became stricter; the *Primus inter pares* concept of the Seven Conspirators (Her III.84) evaporated. The same happened to the constitutional power of the aristocracy, with the immediate execution of Idaphrenes. Despite his distinction in stabilizing the realm (DB 50), and the fact that he simply adhered to his prerogative as one of the Seven, which allowed him to ignore palatial protocol (Her III.118) he was summarily executed with all his family and kin. A more plausible story is that Idaphrenes, who had been introduced to the circle of conspirators by Otanes (Her III.70,2), was considered loyal to the latter and prone to instigate one more coup, possibly towards the rather egalitarian constitution proposed by his mentor (Her III.80,2) and might well have been the third vote against kingship when the Seven voted for the constitution of the Empire (Her III.83,1).

It is an established fact that the power base of Darius was located to the eastern Iran (Waters 2004), as shown by the geographical distribution of the insurrections he had to confront (DB 52), with repeated risings in Media, Elam and Babylon. Cyrus, an Anshanite Persian, had befriended, embraced and promoted the elamitic constituent. He had his own capital built, Parsagadae (Llewellyn-Jones 2012), but the Median capital of Ecbatana retained quite a status, with a detachment of royal guards stationed there; the latter became implicated in the insurrection against Darius (DB 25). It is tempting to assign the Persian insurrections against Darius to the vicinity of Anshan, the birthplace of Cyrus and to a sense of duty to the true kings, who founded the empire, and his line.

Understandably Darius enforces a distancing from Anshanic tradition and elamitic influence (Waters 2004) but he obviously has ties with Elam (DB 23): his mother and his name are elamitic (Henkelman 2011; Waters 2004; Daryaee 2017) and his primary capital was established at the reformed elamitic capital of Susa. The latter is understandable; Darius furthered the role of Sushan against that of

Anshan, which was devoted to Cyrus II (Daryaee 2017). For the same reason, he overlooked Parsagadae, the imperial capital of Cyrus II, and established himself at Susa (a direct insult and injury to Babylon) while he was building his *own* Persian capital at Persepolis (Mousavi 2005). This was a sign of utter disrespect against Cyrus, as his imperial capital is overlooked contrary to those of Media and Elam which were considered imperial capitals as well by the annual rotation of the royal household to them (Daryaee 2017).

Similarly, Darius' religious orientation as an emperor had everything to do with the facts of the insurrection and personal, tribal devotion. Whether it was an effect of, or a cause for the support provided by Zoroastrian areas and sects remains debatable. Median and Elamite practices and beliefs were neither persecuted nor discouraged, but Ahura Mazda, an Aryan deity reminiscent of Judaism, (Henkelman 2011), became supreme in a manner similar to the introduction of the One True God upon the Israelites by Moses. At the same time the name 'Ahura' sounds a bit close to 'Assur', the main god of the Assyrians, the arch-enemies of the Medes and Babylonians.

Darius was very strict when establishing the official national Persian religion and his self-definition and introduction as a Persian and Aryan (DNa) served to differentiate the Persians from the Anshanites. These were a liability due to their attachment to Cyrus and their preferential integration to the empire by him, so as to help overthrow the Medes. But the differentiation was also directed against the Medes, a fact at the epicentre of his coup. At a second stage, by declaring Aryan, he fraternized the eastern Iranians (Aryans) such as the Parthians, and the hardcore Zoroastrian beliefs (Soudavar 2012) in stark contrast to the western parts of the nucleus of the empire (western Elamites/Susians).

Still, in foreign affairs, he was *not* very religious, or at least not offensively and aggressively so, as would be his son. He was rather a pragmatist, as was Cyrus II and Cambyses II (Daryaee 2017), and actually most ancient rulers in Europe and the Middle East (van der Spek 2014). In the Babylonian version of the Behistun inscription, it is the Babylonian god Bel who granted victory to Darius, not Ahura Mazda. Cyrus could not have done better; he had paid homage to the statue of Marduk and declared himself a champion of his to 'liberate' Babylon (Henkelman 2011) and possibly of Yahweh to reinstate the Jews.

Under Darius, the empire was divided into more satrapies, to the number of twenty (Her III.89), with additional officials reporting to the king (Her III.128) and thus sapping the autonomy, power and prestige of the satraps. The precautions on the subject are perhaps attributable to Cyrus, especially considering the 'eyes and ears of the King' (Xen Cyrop VIII.6,16; Lazenby 1993) and the military authorities of a satrapy (Xen Cyrop VIII.6,9). Assignment of satrapy and other positions became semi-hereditary; the spawn of a successful official could be granted his father's seat, and an even more successful ruler or official could be promoted to a better province. Still, the seat was of the Crown to be passed to another individual for exceptional service or to be withdrawn in case of substandard performance.

Last, but not least, Darius reformed the taxation system. His taxation was systematic and heavy – with some notable exceptions and made the Empire a centralized organization producing profit for the Throne (Her III.89) and poverty for subjects and subordinates. It was worse for the Greek colonies in Asia: the flourishing civilization of Ionia died to insignificance after the loss of freedom and liberty. The Ionians, *sensu lato*, had been largely indifferent to the Lydian occupation and later to that of Cyrus and Cambyses, offering only token resistance if at all with few notable exceptions. But now, under Darius, they were facing bankruptcy, which was their worst fear. Trade was now a matter of the state, and the favoured subjects were the Phoenicians. Thus, the Ionians started to feel under immediate financial and then physical extermination.

After all, Darius, contrary to a concerted effort from mainly later sources to present him as an enlightened, moderate and exemplary ruler, had never been very tolerant nor anything like mild (Burn 1962). His cruelty was well-known and feared, and with good reason (Her III.159 & IV.83–4; DB 50; 43; 33; 32). Even if this had not been the case, most of his subjects would rather have had him off their backs, despite any moderation of his.

Loose ends and unfinished business

Thus, the Persian Empire Darius I both inherited and built had its weak points across the compass. Darius I was cruel (Her III.119 & 130 & 159), greedy (Her III.89), definitively embracing lies whenever needed (Her III.70), which was the worst vice for a Persian (Her I.136 & VII.209), arrogant to the extreme, buying his own myth and possibly devious (Her III.119), but by no means a fool. His main security problem was correctly identified to be the subjugated peoples still having free kin across the borders. There were four of them, at the very least. The Indians in the East, the Scythians N-NW, the Thracians W-NW and the Greeks due West. The Phoenicians, a fifth such people, were happily and voluntarily integrated, most privileged among the subjects of the Persians and rather a bridge of understanding with Carthage than a security threat. Lacking geographical continuity to Carthage, they were even less dangerous, below zero.

The Scythians, having once invaded Media (Her I.104 & IV.1) and perhaps weakened it enough for Cyrus to overthrow the Median rule, were the most formidable opponent, remaining undefeated by the Persians. Probably the shape of the earth and correct maps were some decades away and thus Darius ignored the exact size, orientation and position of the Scythian Crescent, from the western coast of the Euxine to the eastern coast of the Caspian Sea (**Map 2.1**). But he was able to recognize a problem when seeing it. Having invaded his lands unpunished and ruled them unopposed some generations earlier; having been defeated and expelled by vice and not by virtue (Her I.106); having slain the first Persian emperor (Cyrus II the Great) who attempted an invasion, and getting away with it (Her I.214), the Scythians were a beacon of the vulnerability of the Persian State and a mockery of the throne's deterrence.

The Thracians were numerous both out of and within the empire (the Bithynians or Asian Thracians, Her III.90 & V.3), warlike, brave and fierce, but militarily insignificant compared to the Persian way of war. An important issue was that they were conveniently positioned to the access routes leading against both the Scythians and the Greeks, and thus killing two enemies in one campaign was an appealing prospect.

The Indians were very numerous and difficult to subjugate, by sheer weight of numbers in terms of population, resources and territory; furthermore, they posed no danger as they showed no real signs of aggression. The *Achaemenid* aggression against them is of dubious date; one possible date being between 519 and 515 (Darius' pacifying the realm and the onset of the Scythian campaign). Another is between 512 and 500 bc, after the failure of the Scythian campaign and before the Ionian revolt. The empire conquered under Darius had significant areas in this direction, but eventually had problems in subduing them and keeping them docile. When Alexander invaded Persia, the Indian territories seem to have veered away from imperial control. On top of practicalities, the sheer size of the Indian nations and homeland made any concept of rounding up their conquest a dubious project (Her III.94 &101 & 106).

Thus, both by urgency, by necessity and by simple realism, the Persian sights were set on the west. By definition, the first target was the Thracians. Indeed, Darius actually subjugated the tribes between the Bosporus and Scythia (Her IV.93); Megabazus did likewise with the more westward ones, towards Greece (Her V.2 & V.10), although, most probably, in no great depth; some tens of kilometers from the north Aegean shore, to Lake Prasias in Paeonia (**Map 5.2**). But what direction would be pursued after the Thracians (Her III.134)? Would it be the formidable and threatening Scythians? Or would it be the fourth neighbour, the Greeks?

The Greeks, contrary to the Thracians, were not very numerous; but they were extremely dispersed throughout the Mediterranean and politically divided. The arid peninsula, their homeland, due west, seemed less formidable and even less threatening than large and populous Thrace. The problem was their dispersion and their disposition. Colonies firmly established from the western coast of Asia Minor all the way around the Euxine and then westwards to the ocean. Moreover, substantial communities were planted in other, alien areas and cities, especially in the Levant, but even amidst the Egyptians (Her II.179), despite the latter being a xenophobic and arrogant culture (Her II.79).

This meant that if only one of their independent states remained free, it could become a nucleus of opposition, sedition and dissension. Furthermore, the most ominous reality was that the mainlanders had already declared war on Persia, when the Spartans, their most prominent war tribe had dared to forbid to Cyrus infringement with the Asian Greek colonies (Her I.152) – although Sparta had sent none in Asia! This spelled problems in the making, a collective identity across the Aegean. Laughed out by a frustrated and infuriated Cyrus (Her I.153), due to his lack of a fleet to deliver punishment, it *was* there and vibrant. It constituted an uneasy and pernicious condition. An open matter, or rather a wound ready to fester, especially once the unwilling subjects of Cyrus, their cousins in Asia, had started spreading and fostering discontent at the edge of the empire of Darius (Lazenby 1993).

Thus, all of the Greek states had to be conquered; and to do so, powerful fleets were needed, making the Persian success dependent on seafaring subjects and accurate intelligence. But that may have still been insufficient. The first-hand intelligence coming by a spying party led by Democides, the personal physician of the Persian royal family (Her III.135–6), which made its way to southern Italy, indicated that the de-Hellenization of the Mediterranean was a gigantic endeavour. Fleets larger than the ones recently acquired by conquest might be needed. This was bringing Carthage, the mega-colony of the Phoenicians, conveniently into play, and perhaps other, like-minded peoples; the Etruscans being the best candidates.

The last and most interesting issue with the Greeks was their accomplished type of warfare, the advent of the Hoplite Phalanx, which enabled their colonial campaigns and resulted in an expanded sphere of influence, not much smaller in longitude and latitude than Darius' own realm. It was though much less cohesive, less co-ordinated – if at all – and definitely more lax: it was the Greek World, in contrast to the Persian Empire (**Map 2.1**).

This military system, at least a century old and possibly close to two, was still successful and ubiquitous enough to be adopted by many of Darius' current subjects (the Phoenicians included) while being exported or simply imitated by a significant proportion of the peoples around the Mediterranean basin, such as numerous Italian nations, tribes and cities. The Greek ilk in the form of mercenaries, colonists and allies had taken the field in Libya, Egypt, Babylon, Cyprus, and Phoenicia, roaming over extended parts of Asia Minor, Eastern Europe, France, Spain and

Italy, reaching the Atlantic beyond the Pillars of Hercules. In the invasion of Egypt, Darius, a royal spear-bearer, would not have failed to notice Greek Hoplite forces fighting for both sides, as subjects of the Persians and as mercenaries for the Egyptians (Her III.1 & 11 respectively).

The Greek Hoplite was an adaptable opponent to be reckoned and respected, although not that aggressive. Still, this could change if given time to consolidate a *panhellenic* state. Then, the resources of the Mediterranean could be funnelled to the east, first to Asia Minor and then to the core of the empire; such concerns (named 'prudence') often drove Roman aggression against nations which were on the eve of forging a political identity, like the Dacians, Gauls and Germans. With the partial failure of the reconnaissance trip of Democides (Her III.138), though, a campaign was not easy to plan. Consequently, the highest priority opponents, to be dealt with right after the Thracians had been taken care of, were the Scythians.

Chapter 5

The Scythian Adventure

Darius is obviously overrated, especially by Herodotus. The intention of the latter must have been to glorify the success and the high moral standing of the Athenians who challenged his authority. Another motive may have been to be fair, if not agreeable to the Persians, who were in his day on friendly terms with the Athenians; the then Emperor, Artaxerxes, must have revered his grandfather Darius I but not his father Xerxes, who had jeopardized, with his palatial machinations and inadequacy, his own life, forfeited the lives of his siblings and undermined the empire.

Indeed, Darius fought and won many battles between 521 and 519 BC to safeguard his throne, but their size and nature should not be overrated. They were mostly counter-insurgency affairs in modern parlance. Then, the empire did expand to India, but there is no record of how, when and under whose leadership this expansion took place.

According to Herodotus, right after the resubmission of Babylon, Darius embarked on the Scythian adventure. This resubmission must have been the suppression campaign where Zopyrus (Her III.158) gained fame. Regarding the latter, the 'right after' is a little inaccurate; once the realm was pacified the new, satrapal administration should have been enforced, matrimonial measures were taken to solidify the new dynasty (Her III. 88), and the proper decorum would have been of the utmost importance and of the highest cost. It must have been at this point that the royal robe changed from Elamite to Persian (Sekunda & Chew 1992), while the person of the king was sanctified.

Darius I had been an Arstibara and to secure his throne he led his forces in person on many occasions, but once emperor, he only once acts as *Karana*, that is head of the hosts (Fields 2007): during the Scythian campaign – or at least this is the only occasion reported to us. In all the other cases he delegated authority, something advisable and with precedents aplenty, as was Harpagus' mission of conquest in Ionia, ordered by Cyrus II himself (Her I.162,1). In any case, the 'warrior' aspect of the king is fading after Darius: he does lead and campaigns in person until he secures the throne, and then things change. The triple identity of the Persian King was Farmer, Warrior and Judge/High Priest. It differs from similar prerogatives, as among the Jews and Assyrians, where the *motto* was Shepherd, Warrior and High

Priest/Judge (Llewellyn-Jones 2012) and means that the Persians were pastoralists to a lesser degree and settled farmers to a higher degree than usually believed.

The personal bravery issue remains steady in the Persian royal lore. Kings declare their mettle, as does Darius who considers himself 'a good spearman/archer on horseback and on foot' (Dnb 9). The king is a warrior chosen by warriors (Fields 2007), although the actual method and procedure of such choice is controversial in the dynastic context. But such prowess stands for their life and career *before* becoming kings, as is the case with Darius III (Diod XVII.6,1–2). In many cases a *Spadapathis* (general-in-chief), such as Artybius (Her V.112,2) or Mardonius (Her IX.63,1) may fight personally, although this is not a rule; Datis did no such thing. But once enthroned, Achaemenid kings may lead their armies, as does Xerxes, but do not fight themselves, despite the fighter status attributed to them by some modern scholars (Fields 2007). Xerxes might have fought when he was Arstibara or even when viceroy, but never engages when taking the field in Greece as *Karana*, and is not even present in the line; there are also no direct reports of Darius I, Cambyses and even Cyrus II engaging in the way Alexander III, Leonidas, Epaminondas, Themistocles, Callimachus and many Greek kings, generals and emperors did (Hanson 1999). Darius III is present in the battle line (Arr Anab II.8,11), in sharp contrast to Xerxes and similarly to Artaxerxes II, but his participation in an engagement is due to the failure of his entourage and army (Arr Anab III.14,3), not to his intention or choice. Cyrus the Younger and Artaxerxes II were to resolve a personal bitterness and once more, only the former actively engaged willfully (Xen Anab I.8,24–6).

More time was spent by Darius in purging the previous administration, as in the satrapies of Sardis (Her III.127–8) and Egypt (Her IV.166,2), and consolidating the new one. For the latter case, the example is the extermination of Idaphrenes (Her III.118), the maverick amongst the Seven; and even more time was perhaps spent on the Indian campaign, if it took place in this period and not later. All these must have taken at least a couple of years, which is hardly 'right after'.

In any case, the lore has it that Queen Atossa, daughter of Cyrus II and mother of Xerxes I, persuaded Darius to choose Greece as his first target to the west. This was allegedly because she craved slaves from these places (Her III.134), but she might have taken a personal insult from the Spartan ultimatum to her father (Her I.152–3). Be that as it may, the spying mission of Democides (Her III.135) to Thrace, Greece and Italy was a total disaster in terms of public relations (Her III.137). As a result, the priorities changed: a massive host was brought across the Bosporus to invade Scythia from the west. In a time of no maps Herodotus thinks of Scythia as practically a square shape (Her IV.101), although he clearly considers the European Scythia, or, in modern terms, central Ukraine. There is no notion of the Scythian crescent and the eastern steppe people, as the Massagetae are considered different than the Scythians. This is not necessarily correct. The name Massagetae is a product of Getae, a Thracian tribe at the Ister (Her IV.93), and the comparison between Scythians and Massagetae rather implies a different federal/tribal system and not a national difference (Her I.201).

Darius mobilized a 600-strong Persian fleet, the standard ever since, and a 700,000 land force (Her IV.87). The latter figure creates questions much more severe than its size proper might have. In this expeditionary force, the Greeks are few but prominent: a Samian engineer bridged the Bosporus (Her IV.87–8), most probably by a pontoon bridge. The Samians were top engineers at the time, having completed back home three magnificent engineering feats: the aqueduct of Eupalinus, the temple of Hera (both mentioned earlier) and the great breakwater at the port of Samos (Her III.60). Furthermore, the imperial fleet is mostly Greek (Her IV.89). One commemorative inscription (Her IV.87), a specimen of the magnificent works Darius had been so fond of (i.e. the Behistun inscription), read clearly at the time of Herodotus that the king led contingents from all over the realm; but the navy, at least once in the Euxine, seems to have mustered Ionian, Hellespontine and Aeolian Greeks and perhaps Carians and Dorians by association (Her IV.138). It is of note that most areas furnishing ships to Xerxes in 480 BC (Her VII.91–95) are altogether absent from this campaign: Egypt, Phoenicia, Cyprus and Cilicia, Lycia, Pamphylia (the whole S/SE of the coast of Asia Minor).

The preponderance and special role of the Ionians might seem ill-advised, but the Persian system was based on personal reckoning and the truth is that it worked fine, with precious few exceptions for many years. Thus, the Greek part of the fleet, the only one with skill and experience in navigating the Euxine, passed through the Bosporus, reached the Ister and prepared another bridge for its crossing (Her IV.89), obviously smaller and less elaborate and, more importantly, modular (Her IV.139).

The Persian army arrived at the Bosporus by a route undisclosed by Herodotus but most probably by the road of Pteria and from there through Gordium to the Bosporus. Once in Europe, the advance must have been W-NW and then turned north (**Map 5.1**), subjugating Thrace with relevant ease (Her IV.93). The Thracian political disunity, though, meant that tribes not along the axis of advance did not surrender easily, and tribes near Greece really felt no reason to do so. Major cities remained independent very near the staging point of the invasion, as described later.

On the other hand, although some bits and pieces of NW Asia Minor may have had yet to succumb to the crown, like Sigeum, conquered by Peisistratus in the name of Athens (Her V.94–5), most of the straits passed safely to Persian hands. This cut off the Greek colonies of the Black Sea from the mainland, independent

Metropoleis, resulting in no more corn trade or imports of Scythian archers, beyond the ones already recruited by Peisistratus and his sons once upon a time (EB Peisistratus 2018). Darius should have had detailed information of Greeks trading with Scythia, at least concerning the Ister, a vein of commerce. Detailed reconnaissance seems typical for the Persians, but especially for Darius as evident from the mission of Democides (III.135).

Crossing the Ister, Darius ordered the fleet to dismantle the bridge and support the advance of the land army (Her IV.97,1). Koes, a Greek captain from Lesbos, advised against dismantling the bridge and sailing (upriver?), for reasons of security and his advice was heeded (IV.97). In this deliberation and arguments, one may detect very interesting patterns and practices of the imperial Persian war machine.

i)   Since the fleet was initially ordered to dismantle the bridge of the Ister and proceed, it must have been the Persian *modus operandi*. The vessels, once released from supporting the bridge, were to assist the invasion. The fleet going *upriver* would mean going *away* from the army. This might have been intentional, so Darius could level the Greek colonies of Pontus without any complications due to the national allegiance of his fleet. Still, there is no evidence of any lack of reliability by his Greek subjects. Perhaps the order was to come up *along the coast of the Euxine*, to assist the invasion as had been the case in Egypt, and not *upriver*; Herodotus' reporting may be erroneous or corrupted but the actual orders and intentions of Darius might not have been.

ii) Thus, the bridge over the Bosporus should have been dismantled as well. Was it constructed by the Greek part of the fleet, which carried on in the Euxine, or by any other squadrons, which afterwards disappear from the narrative? Maybe the non-Greek part of the fleet was left in Propontis to survey the area and keep it secure, while the actual expeditionary fleet served both as an invasion arm and as a massive hostage camp to ensure the behaviour of the area. This sounds perfectly Persian but it is a patent misuse of resources. The possibility of a mainland Greek naval challenge is far-fetched, as the political organization of the mainland did not allow such ambitions, nor was there a state of war with the Empire – with the possible exception of the Spartan ultimatum to Cyrus (Her I.152–3).

iii) By the same token, the bridges of Xerxes in 480 BC should have been dismantled and their ships put to good use, and not destroyed by tempests. This would explain the safe-keeping of the cables of the bridges in Sestos (Her IX.115). It was the result of a fully organized and scheduled dismantling, not the salvaged remains after a catastrophic gale.

Darius was an experienced monarch. After his taxing ascendance, he must have taken notice of the character of the Greeks. Without them, he could not have attempted the expedition, as their ships were only a small part of their actual contribution: knowledge and intelligence regarding this area were their absolute prerogatives, as the Phoenicians had never ventured in the Euxine. Even more important had been their wholehearted participation in the expedition and the imperial ideal in general, as Darius had conceived it (DB 63). They guarded the Persian rear and did it dependably and efficiently. This support was actually a service against their folk in the Euxine colonies and was offered with precious little enticement. More of such services could be expected in any endeavour against their Metropoleis, provided that petty rewards would be offered by their master; in some cases simply spiting a fellow Greek neighbour or antagonist. The Samians, for example, had been massacred by Otanes, but they provided excellent services like the bridging of the Bosporus. Their traitorous, selfish behaviour during the Ionian Revolt does not suggest that such support was intended to keep the Persian threat away from the Metropolis and the Persian troops as far away as possible from their own cities. In short, their demeanour compares poorly with the valiant and concerted veto of the Phoenicians to Cambyses (Her III.19), which saved their colony, Carthage, and established them as *privileged* subjects (Holland 2005) and may, just may, be explained by some or other social/class struggle or upheaval within their island, with some strata having reaped rewards or just benefits from the Persian atrocities and subsequent overlordship.

The Scythian expedition was an uncompromised disaster (Grundy 1901). A highly mobile Scythian retreat and scorched earth strategy (Her IV.122), coupled with swift cavalry onslaughts (Her IV.128,2–3), harassed, demoralized and starved the Persian host and finally threw it back in full retreat if not outright flight (Her IV.135). Miltiades, an elected – actually selected – tyrant in the European part of the Hellespont, possibly a vassal and not a subject of Darius, proposed the demolition of the bridge of the Ister, kept and guarded by the Ionians alone, so as to trap the Persian army in Scythia and undermine the Empire then and there. Scythian messengers had infiltrated the Persian rear to request exactly what kind of action was required (Her IV.136). An imperial army with the bloodthirsty emperor and his top warriors would vanish without a drop of blood of his mutinous servants. No risk, innumerable gains. In retrospect, huge areas were ready to revolt given *half* a chance, from the belt of Greek colonies and the European shore of Thrace to Egypt and Babylon.

Too good to be true. The tyrant of Miletus, Histiaeus, reversed the commotion by appealing to the political instincts of survival of the assembled tyrants (Her IV.137). Thus, the bridge was kept intact from subversion by his fellow Greeks and safe from any Scythian incursion (Her IV.139). He literally saved the empire, and thus became an iconic figure throughout the ages for selfishness and self-interest; he also became Darius' personal hero (Her V.11 & VI.30). Miltiades, on the other hand, became blacklisted; understandably so, since discretion has never been a Greek virtue.

To assess the result of this campaign one turns to the accomplishment of declared or inferred objectives. Darius wanted to subjugate the Thracians as there were Thracians under his rule in Asia, such as the Bithynians (Her VII.75), and free brethren of one's subjects across the border always means trouble (Grundy 1901). Did he do so? He moved along the coast, to skirt Haemus and Rhodope ranges; so a wide swath must have succumbed directly. The point is, though, his westward progress (**Map 5.1**). The mountain ranges of Haemus and Rhodope are inaccessible and there is no hint of tribes residing on them having bent the knee; mountains were a constant vulnerability of the Achaemenid empire, as practically independent tribes could be found even in the Persian heartland, as were the Uxians, who were collecting tolls and presents from the King of Kings to provide 'road security' for the royal household through their mountains (Arr Anab III.17,1). The question is what happened with the wide plain inbetween the two mountain ranges, in modern-day Bulgaria, and then his proceedings in modern-day Romania. How much time did he spend subjugating these vast plains? It is possible that the tribes there sent proxies to pledge submission due to mere awe and terror.

Still, when Miltiades was kicked off his fief, he was able to seek refuge near Olorus, his father-in-law, a Thracian king (Her VI.39–40) lording over territories of unknown size. This suggests that the king was not aligned with the empire, since Miltiades was a wanted man (Her VI.133,1). Additionally, the campaign of Megabazus (Her IV.144), which is discussed later, seems to have been intended to secure some depth along the Aegean coast of Thrace. Whether additional campaigns were to follow is open to question. From the successful, or 'successful', completion of Megabazus' campaign (Her V.16) the area remained relatively quiet for a decade (Her V.28). The sole exception was some mopping up by Otanes (Her V.26), which was focused on the geographical system of the Straits, from the offshore islands of Imbros and Lemnos to Byzantium (**Maps 5.1 & 5.2**). There is no indication of imperial occupation north of the Rhodope range at this time, nor after the operations of Mardonius in 492 BC and, according to the traditional interpretation, nor during Xerxes' invasion. It was as if the empire was Greek, or Phoenician-minded and was seeking occupation of coastal areas.

As Darius flees with the remnants of his army, mutiny must have followed suit. Darius crosses from the Hellespont by ship (Her IV.143) and stays for a time at Sardis, to (over)see the containment of the mess of the Scythian expedition.

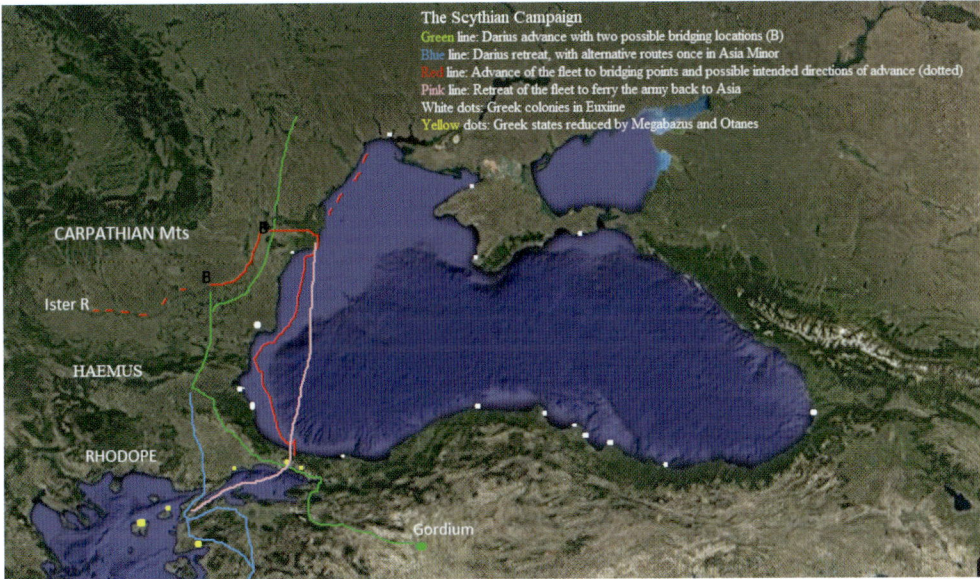

The Scythian Campaign
Green line: Darius advance with two possible bridging locations (B)
Blue line: Darius retreat, with alternative routes once in Asia Minor
Red line: Advance of the fleet to bridging points and possible intended directions of advance (dotted)
Pink line: Retreat of the fleet to ferry the army back to Asia
White dots: Greek colonies in Euxiine
Yellow dots: Greek states reduced by Megabazus and Otanes

Map 5.1.

Megabazus is left behind in Thrace, with 80,000 troops of the Persian host, to conquer the Hellespontine region (Her IV.144) and Thrace (Her V.2,2) due west, or to keep in check the Thracian areas subjugated previously, up north, or both.

The army size becomes relevant at this point: Megabazus seems to command two army corps at standard expeditionary strength of two-thirds each; 40,000 out of 60,000, for an active force of 80,000 all told (Her IV.143,3). His first and major success is the reduction of Perinthus (Her V.2), sitting in the middle of the northern

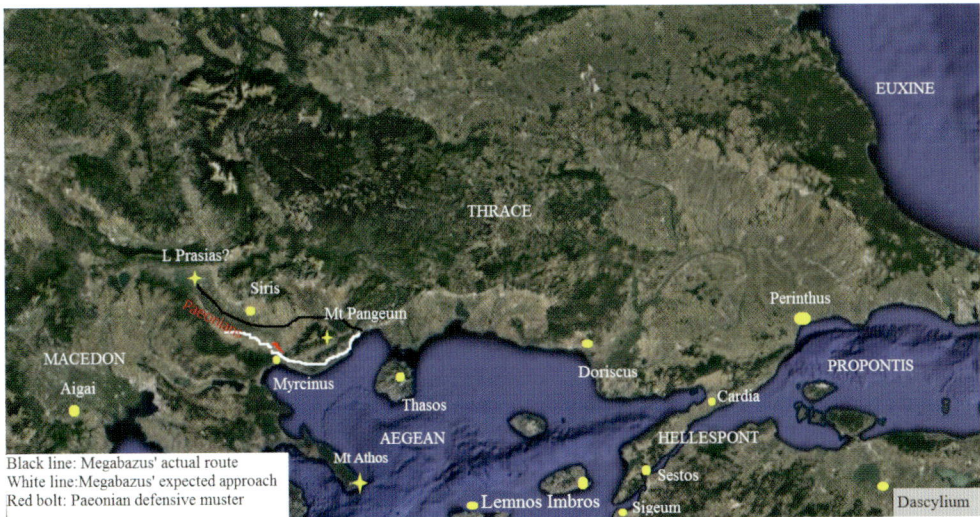

Map 5.2.

shoreline of Propontis, followed by an advance to the Thracian mainland to the west (**Map 5.2**). Megabazus thus rounds up the reduction of one of the Persian geopolitical loose ends. His advance reaches Paeonia up the Strymon valley, to stop north of Mount Pangeum and Lake Prasias (Her V.16). Although the coastal Greek cities were not reduced, the kingdom of Macedon under the House of Temenids now borders with the empire and perhaps becomes tributary (Her V.17–8). It is not governed by satrapal decrees, but the area of Myrcinus at the mouth of Strymon, near next-to-be Amphipolis, is Darius' own to gift to Histiaeus as recognition for his good services at the Ister (Her IV.141).

Megabazus declares his mission accomplished and returns to Sardis, bringing along the Paeonian tribe as prisoners, due to Darius' whim for industrious slaves (Her V.13–4). Megabazus counsels Darius in Sardis to keep Histiaeus under surveillance (Her V.23) and Darius lures the latter from his new fief in Myrcinus to Sardis and includes him in his retinue as he moves the court to renovated Susa, his royal city and capital, where he retires once the western border is declared more or less secure and Thrace subjugated (Her V.24). In his stead, he leaves as general on the coast Otanes son of Sisamnes (Her V.25,1). The latter is a different and younger man than Otanes son of Pharnaspes, the general who subjugated Samos and was a member of the Seven (Her III.141). The seat at Sardis, once kept by the mutinous and murderous Oreites, who beguiled and murdered Polycrates and conquered Samos, is presented to Darius' brother Artaphrenes (Her V.25). Otanes expediently brings some northwestern areas into Persian control with the help – especially in vessels – of the very loyal friend Koes (Her V.26) who is installed, after Darius' return to Asia, as a tyrant in Lesbos. This seat was a recognition of his good services to the throne, mainly his advice not to dismantle the bridge at the Ister after crossing to Scythia, so as to maintain a ready point of retreat (Her IV.97). Thus, Imbros and Lemnos succumb, thanks to the lesbian fleet, as do some areas of lesbian overlordship in NW Asia Minor and, most importantly, the mutinous Byzantium (Her V.26). Only the Sigeum, a protectorate of Athens (Her V.94–5), remains outside the Persian border.

Megabazus is a person of interest for the developments of the next decades. Most probably he becomes satrap in Dascylium. After the fall of Miletus (circa 493 BC) the satrapy is in the hands of one Oebares, son of Megabazus (Her VI.33,3), and at 478 BC of a Megabates; the very one who campaigned against Naxos in 500 BC (Her V.32). This latter sired a Megabazus and thus, he was the son of one and, consequently, brother to Oebares. Thus, the line might have been Megabazus I – Oebares and Megabates – Megabazus II. The latter must be one of the four district admirals (Her VII.236) during the campaign of Xerxes, and probably last of his line, as the satrapy eventually came to the maverick Artabazus (Diod XI.44,4).

In any case, the pompous title of Megabazus I, 'General of Europe' reported by Herodotus (Her IV.143,1) and the alternative one, 'General of Thrace' (Her V.14,1) may be two different free translations of the original Persian, which might refer to Skudra, the Persian lands in Europe. More complex analysis (i.e. as in Boteva 2011) might be needed on the subject of slightly different titles. Skudra was possibly under the surveillance of the Satrap of Dascylium or under a new, non-satrapal administrative unit based at Sestos (Her VII.33).

The sum of the western Scythian campaign was very different than the almost easy subjugations of eastern parts of Scythia (DB 74), some Indian territories (DB 6) and other late acquisitions. Of the four geopolitical threats, only one was efficiently dealt with – the Thracians; the Scythians had survived and were contemplating revenge (Her VI.84,2). Furthermore, an initial rounding-up of Greek territories would unmistakably lead to war eventually, as was the idea and the wish of the Queen (Her III.134) before the Scythian expedition.

Chapter 6

Towards the Ionian Revolt

The return of Darius I back home was not uneventful. He had his fleet following his steps but did not cross the Bosporus back to Asia, nor from anywhere in Propontis. He took his battered and hungry army all the way to the Hellespont to make the crossing (Her IV.143,1). This means one thing only: that the more suitable areas for such crossing were in revolt – a revolt possibly engulfing some Asian territories, such as the ones inhabited by Thracians and close to the Hellespontine region (*sensu lato*). This assumption fits well with Megabazus' first target, Perinthus (Her V.1,1) which lies very near Byzantium and had been left unconquered at the rear of the expeditionary force, while the Hellespont is also explicitly mentioned as not entirely docile and conquered by him (Her IV.144,3). Similarly, the proclamations of his replacement, Otanes, when (re)conquering Byzantium and Chalcedon, that they harassed the royal army during its return from Scythia (Her V.26) also indicates a revolt.

Miltiades' proposal to entrap Darius and his army in Scythia might have been brought about by news or advance knowledge of such events; alternatively, it might have triggered them. There is no question though that the situation was clearly critical, so critical that Darius spends quite some time in Sardis; there was ample time to grant Histiaeus his wish about Myrcinus and for the latter to go there and start organizing his fief (Her V.23,1). Darius relocated himself and his court at Susa only when the situation was firmly under control (Her V.25,1). The time sequence is a bit lacking and unsure, but it is certain that once he moved to Susa, he had filled the two satrapal seats in western Anatolia that were vacant after the elimination of the treacherous Satrap Oreites (Her III.128,5), who had been established at Sardis by Cambyses. The satrapy of Dascylium was presented to Megabazus, probably after his triumphant return to Sardis with his prizes, the Paeonian captives being prominent amongst them (Her V.23,1). That this triumphant return was through the Hellespont might imply that Byzantium and the whole area around the Bosporus was still in revolt.

The satrapy of Sardis was assigned to Darius' brother Artaphrenes (Her V.25,1). And it is exactly then, between Darius' departure for Susa and the eruption of the Ionian Revolt, that ten whole years are missing from the account of Herodotus. Trying to fill the lacuna, one may suppose that Darius undertook his pharaonic projects in Egypt and Persia and additional conquests to the East, especially in India, during this time. Such a timeline would have accounted for a successful kingship, overcoming the adverse results of the Scythian expedition and establishing firmly the realm before the eruption of the Ionian revolt. The latter was to initiate a spiral decline of the empire; a long and torturing spiral. The missing decade accounts well for the creation of the shiny empire inherited by Xerxes, which was much more than the one Darius appropriated from Cambyses and Bardiya/Smerdis.

Histiaeus was dwelling at Susa, in a golden cage for ten years, enjoying sincere respect and privileges; he also understood he was never to see the sea and his fief at Myrcinus. Aristagoras, his lieutenant, is comfortably seated in Miletus and develops aspirations for his own kingdom within the empire. The Athenians depose their tyrant, Hippias, who eventually flees to Persia, adding the last missing part in NW Asia Minor, Sigeum, to the king's estates; *last*, after the campaign of Otanes, which resulted in the subjugation of two islands, Lemnos and Imbros and most of NW Asia Minor under the pretext they opposed the Persian endeavour against the Scythians (Her V.27,2). This pretext for invading Lemnos could only mean that the Lemnians were officially bound to participate and thus under an already established Athenian overlordship. Miltiades was also participating in the endeavour and there is no other context explaining the Lemnians' duty to this end.

The role and status of this Otanes (son of Sisamnes) is very crucial as he has evidently nothing to do with his namesake, Otanes, son of Pharnaspes (Her III.68,1). The latter had probably been uncle and assuredly father-in-law to and older than Cambyses (Her III.2,2 & 68,3 respectively). He partook in the Coup of the Seven and then conquered Samos (Her III.147,1). The former Otanes is explicitly mentioned as the replacement of Megabazus (Her V.26), but his title is General of the Coast (Her V.25,1), not of the Hellespont (Her IV.144,3), Thrace (Her V.14,1) or Europe (Her IV.143,1), as was Megabazus. The variability of the latter's titles prompted an elaborate reshuffling of the timeline of events (Boteva 2011) but may be explained by different Greek translations of the Persian concept of Skudra and the latter's evolution and transformation within the Achaemenid administration. Otanes, on the other hand, is never mentioned as operating in Europe, except for the two aforementioned islands (Her V.26), which are quite accessible from the NW Asian shore and less so from the peninsula of Helle. He also subdues Byzantium, just across the straits. This implies a different area of responsibility than Megabazus, despite Herodotus' understanding that he was the replacement of the latter. Neither his area of operations nor his title seem to confirm the statement of Herodotus (V.26) and are much more compatible with his performance during the first phases of the Ionian Revolt (Her V.116 & 123).

The Coast is a puzzle: mentioned by Herodotus again as under Artaphrenes in *circa* 500 BC and under Hydarnes in *circa* 483 BC (Her V.30,5 and VII.135 respectively) and present in the Behistun engraving (DB 6), it cannot be identified properly. Herodotus defines it as a proper satrapy, a view supported by the tribute list (Her III.90,1) and its border with Cilicia to the SE of Asia Minor. This description little adheres to Behistun (DB 6), where it is a different entity than Ionia and the Islands. Moreover, a capital for it, a satrapal seat, is never mentioned, nor a satrap; the overlord reigning over it is the satrap of Lydia, Artaphrenes, who is specifically mentioned by Herodotus to be in command of the Coast (Her V.30,5). He handles all issues in the near Aegean and treats Aristagoras in Miletus as his direct subordinate (Her V.31,1 & 4). As the satrapy of Artaphrenes provided land forces under Xerxes (Her VII.74), forces led by his son, Artaphrenes the Younger, the vessels of Ionians, Carians etc., by any account, should have been the quotum of another satrapy. Still, it is Artaphrenes the Elder who authorizes and prepares 200 vessels for the campaign against Naxos engineered by Aristagoras (Her V.31,4).

The contributions of ships to the Grand Fleet of Xerxes show that Sardis may still claim 200 from the coast of Lydia, inhabited by Ionians, Dorians and Carians (Her VII.93–4). Another 160, probably brigaded with the aforementioned 200 towards a regional fleet of a Naval District were furnished by coastal communities attached to Dascylium. These would be Aeolians and Hellespontines (Her VII.95). This arrangement might apply to the Scythian campaign and/or to that of Marathon. It must be noted that the satrapy of Dascylium (at least as inferred in Her III.90,2) provided land forces to Xerxes (Her VII.72–3) as well.

Similarly, the seat of Dascylium had been assigned to Megabazus and then to his offspring (Her VI.33,3). The Coast nominally extends to his shores as well, and Otanes operated there, including Byzantium (Her V.26,1). It is more than obvious that the new conquests in Europe are assigned to Megabazus not to any other satrap or governor, as nothing of the kind is mentioned. Megabazus conquered such lands for the crown and his bloodline remained active in the region. His son Bubares was investigating the disappearance of an embassy to Macedon (Her V.21,2) and became betrothed to the daughter of the King of Macedon, Amyntas (Ibid). His exact status is not declared in Herodotus, but he oversees the digging of the Athos canal (Her VII.22). One could surmise that the invasion project of Xerxes was assigned, at least for its local preparations module, to Dascylium and that Bubares was not an overseer, but the lord of the European lands in whose territory the work was taking place.

Artaphrenes, possibly jealous of the conquests of Megabazus and Otanes but also clearly attuned to the insatiable appetite of his brother Darius for conquests and loot, induces the Athenians into voluntary submission (Her V.73,2) and sanctions an amphibious campaign to conquer Naxos (Her V.31,1 & 4) and ostensibly the other nearby Cyclades islands (Her V.31,2) with a clear view to Euboea, the door to central, mainland Greece (Her V.31,3). These arguments, presented to him by Aristagoras the Milesian by 500 BC but wholeheartedly accepted both by him and by Darius, show that the preying eye of the monarch was set due west before any provocation. This corroborates the intentions behind and the implications of the reconnaissance mission of Democides (Her III.135,1–2) and the perverted longing of the Queen for Greek slaves (Her III.134,5); perversions too familiar in the context of the Roman Empire and later European monarchies.

The last and capital figure is Miltiades. Being the last from a line of imported sovereigns both invited by the locals and sanctioned by the Athenian government under Peisistratus and his sons (Her VI.34–6 & 140), he rules over the Thracian Chersonese, a strategic area which forms the European shore of the Hellespont. This dynasty tried to extend their hold both to the Asian coast (Her VI.37,1), being on excellent terms with Lydia and Croesus (ibid), and to the nearby islands (Her VI.140). The latter issue is open to speculation, as Herodotus' wording may imply that the actual inhabitants of the island of Lemnos were independent both when attacked and subdued by Miltiades (Her VI.140) and when attacked and subdued by Otanes the Persian (Her V.26–7). Necessarily, one subjugation predated the other. It is more believable that Miltiades was first there as a conqueror in the name of Athens (Her VI.136,2). After Darius' return from the Scythian Expedition, such lands of Miltiades were attacked and seized by the empire, most probably by Otanes as he had been declared its enemy (Her IV.144,3). The islanders, left to their own devices, offered stiff resistance against the oriental terror (Her V.27). The Athenians had allegedly driven away the original inhabitants, but that was only for the ones that *did* abide by the convention; the ones declining and finally subdued by force (Her VI.140,2) were most probably reduced to vassalage if not servitude and thus must have been present when Otanes landed (Her V.26–7).

The alternative is that Miltiades attacked the island much later, while it was officially Persian during the Ionian Revolt (Burn 1962). This means he had to overcome the resistance of the locals, after their rebelling and disposing of the stranger (Samian) Lycaretus, who had been installed as a tyrant by the Persians under Otanes (Her V.27). Under such circumstances, the need for an ages-old pretext by Miltiades sounds unconvincing (Her VI.139–40). Even more perplexing is the issue of how this new territory, hitherto an Achaemenid fiefdom, was found under Athenian sovereignty (Her VI.136,2) while Athens had decided to desist from any further hostilities with the empire after the battle of Ephesus (Her V.193,1).

With the Thracian Chersonese as his personal fiefdom, Miltiades is situated opposite Sigium, the personal estate of the Peisistratids (Her V.91,1 & V.94–5).

In this way, between themselves they established an Athenian gate to the Euxine despite some reverses when trying to expand and consolidate it (Her VI.37,1.). Thus, Miltiades was comfortable as long as the Persians were occupied elsewhere, despite the more autocratic turn of the Athenian government under Hippias. But he participates in the Scythian expedition with Darius I (Her IV.137), and this makes him either an ally, probably by fear to be invaded eventually, since at this age the Persians do have fleets, or a vassal. The latter might have been the case if Darius' campaign in Scythia had been preceded by a limited local campaign of establishing a bridgehead in Europe, possibly by Megabazus (Boteva 2011).

However, much more probable is that his participation in the Persian expedition was part of an extended network of loose dependencies built by the Persians in times of war. The similarity with European Thracians flocking under the standards of Xerxes in 480 bc to participate in a looting excursion to the south, to Greece (Her VIII.116) is telling. Last, but not least, an understanding between Athens and Persia might have been established early on, as the Athenian fiefs in Asia Minor seem to be almost autonomous if not independent areas just next to the realm of the King of Kings and more specifically, next to an area subdued duly a generation earlier by Harpagus the Mede (Her I.174,1). If this was the case, Miltiades, a vassal of Athens, joined the massive campaign of Darius against the Scythians as the allied contribution of Athens to an all-powerful neighbour, and was thus subject to the Persian High Command (Her IV.98) and military law.

Darius' opting for the Hellespont implies that during this epic retreat, Perinthus was closed to the Persians, harbour and shores. Either it was steadily defiant from the beginning of their invasion, or it probably rose in revolt along with Byzantium, Chalcedon and a great part of Thrace.

In the Scythian campaign, Miltiades deliberated to cut off the Persian royal army at Scythia, so as to destroy the empire with one swift blow (Her IV.137,1). It might have been something more than an idea. As Darius returns, a revolt seems to have been triggered, making him return to Asia through Sestos in the Hellespont (Her IV.143,1) and provoking a retaliation and suppression campaign by Otanes (Her V.26–7). Miltiades' hand in the uprising cannot be assessed, confirmed or rejected as a possibility. Still, he is not a major player; Darius' chose to cross to Asia from within Miltiades' own fiefdom in Chersonese (Her IV.137,1). Thus, it was considered suitable and rather safe. Due to the sheer size of the royal army? Or because Miltiades was still with the royal fleet, a hostage for all practical purposes, but evidently before his hostile intentions were brought to Darius attention? Herodotus' narrative for the conquest and suppression campaigns of both Megabazus and Otanes mentions nothing concerning Miltiades, which implies that formally he remained a subject and thus actual operations against him were not undertaken; but such operations *are* mentioned against (some of) his territories, certain Hellespontine cities (Her IV.144,3).

But knowing Herodotus' bias against this family, due to his sponsor Pericles, it is possible to notice that Otanes attacked and subjugated Lemnos during his punitive expedition (Her V.26); this colours the island as either a neutral or a rebellious state during the ebb of the Scythian campaign (Her V.27,2). This detail is important; Herodotus clearly mentions that Lemnos had been brought under Athenian sovereignty thanks to Miltiades (Her VI.34–6 & 140) and this cannot have happened, according to the story, *after* it had been invaded and conquered by the Persians (Her V.26) as already discussed. It seems it was considered enemy territory (specifically by Miltiades) and was invaded as such.

This perspective leads to some interesting conclusions and suppositions. It is possible – if not a matter of fact – that Darius eventually heard of Miltiades' plot and treated his territory as hostile ground. Miltiades might have resisted against both Megabazus and Otanes; thus the former's campaign against the Hellespontine cities (Her IV.144,3), and the latter's against Lemnos (Her V.26). Herodotus does not report it; even if he knew he would avoid glorifying Miltiades and thus displeasing Pericles. Miltiades might have failed to defend the land border of the Chersonese, but keeping (most of) its cities out of any direct Persian control, and the rural areas inhospitable for casual Persian presence and use, would have been quite a feat and plausible at that. Incursions for plundering and transition of major armies would have been possible and perhaps probable, given the limited resources of the region. This may explain Megabazus' passage back to Asia from this area, even if it were not fully pacified. Another alternative is that Megabazus crossed back to Asia from the Hellespont (Her V.23), which in this case must be understood to *include* Propontis, thus making Perinthus the obvious choice.

The heart of the problem is this: Darius must have learnt of Miltiades' attempt the moment he set foot – or hoof – on the south bank of the Ister, not some time later. Otherwise, his debt of gratitude to Histiaeus (Her V.11,1 & V.23–4) is a mystery. He would have been, in Persian eyes, a mere vassal who did well in a not too demanding task (Her IV.98), along with many others. If Darius had indeed been informed early enough, how did he not follow his first impulse, which would have been, according to the reading of the inscription of Behistun, to flay, gut, crucify or at the very least decapitate Miltiades on the spot? Not only that, but he travels to the latter's territory and crosses from there (Her IV.143).

The only logical recreation of the events is that Darius heard of Miltiades' attempt at high treason once south of the Ister, and Miltiades took flight promptly – or had already done so the moment he understood that Darius' return was imminent and the bridge would be thrown back into position and function. The informer was obviously Lysagoras the Parian, whom Miltiades so loathed that he led the Athenian punitive expedition against Paros after Marathon (Her VI.133), an endeavour which proved fatal for him (Her VI.136). The Scythian disaster caused a revolt, which erupted in the vicinity of the Bosporus (Byzantium, Chalcedon) if not throughout Thrace and culminated in the destruction of the bridge over the Bosporus (Ktesias 25) but this must be taken *sensu lato*, as the bridge might have been dismantled already. Furthermore, it made the area unsuitable or even pernicious for the Persians to cast another bridge or embark to cross back to Asia. Accordingly, Darius had to board somewhere else, preferably with a small width of sea to cross. Thus, Darius and his troops advanced to the Hellespont, the fiefdom of the now renegade Miltiades, and crossed from there as fast as possible, confident in the size of their army, but without thoroughly (re)establishing control over the region. Megabazus was left behind to reinstate the *Pax Persia* by subduing rebels and independent states and tribes, especially the Thracians to the west, among whom must have been the father-in-law of Miltiades, where he must have found refuge and a base for his machinations. But the first task of Megabazus was to sack Perinthus (Her V.1,1) in order to acquire a suitable port on the European side so as to establish a proper, effective and secure line of communications with Asia.

Megabazus campaigned successfully all the way to Macedon (Her V.18,1), which he made tributary but not vassal, secured his hold there through matrimony (Her V.21,2), and returned to Sardis, to be presented with the satrapy of Dascylium (Her VI.33,3). Only then did Darius feel comfortable enough to move back to Susa (Her V.23–5). As Megabazus had made a tributary out of Macedon, or at the very least an 'ally' by matrimony (Her V.21,2) the empire had established a narrow but continuous land corridor leading to the northern gate of Greece (**Map 5.2**).

Otanes' operations developed *behind* the theatre where Megabazus had been active and this raises some questions. It probably implies that Darius had no other army at his disposal when he crossed back to Asia and assigned priority to the campaign in Thrace as a means of stabilizing the frontier (Her V.2,2) and the border territories. Quelling all sparks of the revolt in Asia Minor was left for a later time, at ease, once the situation had been stabilized and was assigned to Otanes.

Otanes was named general (Her V.25,1). He must have been *Spadapathis*, foremost military commander in a theatre. Once confirmed, Otanes operates in Troad, off Troad, to the nearby islands including the Athenian outpost of Lemnos and in the vicinity of the Bosporus, bringing into line the revolting or unruly cities (Her V.26; Ktesias 25); his jurisdiction is usually understood to have been both sides of the Straits. This is a most definite indication of a massive loss of imperial prestige and power, directly attributable to a major reverse (Grundy 1901; Burn 1962).

Part II

When First They Met

Chapter 7

The First 'Quest for Freedom': The Facts of the Ionian Revolt

The fiasco that was the Scythian campaign had some unforeseen long-term results. The empire had some territorial gains, having conquered lands in Thrace; the campaign though had been an unqualified disaster, as becomes obvious by the rebellions in its wake, especially of Byzantium, which made Darius cross back to Asia by veering to the west, at the Hellespont and also made prolonged Imperial counter-insurgency campaigning in the area a must. This phase went better and Darius was able eventually to retire at Susa and perhaps his new capital, the secret city, Persepolis (Mousavi 2005) – a city unknown to the Greeks until the invasion of Alexander the Great, or shortly before.

In Susa, or rather with the Persian court, resided Histiaeus the Milesian, as the token of gratitude he asked for saving the Persian army at the Ister, the fief of Myrcinus at the (literal) Far West of the Empire, had been deemed risky for the interests of the Emperor (Her V.23,2). The prize was granted, but the opportunity to enjoy and make good use of it was denied. Histiaeus, after at least ten years in this golden cage, knew he was never to see the sea, nor to achieve his ambitions of becoming something more than a Persian puppet tyrant (Grundy 1901); perhaps a vassal king. Herodotus has him instigating the Ionian revolt on these grounds. His son-in-law and cousin Aristagoras, governing in his stead, on the other hand, had no reason to do so, ruling practically alone for a decade thanks to the Persian spears. Herodotus understands that Aristagoras found himself poised to revolt due to his unenviable position after a failed campaign (see later), when his Persian colleague/co-commander, or rather supervisor, Megabates, was bound to file complaints against him. Additionally, Aristagoras was expected to pay the expenses of the failed expedition himself (Her V.35,1), since the Throne gave him credit, sanction and help but did not take over the costs (Her V.31,2). As the fleet was at anchor, just after the ignoble return (Her V.36,2), Aristagoras revolted, seized the expeditionary fleet (200 galleys minus any possible casualties due to accidents, as there was no sea-fight in the campaign) and relinquished his tyranny (Her V.37,2). This set the whole of Ionia on fire and Aristagoras went to seek help abroad (Her V.38,2).

Concerning the Ionian Revolt, Herodotus is at his worst. He is clearly biased against the rebels, presenting them as troublemakers who caused evil to both Greeks and barbarians (Her V.97); who marred the perfect nirvana of the eastern Greek world, which was flourishing under a spirit of co-operation and understanding within the bosom of the benevolent Achaemenid empire; undisciplined; militarily inept at times; when they shirk engagement, cowards and when they do not, definitely stupid or.... irresponsible (Grundy 1901; Burn 1962). Of course his Carian- and Dorian- bloodline had this kind of feud with the northern neighbours embedded in the DNA. But Herodotus is also a devoted Atticiser and promotes an argument to the tune of 'serves them right' regarding the Athenian oppression and milking the Asiatic Greek cities of his era (Burn 1962). In these chapters, Herodotus seems not simply neutral, or even distanced, but demonstrably pro-Persian, speaking for the wrongs the Ionians did to the king, in daring to rebel and helping some of his captives (the Paeonians) to escape back to their homeland (V.98,1). This absurd stance, noticed and severely criticized since antiquity (Plut De Her Mal 24) is going to change in his narration only when it is the Athenians who reconsider their position from that of spontaneous dependence to resilient resistance or, rather, rebellion.

In truth, although his animosity and bias are declared and self-evident, there were objective difficulties he faced regarding the facts and their interpretation. He must have been unable to find precise info, as in his day the then rebellious teenagers were 60+, and the adults of the years of the Ionian Revolt, with a somewhat clearer view on events, were long gone. The timing of the events, especially the temporal sequence of events unfolding at different locations, is extremely problematic despite his best intentions and efforts. In spite of these facts, his account, in terms of objectivity and historicity, is infinitely better than the surviving Persian historical accounts of any event, exemplified by the Behistun inscription that mentions dryly 'he lied to the people'; 'great host'; 'I ordered my slave to go smite these followers of the Evil'; 'Ahura mazda willed it thus'.

The Ionians had some tribal characteristics: they were not very warlike for some generations; they were refined and kick-started the classical Greek civilization, by nurturing sciences, philosophy and the civilized life in general. They were merchants; most of them, after a more or less decent resistance, became privileged subjects of the Lydian kings, functioning as liaisons with mainland Greece and reaping profits from commerce within the Lydian Empire and its network of allies and partners. They were becoming rich, and although Cyrus denied them their previous privileges, the commerce within the much larger, Persian empire was fruitful. Many of them were very happy being loyal subjects in a multi-national experiment, even if they were nowhere near the master race.

Another thing is that the Ionians had developed a new form of self-government, much more representative and equalitarian; it was Democracy in all but name, which is erroneously attributed to the Athenians. The Ionians had a considerable proportion of names ending in 'agoras' like Molpagoras, Aristagoras, Pythagoras and so on; this suffix indicates the *Agora* marketplace, fomenting not only commerce, but also politics. Their progress on the subject can be followed by Cyrus' answer to the Lacedaimonian embassy sent to warn him against meddling with the Greek colonies in Asia. Not knowing the Spartans proper, he declared that he had no fear, especially of people who constitutionally lied and deceived each other as a form of government (Her I.153,1). Sparta had nothing to do with this; Athens was a side note in the pages of history, and deep under the aristocratic brawling which culminated in the rule of Peisistratids. But the Ionians were exactly what Cyrus had in mind... He was right in principle, wrong regarding the subjects. The Spartans were fearsome...

Cambyses was no Cyrus, but there is no indication of any friction between him and the Ionians. On the contrary, their competitors, the Phoenicians, seeing the Ionian profits within the empire, surrendered spontaneously (Her III.19,3) to become loyal subjects and take a portion of the pie. They did well in both; still, Cambyses had no preference for them, as the Ionians were loyal and had precedence. The flat Phoenician refusal to campaign against Carthage (Her III.19,2), although without immediate, harsh disciplinary action, must have been noted for further use by the emperor. With Cambyses, the Ionians were at their best, give or take, as he had no grudge against them as had Cyrus, whose overtures to them against Croesus had been rejected (Her I.141,3).

With Darius, things changed. Taxation became systematic and extremely heavy (Burn 1962). Herodotus' list proves that a tiny strip of land paid a yearly tax of 400 talents of silver (Her III.90,1), when Cyprus, Phoenicia and Syria together paid 350 (Her III.91,1). It is no accident that after the Ionian Revolt Artaphrenes revised the quota (Her VI.42,2). The Phoenicians gained precedence over the Greeks, and, even worse, Darius' wars closed markets and resulted in contributions on top of regular taxes. The Ionians were impoverished, while the Persians, with a natural detestation of everything equalitarian, used to govern through networks of personal acquaintances and relationships of personal trust. Thus they established tyrannies in Ionia; not the tyrannies of the mainland or of western Greece, which were starting as a public rising headed by a champion against the aristocrats to degenerate to authoritarianism at a later stage. In Ionia, the tyrannies were clearly a step back to totalitarian, unconstitutional regimes. Combined with impoverishment, the Ionians had had enough of Darius' greedy benevolence (Burn 1962).

And greedy he had been: either as a personal opportunity to aggrandizement, or to find a pretext to mobilize the Ionian fleet and thus hijack it and initiate revolt (Grundy 1901), Aristagoras proposed a campaign against Naxos to Artaphrenes (Her V.31,1–3), in terms of pure conquest and looting. Naxos had delivered no harm, but was rich and a nice step towards the even richer Euboea and the Greek mainland. Artaphrenes had been watching his northern neighbour, seated in Dascylium, adding new conquests: the fiefdom of Miltiades at the peninsula of Helle (Her VI.36,1) in Thrace, the fiefdom of Peisistratus at Sigium, granted by Hippias to the Crown (Her V.96), and the islands just to the west, conquered by Otanes (Her V.26). Compared to these, Artaphrenes had procured the official but not factual subjugation of the Athenians, who were the nominal overlords of both the above fiefs (Her V.96 & VI.140,1), but little else, as they were far away. To claim Athens, he needed an approach, and this enterprise of Aristagoras was a nice chance. He had to ask for Darius' permission and, as expected, the greedy monarch sanctioned the campaign, and doubled the expeditionary fleet to 200 galleys, from the 100 which were requested by Aristagoras (Her V.31,4). Why 200? This must have been the fleet proportion of the satrapy of Artaphrenes (Burn 1962) since this was in fact a local, border action. The balance towards the Ionian fleets of independence or the Ionian quota to the Imperial grand fleet of Xerxes must have come from the northern satrapy ruled by the line of Megabazus, or Megabazus himself, seated at Dascylium.

The attempt at Naxos

The royal sanctioning for the expedition at Naxos was granted and a task force with a Persian nucleus expanded by 'allied troops' (Her V.32) – probably Iranians – was sent to meet and board the 200 vessels prepared and manned by Artaphrenes (Her V.31,4). The crews were Ionians, as were most of the marines, but for the imperial troops sent by Darius. In this Herodotus might be mistaken; the dispatch of the troops would take some time, and sanctioning a local muster from satrapal forces and military fiefs within the satrapy of Artaphrenes is a much better guess. The army, if not the expedition as a whole, is commanded by a royal cousin, Megabates (Her V.32), which most probably means he was the son of Megabazus (see Chapter 6) and a sister of Hystaspes, father of Darius and Artaphrenes. There was friction between Megabates and Aristagoras, the soul of the operation (Her V.33–4), which culminated in disaster.

The fleet sailed from Miletus north, allegedly for the Hellespont (Her V.33,1), which directly implies a volatile condition there despite the operations of Megabazus and Otanes (Her V.2 and V.26 respectively). When it had reached Chios, it suddenly turned southwards, so as to catch a north wind and approach Naxos fast and unexpectedly (Her V.33,1). But despite such precautions, the element of surprise was lost. Whether Herodotus has it right and Megabates sabotaged the operation to get even with Aristagoras (Her V.33,4), or Aristagoras and some friends did it to leverage events which were to ignite the revolt, long-planned beforehand (Grundy 1901), the islanders were tipped off and had taken every precaution for a siege. The legendary Achaemenid efficiency (and proficiency) in siege warfare must have taken a vacation, as after a prolonged four-month siege Naxos was still holding (Her V.34,2). Money, supplies and morale failed the raiders who simply fortified a position for their local Quislings (Her V.34,3) and left for Asia in disgrace, calling at Myous (**Map 7.1**), near Miletus and landing the troops. The latter either started the return trip to Central Asia by the king's road or were demobilized locally to their fiefs for the winter, while a similar order was expected for the fleet. But before the order arrives, a pre-existing ring of Ionian conspirators convenes in Miletus and takes the chance: they go to Myous and raise the Ionian crews and boarders of the fleet to revolt. And they do it with utmost success (Her V.37,1). By this move the

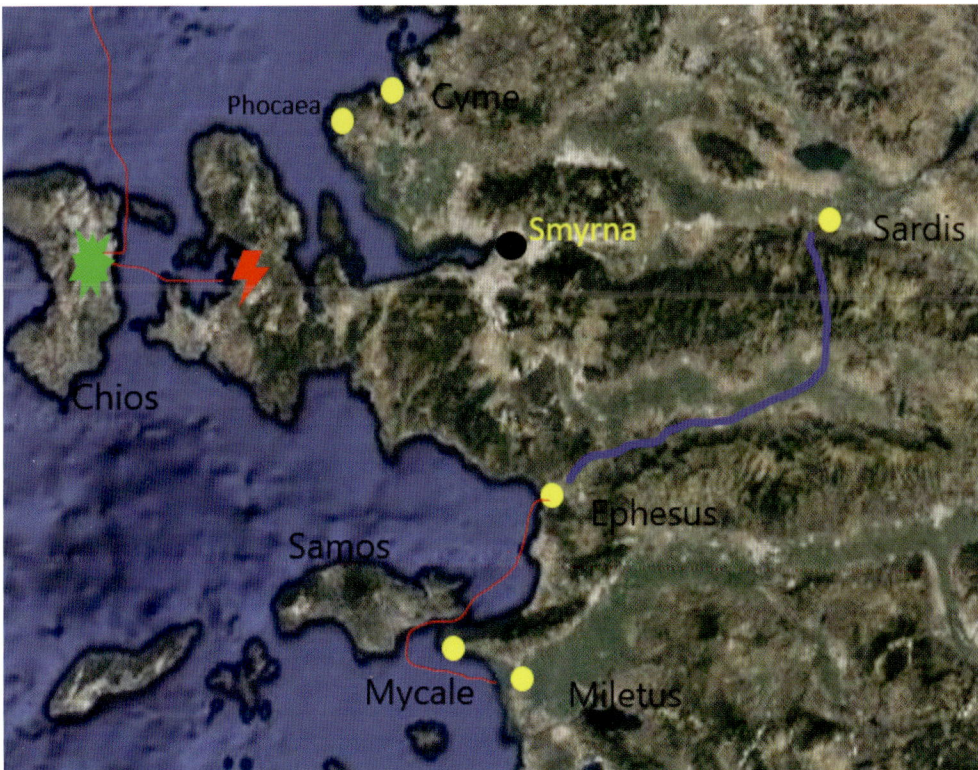

Map 7.1. The opening moves. The rebel fleet (red lines) draws enemy cavalry masses off position and lands a Milesian-led army near Ephesus to attack Sardis stealthily (blue line) as the imperial cavalry are drawn out of position (red lightning), chasing the escaping Paeonians (green blast) who boarded the rebel fleet opposite Chios to Europe.

eruption of the revolt happens while the imperial loyalists (the land army element) are away, the insurgents are concentrated and in position, and most of the imperial commissaries, that is the tyrants of the various Ionian and Carian cities, are still gathered in one place and unsuspecting with their squadrons (Her V.36,4) while getting ready for the trip homewards.

The insurgency erupts

The first move of the insurgents, after capturing but not slaying their tyrants (Her V.37–8) – a most grievous mistake – was to launch some propaganda and secure some advantages. Sparing the tyrants made the uprising look humanitarian in the extreme. To double this impression, the Ionians got in touch with the deported Paeonians who were abducted by Megabazus and carried to Asia on Darius' whim (Her V.98,1). The Ionians offered them sea transportation to Thrace, had they had the guts to approach the sea by themselves. The deal was struck and the Ionian fleet first took the Paeonians from Asia Minor to Chios (**Map 7.1**), which was nearby, to save them from the royal pursuit and then, more leisurely, took them to Lesbos and from there to Doriscus in the coast of Thrace (**Map 7.2**), whence they returned to their motherland on foot (Her V.98,2–4). Offering the wretched expatriates, or rather deportees, such assistance was a propaganda triumph, as the subjects of the king could believe that their salvation was coming from Ionia, should they simply do their part. The Thracians and all of Europe were witnessing the Ionian benevolence and magnanimity (Grundy 1901). Additionally, the external assistance from the mainland, forthcoming in limited numbers (Her V.97,3 & 99,1), almost insignificant, was still even better propaganda; the rebels were not alone.

And then, the masterstroke: Herodotus considers the liberation of the Paeonians an act of pure malice against the king (Her V.98,1). That the enslaved men were free and back at their hearths counts for nothing in the age of the Athenian Empire, except if these were Athenians. This is obvious. What is *not* obvious is that in this way, beyond the propaganda spinoffs, all the available Persian cavalry was pursuing the fugitives towards the coast, most probably opposite to Chios (Her V.98,4). And its whereabouts could be deduced by the rebels as they were keeping track of the trail of the Great Escape, more or less. Thus, the insurgents formed a task force at Miletus, the headquarters of the rising, from where the fleet of the rebels ferried them to Ephesus by sea, away from any imperial detachments converging to isolate or besiege Miletus, the nest of the rebels (**Map 7.1**). From Ephesus, taking local guides (Her V.100) the rebels marched inland and up the river Caicus out of Persian eyesight, as the operational eyes of the Persian high command, the cavalry, were engaged in the pursuit of the Paeonian fugitives. Then, the insurgents crossed the

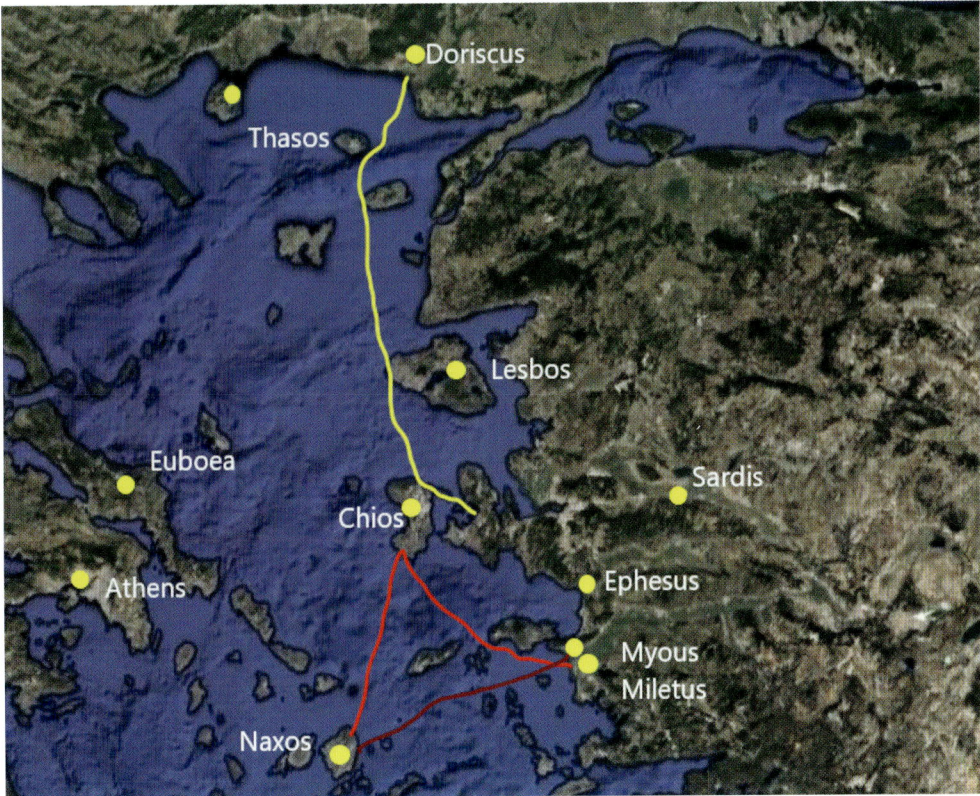

Map 7.2. The operational foreplay. The imperial raid to Naxos (red) and the embarrassing return (deep red) brought the Ionian squadrons at Myous, where they rebelled and subsequently transported the Paeonians from across Chios to Europe (yellow line).

Tmolus mountain range (Her V.100) and found themselves conveniently outside Sardis, the seat of Artaphrenes, the Satrap of Lydia and actually western Asia Minor, the brother of the king.

The surprise assault of the rebels had caught everybody sleeping (ibid) and in the panic that followed the taking of the lower city of Sardis, a fire started. Greeks, through Herodotus, attributed it to accident, due to the panic of the inhabitants; a lamp in a household was dropped and started the fire. The Persians preferred another story, that this was done intentionally – a perfect reason to exact revenge and to fraternize fully with the Lydians, who were supposed to rise to assist the Greeks. In truth, it might have been initiated by the defenders as a barrier against the aggressors; in any case, it was due to the Greek attack, no matter what the details – and one should remember that some Ionians might have nourished a grudge against the Lydians, their previous overlords, no matter how light the occupation had been (a subjective assessment, no doubt). The other fact was that the whole lower city was burnt, including the most revered temple of Cybele. The Greeks paid homage to this particular deity and had adopted her in their own Pantheon. Moreover, the burning of temples was considered by them uncivilized, petty and sinful. Arson by premeditation is not unthinkable, but rather implausible on their behalf; the later Persian allegations that they were burning the Greek temples in revenge were pretentious in the extreme (Her V.102,1). They were burning everything for reasons of religious nature relevant to the version of Zoroastrianism forwarded, or rather imposed, by Darius and Xerxes.

On top of an existential insult to the Lydians and a lasting pretext to the Persians, who felt responsible for the outrage against the deity of one of their subjects (Tuplin 2017), the fire had one more reverse effect: it herded the Lydians and Persians of the city so they formed up and presented, *ad hoc*, a formidable resistance which repulsed the Greeks (Her V.101,2–3); the latter stood no chance of storming the citadel, once its guard stayed put and was reinforced by the lower city dwellers. Knowing that further reinforcements would converge, they withdrew the way they came (Her V.101,3). The city where the satrap was seated being burnt to ciders, even by accident, was a huge blow to imperial prestige and a massive bonanza for the rebels. Before any particulars were made known, the rebellion, fed by the mainland metropolis, had the chance to spread more or less spontaneously. From the unenthusiastic and previously battered Hellespontine region at the north, where some persuasive arguments in the form of the rebel triremes and marines were needed (Burn 1962), to the Carian cities at the south and in Cyprus (Her V.103,2 & 104).

Still, the Persian administration and military power at Sardis was left intact, despite heavy material damage to go with the collapse of Persian prestige; the Greeks had stolen the picture but not the substance. They had no victory to show. As they were retreating, the Persians caught up with them before they had time to get to their ships and leave. They may have not been on to this idea, but their retreat made Herodotus draw this conclusion. In any case, a set-piece battle took place out of Ephesus, the best possible battleground for the Greeks. The Persians of Sardis, their Lydian allies and the reinforcements which converged from the other satrapies perhaps outnumbered but definitely outdid the rebels. Herodotus speaks of a disaster (Her V.102), with the Eretrians losing their general (Her V.102,3) and the Athenians, after the defeat, leaving with no booty (Sekunda 2002) or rather deserting the rebels, never to return (Her V.103,1). It is possible they were recalled by a new, pro-Persian Athenian government (Burn 1962), actively (by a direct decree/order) or by default; the expeditionary period was over and their mandate not renewed. Still, the events that followed show that the defeat was not decisive; the rebels were able to retain the initiative to help the Cypriots and try to interdict Persian reinforcements and onslaughts (Grundy 1901). But contrary to Aristagoras' assertions to the Spartans (Her V.49,3–4) – and most probably to the Athenians as well – and to the belief of all Greeks, mainlanders and colonial rebels alike, the imperial land forces were not easy to defeat and kill; they overpowered the urgently mustered Hoplites.

The troops sent by Eretria and Athens seem a trivial contribution in terms of numbers but this is but one reading. True, twenty vessels from Athens and five from Eretria, the latter triremes according to Herodotus, the former not explicitly so (Her V.99,1) and thus conceivably pentekonters (Haas 1985), were a very small fraction of the fleets involved. The initially mobilized Ionian fleet consisted of 200 vessels (Her V.31,4) and at Lade, it was a staggering 350 (Her VI.8,2). But they were a hefty 40 per cent of the Athenian fleet, at a moment when the relations with Aegina were once more only just short of open war. The five Eretrian vessels, new technology triremes, were the contribution of an old ally to another, settling a debt from the War for the Lelantine Field (Her V.99). After the rough handling of Chalcis by the Athenian democracy (Her V.77), Eretria must have been a major sea power once again, and definitely the major one in Euboea. It may have exercised influence over several of the Cyclades and its navy may have dissuaded Aegina from further humiliating Athens (Burn 1962).

Once Darius learned of the events, and being aware thanks to his postal service with just a weekly delay, he made several moves, the first being the mobilization of the nearby satrapies. But, possibly without expecting his orders, the near satrapies had already mobilized and ran to the rescue, this implying definitely Cappadocia and possibly Armenia as well. Otanes was also moving to Sardis, and he must be considered as a purely military commander rather than the Satrap of Dascylium. At the same time, Artaphrenes perhaps moved as well against the rebels to besiege Miletus (Plut De Her Mal 24), although this may have been a corrupted tradition of his sending troops to do so, not leading them himself. These troops may have been local levies of his satrapy and/or the troops of the expeditionary force who were demobilized or returning to central Asia and were recalled while on the march.

The second move of Darius was to send Histiaeus to try to contain the explosive progress of the revolt. The timing is uncertain; he may have done it immediately, but he may have thought the uprising a matter of course; he had been quelling rebellions for sport by now, it was the trademark of his reign. Thus, it is also plausible to have reverted to such a move only some years later, definitely after the events at Sardis on which he deliberates with Histiaeus, and because of subsequent, much more negative developments. In any case, Darius had singularly misjudged his man, as Histiaeus wanted exactly this thing (Her V.107); still, perhaps the Milesian vagabond had a number of alternative plans and he was not committed to betraying his benefactor and captor. But arriving at Sardis, understandably, as a senior officer by the King's

Road with a more than handsome retinue, he was confronted, in a friendly chat, by Artaphrenes who told him flatly that he considered him, not Aristagoras, the kingpin of the revolt (Her VI.1,2). Histiaeus perhaps intended to help the Imperials contain the revolt and become thus a hero once more; there was no other, really promising, prospect for him. But caught in panic he made his escape, being well manipulated by Artaphrenes, and thus showed his hand. He had to escape to the rebels, who, of course, really had no intention of receiving him (Her VI.5,1). They hated him for his Medizm, for his tyranny, for his bad breath but they also distrusted him, considering him an agent of the king (Her VI.2,2), as the king himself kept doing (Her V.108,1). The rebels, learned men and travellers, might have been informed of the story of Zopyrus infiltrating the rebellious Babylonians only to betray them to his master (Her III.158) a mere twenty years ago.

Herodotus reports a conspiracy between Histiaeus and prominent Persians at Sardis, who were apprehended and executed after Histiaeus' messenger betrayed the correspondence to Artaphrenes (Her VI.4). Both the exact content and the timing of Herodotus may be doubted. Indeed, a dissension within the Persian aristocracy is by no means impossible, especially since the previous Satrap Oreites had been eliminated by Darius (Her III.128,5), who later appointed his own brother Artaphrenes. Herodotus implies that the letters to the conspirators were written after Histiaeus had escaped, but this is less probable than the opposite. Thus, Artaphrenes would have not merely been saying that he considered him culpable of treason but would be proving it to be so. The time from sending Histiaeus to the coast under imperial mandate (taken as just after the fall of Sardis) till his execution is six years, and his proceedings among the rebels until his demise, as recounted by Herodotus, do not seem to account for so long a time. This implies a time of sojourn near Artaphrenes, before the latter exposed – or rather trapped – the devious Milesian.

The third move of Darius was to send reinforcement army/ies. Being nepotistic by conviction, Darius dispatched three sons-in-law, husbands of his daughters (Her V.116), supposedly each in command of a separate force, although all three of them moved together as fast as possible, probably following the King's Road. The event is in doubt; very possibly these armies were the product of the mobilization of the nearby satrapies, as already mentioned. The timeframe is also problematic. Herodotus probably compresses the timeline; he is often accused of doing so almost by choice, as his wording more than encourages such a feeling. The clearest example is the time between the abortive Greek expedition at Tempe, by his own account late spring or early summer of 480 BC (Her VII.174 & 37.1) and the following one to Thermopylae, definitely within August of the same year (Her VII.206); in Herodotus' wording one tends to believe they were in quick succession (Her VII.175 & 177).

A possible timeline for the eruption

The revolt must have erupted in early autumn, as the fleet had retired from Naxos to Myous, near Miletus (**Map 7.2**), but was not yet disbanded (Her V.36,4). The weather would have made the Imperials leave before the autumn gales as their supplies would have been dangerously low, being gathered for a rather short border action and not for a prolonged campaign. Such timing allows for the whole winter to be used by the rebels to get organized and find accomplices within the empire; to conspire with the Paeonians; to request assistance mainly, but not exclusively, from their mainland brethren (Her V.38,2) and have it delivered by ship (that is at the opening of the sailing season), plus to instigate Caria, Cyprus and the whole of the Hellespont (Her V.103,2). Darius would have learnt the events in less than ten days from any dispatch, which would have been sent from Myous, Miletus or any other rebellious city by the Persian garrisons and their collaborators through Sardis. This means that if Darius had permanently mobilized or high-readiness forces and could dispatch them immediately, they may have appeared in-theatre by mid to late winter. Any time needed for further preparations by royal forces would move the ETA (estimated time of arrival) accordingly. Satrapal forces were nearer but might still require mobilization.

The season was the most important factor. Although Darius had possibly conducted at least one winter campaign during the year of his consolidation (Holland 2005), it is a given that such proceedings were ill-advised, as transportation would be much more difficult and of greater volume to include provisions of fuel and winter clothing, blankets, tents and footwear, plus the provisioning for man and beast with higher calorie rates per day. For the man, it is always the same, as summer or winter the expeditionary force would draw from depots, be they friendly or non-friendly upon invasion, although at a somewhat higher rate in winter. But the beasts would have to be supported wholly, especially the horses, during a season with no available grass to graze. Thus, winter campaigns do not happen during the Persian Wars, with very few very late autumn – not proper winter – exceptions, as was the siege of Sestos in 479 BC. This was the main idea: initiate the revolt so as to have a whole winter to consolidate, despite some modern scholars believing that during wintertime the Imperials, especially the local authorities, started containment measures such as a prompt attack and siege – or, rather, investment – of Miletus (Grundy 1901) by the local loyalist forces. Even in this scenario, as operational moves are by definition limited due to supplies and weather, the immediate response of the Empire would have been limited and any off-theatre reinforcements, which would have to be mobilized out of season and expeditiously, and would have been relatively few as well. The exception was, as already noticed, the expeditionary force of the Naxos' campaign, which already could not have been very far away.

This is the time of the Great Escape of the Paeonians. The time is earlier than wished for by the imperial cavalry to feel comfortable giving chase, but at least as late as needed for the fugitives to be able to negotiate the road on foot, and for the Ionian vessels to be able to sail the, understandably short, distance for a mass evacuation, and later for a mass transportation to Doriscus. Still, transporting the Paeonians to the Thracian shore means there was no Persian force worth its name to impede the disembarkation on the spot, although Doriscus (*the* spot) was a military establishment since the campaign against Scythia (Her VII.59,1). Nor would any other Imperial force, had it been available, be there to intercept the overland march to their homeland. It was as if there were no Persians/Persian forces in Europe.

The Imperial cavalry, which ultimately gave chase while the fugitives were still on Asian soil, had been enticed out of position. Thus, it is in early spring that the rebels attacked Sardis (**Map 7.2**), burnt it and then retired. Conceivably (Grundy 1901) but not probably, they had already been besieged in Miletus by local, satrapal forces, and with this move, they both outmanoeuvred the mass of the Imperials and compelled them to abort the siege so as to save Sardis (Plut De Her Mal 24).

The news of Sardis, the westernmost Imperial capital, where the Great King himself resided for some time perhaps a dozen years previously (Her V.11,1), being ablaze sets Caria on war footing, and perhaps this was the catalyst for Cyprus as well. There is a tradition that a Phoenician fleet had been intercepted and crushed off Pamphylia (Plut De Her Mal 24), possibly manned by the Phoenicians of the island (Burn 1962). Such a fact allowed freedom of action in Cyprus for the local rebels and for the Ionian fleet in the western waters (Grundy 1901), making a seaward suppression effort impossible for the empire at such an early stage (Burn 1962). How the rescue operations of the Paeonians, this naval battle and the amphibious attack at Sardis are interwoven in a temporal continuum is a tough question, but the naval engagement must have taken precedence as the other operations required naval superiority if not sea dominance and the Phoenicians would have prepared through the winter to launch at the first sign of spring.

The possibility of the Eretrian fleet scoring a blow to the Phoenicians (Burn 1962) must not be rejected. The event is reported to have happened just before the amphibious attack at Sardis and implicated the Eretrian fleet delivering a decisive blow at the Pamphylian sea, the SW corner of Asia Minor, against a Cypriot fleet, (Plut De Her Mal 24), obviously moving NW to intervene in the rebellion and coming from the Phoenician cities of the island who were the closest *reliable* naval power to the rebellious area. Such an event would have proved that the mainlanders were in for the ride and in quite a capacity and accounted for the disproportionate weight the otherwise minuscule mainlanders' contribution seems to have made to Darius' risk assessment (Her V.106,1).

The Hellespontine region may have been more enthusiastic and joined in, or less so and needed to be coerced by an Ionian naval expedition (Burn 1962). In any case, in a little more than six months from the eruption and being in its second calendar year, the rising seemed an unqualified success, stopping at the southern shore of Asia Minor, where Lycia and Pamphylia were not participating – but they might. No real military success had come to date; Lydia, the most powerful prospective ally and accomplice had been alienated by the burning of Sardis (Grundy 1901); an event so beneficial for the Persian cause that one would be tempted to pin it to the most machiavellic Persians.

Early suppression efforts

The withdrawal of the rebels from Sardis must have been the result of the reinforcements converging there. Herodotus mentions three Persian generals, all married to Darius daughters. One of them is Otanes, probably not one of the Seven, nor his son who will partake in Xerxes' invasion as commander of the Persian home troops, but the one last mentioned ten years before as taking over the command, or rather the army of Megabazus to mop up NW Asia Minor and invade the islands of Imbros and Lemnos (Her V.26). Thus, contrary to some scholars who perceive these three generals as commanding reinforcements from the imperial heartland containing royal troops (Grundy 1901), it might be that these generals are provisional military commanders of nearby satrapies, the two-Hymaes and Daurices probably accounting for the provisional forces converging from 'beyond Alys' (Her V.12,1) and Otanes from the neighboring satrapy of the Coast, i.e. the Hellespontine and the Black Sea coast.

Their armies must have included Persian garrisons and fief holders from the local Iranian – or strictly Persian – military colonies (Lazenby 1993) planted in these satrapies plus, conceivably, native troops mobilized by the respective satraps; Myrsus, of Lydian royalty perishes later in the service of imperial forces (Her V.121). This reading complies with some known facts: Darius I, following Cyrus II, had posted a military commander in each satrapy, who must have been responsible for the Persian fief-holders (and other Iranians) planted there. This practice was standard for conquered lands, not for voluntary submission, and thus Miletus, which yielded voluntarily to Cyrus (Her I.169,2) had been exempt before the rising but included in the programme after the suppression of the revolt (Her VI.20). Darius, a staunch believer in the sanctity of family ties, along with most Persian aristocrats and especially the other six conspirators (Her III.84,2), tended to assign this post to members of his extended family. This suggestion implies that the commanders of the individual contingents which made up the army of Xerxes were not the respective satraps, but the generals of the satrapies, although some arrangements had to be made eventually to this scheme.

The timeline of Herodotus, without giving any definite duration for the operations around Sardis, clearly mentions that the Persian reinforcements gave chase, caught up with the withdrawing Greeks outside Ephesus and engaged them; the wording gives the impression of very tight temporal succession, almost immediacy (Her V.102,2). The 'catching up' is somewhat disputable; the fact is that the two sides engaged, which means the rebels did not seek refuge behind the walls and might thus have been waiting for this engagement with confidence. It must be noted that the Persians were victorious and the Persian cavalry is not mentioned. Any attempt to reconstruct such a battle is pure speculation and attempts to guess numbers, battle order and succession of events (Ray 2009) are unsatisfactory. Indeed the rebels, including the contingents from the mainland, were soundly beaten; the Eretrians were mauled much worse than the Athenians, having lost their commander. It is the first *recorded* set-piece battle between Hoplites and Persian line infantry plus imperial subject troops.

Herodotus speaks of a great disaster, but this is mainly to exonerate the Athenian retreat and the refusal for any further assistance until after the battle of Mycale (Her V.103,1). His account (Her V.102,2–3) is exaggerated (Grundy 1901); Ephesus may have been knocked out and ever since not participating in – or even actively counteracting (Her VI.16,2) – the rebellion. It is true that Herodotus *never* specifically mentions Ephesus as taking part in the rebellion. Actually, when the rebels raided Sardis they left their ships at the *territory* of Ephesus (Her V.100), not at the port of the city – a note which invites a great Why. The assault force took *guides* from Ephesus (ibid) but there is no direct mention of Ephesian troops rallying under the standards of the rebellion and boosting the numbers. Even when joining battle with the Persians, it is not mentioned specifically that the rebels were admitted within the city walls before or – and this is important – after their defeat. Herodotus simply states that the defeated fled to their cities (Her V.102,3). A really laconic and out of context later comment is clarifying that the Persian victory sent the rebels running to their ships (Her V.116) and obviously this was their exit strategy which allowed them to return to their different countries and cities (Her V.102,3).

Athens did exactly the same – extracted her troops back home. The defeat was a perfect pretext for what must have been a new, pro-Persian if not actively medizing government, possibly of Cleisthenes' medizing party (Grundy 1901). It might have held sway until 493 BC or so, as heavily fining a tragic poet for causing guilt and consternation to the Athenians for their treason of the Ionians (Her VI.21,2) is only understandable under this light. On the other hand, both the Athenians (Grant

2012) and the Ionians (Grundy 1901) were thinking that their Hoplite prowess was eminently superior to the effeminate oriental battle practices and the result of the battle woke them up to most unfortunate prospects (Grundy 1901). The former retired in haste across the Aegean and the latter made preparations for mass evacuation to one refuge or another, considering Sardinia, the island of Leros and finally Myrcinus, the fief of Histiaeus in Thrace. The latter implies the place was considered at the time a safe haven from the threat of the imperial forces (Her V.125). The operations continued for quite some time, actually almost four years if not more, thus the Persian victory was not decisive. There is another indication, rather conclusive: after their victory, the Persian generals divided the theatre of operations and each took over an area, but one of them, tipped that Caria revolted, turned his attention there (Her V.117).

This particular development shows clearly a number of events and associations: the Sardis expedition was within the same expeditionary period, despite the somewhat hazy timeline of Herodotus. Some scholars (Grundy 1901) firmly believe that the division of the rebellious areas among the Achaemenid generals and the suppression missions took effect after one more year.

Caria revolted after the battle of Ephesus (Her V.103,2), which was a clear Persian victory. Thus the rising happened *after* the news of the burning of Sardis, possibly a bit exaggerated, had time to get there and sink in. The Ionian victory at Sardis, no matter how insignificant, primed the Carians and the defeat off Ephesus was not important enough to make them reconsider; alternatively, they might have rebelled *before* the battle occurred, or, as noted above, before the *news* of the battle came to the attention of the citizenry. Thus, one of the Persian generals, Daurices, was diverted to quell Caria. Most probably the Hellespontine region had rebelled before the battle of Ephesus, with some persuasion from the rebel fleet, and Caria after it. The Achaemenid general assigned to the Hellespontine region had been diverted to assist the threatened satrapal capital, Sardis, which had been left exposed perhaps due to an early attempt of its home troops against Miletus. This allowed the rebels to ignite the rebellion at the Hellespontine region, which was also bereft of troops. Once Sardis was safe and the rebels soundly beaten on land, Otanes remained in the vicinity while his colleagues from further east were diverted to operate at his original, wider area of responsibility. Actually, the Hellespont was the theatre of much more intense counterinsurgency than Ionia and Aeolis, the core areas of the rebellion, at least during the opening Persian moves.

The Carians were soundly beaten by the army of Daurices that descended upon them, leaving his campaign at the Hellespont unconcluded. This was another field victory for the Imperials achieved without any mention of cavalry and with the Persians advancing confidently and crossing a river before attacking the lined up

Hoplites (Her V.119,1). This is in stark contrast to Mardonius' skulking *behind* a river in Plataea, 479 BC, and expecting the Greek Hoplites to cross and attack him (Her IX.40). The defeated Carians retreated in despair (Her V.119,1), but were reinforced by Ionian forces, especially Milesians, gave it another try but were again decisively defeated (Her V.120). Although once more the effort to recreate the battles is unconvincing, the proposal that after these brilliant results the Persian commander tried to seize the opportunity, invade Caria and perhaps subjugate it anew before the rebellion became stabilized there is persuasive (Ray 2009). But this time his confidence, maximized by the string of three battlefield victories, took him into the jaws of defeat. A night ambush by the remaining Carian forces practically exterminated his command, himself and his colleagues – or lieutenants – Amorges and Sisimakes (Her V.121). Ray (2009) believes that a healthy fraction of his troops survived but this is debatable after a night action in a foreign, hostile country without many friends around. On the other hand, it is indeed possible that a bait of some kind, as later in Salamis, was used to lure the Imperials into a careless advance (Burn 1962), as they usually refrained from night operations but for the most expedient cases, as with the night flanking manoeuvre of Hydarnes in Thermopylae (Her VII.215).

If one reads Herodotus without prejudice, the conclusion might be that the campaign of Daurices in Caria took place in the next expeditionary season than the battle of Ephesus, with Daurices reinforced by the other two Persian commanders previously mentioned (Her V.121). The participation of Myrsus, Lydian royalty and obviously a loyalist, means Lydian satrapal levies were included in this task force, which is weird, as the Satrap Artaphrenes would have good use for these troops in-theatre. It is possible, but highly improbable, that Daurices was the military commander of Artaphrenes' satrapy (and thus the commanding officer of Myrsus), leaving Otanes for the same role at Dascylium and Hymaes at Cappadocia. This makes for only one army group coming from beyond Halys to succour Artaphrenes in the first phase of the revolt. Of course, there is also a possibility that Amorges and Sisimakes were, in fact, satrapal generals from further east in Asia Minor who came to the rescue and not Daurices' lieutenants.

Herodotus' narrative at this point captures most probably two (Ray 2009) but conceivably three years of the Ionian revolt. There are three other lines of events that may have developed simultaneously and desperately need some kind of alignment. The first is the revolt of Cyprus (Her V.104); the second is the fate of the protagonists, Histiaeus (Her VI.30) and Aristagoras (Her V.126,2). And the third is the developments in the peninsula of Helle, the fiefdom of Miltiades, and the expedition of the Scythians in these territories (Her VI.40).

Cyprus: a decisive sideshow

The revolt of Cyprus must have taken place before the battle of Ephesus (Her V. 108). Instigated by Onesilus of Salamis, younger brother of the steadily pro-Persian King Gorgus whom he deposed without exterminating (Her V.104,2) – a common but lethal mistake of the insurgents (Her V.38,1 & VI.9,2–3), it spread throughout the island. Salamis was situated at the heart of the eastern bay of Cyprus, and the rebellion was countered by the Phoenician cities of the south/southeast, Amathous reportedly (Her V.104,3) and Kition probably (Burn 1962). The imperial force tasked to suppress it was mustered under Artybius at Cilicia and crossed to Cyprus on Phoenician vessels (Her V.108), most probably by landing to Kerynia at the northern side of the island, to outmanoeuvre the Ionian fleet sent for assistance (Her V.108,2). The latter was probably patrolling off Salamis, the epicentre of the revolt of Cyprus, as was the case with Ionia, where the fleet was assembling at Miletus. As a result, the Persian army had to cross the mountain range of Pentadaktylos to approach Salamis and make contact or relieve Amathous (Burn 1962).

The satrapy of Phoenicia must have contributed vessels, marines and crews but not land forces; still, Persian troops stationed there might have been mobilized and participated. The forces of Cilicia, Persian and native, must have been the backbone, under Artybius, who must have been the general of the satrapy, as Cilicia was self-governed by the local *Syennesis* line of rulers (Her V.118,2). It should be noted that Behistun does not mention Cilicia as a satrapy; nor Phoenicia; the latter must have been included either in Arabia or, less probably, in Assyria. It is not very clear which timeframe of the Persian state is commemorated in the list of Behistun, but 23 lands are mentioned while Herodotus mentions 20 satrapies returning taxes plus Persis, and Xerxes' army included 29 commands based on territorial muster and conscription.

Irrespective of the exact administrative background, the possibility that Artybius led an imperial relief force coming from the heartland of the empire to quell the rebellion in Ionia or Cyprus (Grundy 1901) cannot be dismissed either – and local forces might well have been herded to enhance it. The imperial officers had recruited subject militias massively to boost the numbers of crack Persian troops (Her V.110), a clear precedent of Marathon and possibly a standard operating procedure for the imperial administration. Loyalist troops in Cyprus might have joined, but not necessarily so; they were the militia of one city only (Her V.104,3) or, at most, of a few plus some exiles from the other cities and the rebel army might have been positioned so as to interdict such moves. It is important that once more there is no mention of Persian cavalry, but for the mount of the commander (Her V.111). In Cilicia, there was a special cavalry division of Rapid Deployment Force character

(Her III.90,3) but probably it could not be readily transported; this must have been the reason for the later design and construction of horse-transports by the imperial shipwrights (Her VI.48,2), as in Cyprus the local chariotry (Her V.113,1) may well have been the only cavalry force of any consequence (Burn 1962).

Artybius crossed and disembarked his army uncontested, before any intervention from the rebels. But an intervention did occur, although belatedly. An Ionian fleet of unknown size appeared, took some counsel with the natives (Her V.109), engaged and defeated the Phoenician navy (Her V.112,1). The latter, after having disembarked the invasion force, sailed round the NE promontory of the island probably, to approach Salamis. Its defeat and rout left the Persian land army stranded on the island and set the stage for a spectacular disaster for the Imperials. The early demise of the invading general during the decisive clash by the hand of the rebel commander (Her V.112,2) advanced this possibility. Alas, a massive defection turned the tables (Her V.113,1). It was initiated by the chariotry of Salamis proper (Her V.113,1) showing the pro-Persian sentiments of the upper class, evidently friendly to and aligned with the deposed Gorgus. They were swiftly followed by the contingent of Curium (Her V.13,1). The rebel host was disintegrated. The victorious Ionian fleet left in the wake of the decisive defeat of the land army (Her V.115,1) or due to the more or less spontaneous submission of Salamis, once Onesilus and his supporters had been beaten and killed in battle (Her V.113,2) and the Salaminian loyalists, surviving from the battlefield, returned home uncontested.

This development must have been interpreted by the Ionian fleet as a good reason to retire to its home ports and bases (Burn 1962). Thus the naval supremacy was forfeited by the rebels and the vanquished imperial navy resumed operations to support the victorious land army and the replacement of Artybius, never mentioned by name, possibly reinforced from the Asian mainland, was able to reduce the isolated cities one by one with siege warfare. Of course, any number of Cypriot cities must have capitulated readily and were not stormed (Her V.115,1). The end result was that Cyprus was reconquered rather fast; Soloi, the most reliable and eager ally of Onesilus, its contingent being deployed along with the Salaminians against the Persian division of the army of Artybius (Her V.110), was the last city to be reduced. It withstood a siege for five months, but eventually fell (Her V.115,2). Conceivably the successful Persian sieges were simultaneously carried out against a number of cities in order to finish with the rebellion in Cyprus as fast as possible (Her V.115,1), thus accounting for a full campaigning season to pacify Cyprus (Her V.116,1) but no more than that.

The (lack of) use of Cilician shipping during the campaign, which featured prominently in the invasion of 480 bc, is as weird as the silence on the subject of Cypriot fleets, which were even more prominent in the 480s. The former was smaller than the Phoenician one, but could have provided most welcome assistance and was in-theatre from the first moment. Perhaps its size made Artybius wait for the main, Phoenician naval force and then the Cilician contingent was never mentioned even if participating. For the Cypriots it might have been an issue of managing manpower; the need for troops on land might have undermined their ability to man their fleets, or such fleets may have been underdeveloped or politically unavailable if skippers and owners were loyalists which is the most probable interpretation. The question is the Ionian fleet. It represented a massive effort in terms of human resources with 20,000 mariners required for the manning of 100 vessels. If the operations in Cyprus unfolded simultaneously with the battles of Ephesus or the events in Caria, the rebel land forces would have been depleted or, at least, lower than standard. This would apply to the field armies and to the garrisons defending the walls of the rebellious cities.

The joker and the schemer

On the subject of the instigators, Aristagoras must have been killed in action after the battle of Ephesus, while trying to secure the European fief of Histiaeus (Her V.124,2), against the natives' bitter resistance (Her V.126). The effort was to secure a refuge, since the land operations looked like a huge disappointment. At the same time, Histiaeus must have been nearby. His usefulness for Darius, a master in quelling and suppressing revolts (DB 52–4), would have been early after the onset of the rebellion, to allow for imperial mobilization and to contain the spread of the revolt. Alternatively, he would have been invaluable if the immediate containment efforts had failed and things were going sour. The latter version implies that he was dispatched after the fall of Sardis and the disaster of Daurices and supports the suggestion of a Babylonian revolt at this approximate time, instead of shortly before the campaign of Xerxes in Greece (Gertoux 2018), as it would account for the inability of the Empire to send more household troops.

Histiaeus was an important imperial official, on a grandiose mission (Her V.106), thus he must have had with him a considerable retinue, especially a bodyguard. Once at Sardis, Artaphrenes challenged him, but at this point, Herodotus' timeline must be off: Histiaeus was a brilliant opportunist and wily plotter and would not have been uncovered that easily. Possibly he had a dispute with Artaphrenes over his mandate and the latter's inadequacy in preventing and containing the uprising. The issue is recurring, as Aristagoras' troubles with the imperial administration started in a similar way (Her V.33,4 & 35,1), over the specifics of the chain-of-command shared between a foreign dignitary of high status within the empire and a Persian and member of the extended family of the monarch (incidentally,

Artaphrenes' nephew). Histiaeus must have sent letters to prominent Persians (Her VI.4,1) while he was still at Sardis, *not* after he had escaped. His intention must have been to introduce himself as the supreme commander in theatre, *Karana*, and call for their support, acceptance and loyalty based on the imperial mandate bestowed upon him. Artaphrenes must have executed without trial everybody sympathetic or responsive to such a call (Her VI.4,2). Subsequently, Artaphrenes accused the isolated Histiaeus of conspiracy. He was not guilty, but would have no chance to prove his case, nor a hearing by the king; and so he changed sides (Her VI.2,1). His capture and death occurred after the fall of Miletus (Her VI.28–29), thus he was active in the vicinity of the Bosporus for quite some time (Her VI.26), perhaps counted in years.

What were his actions? He tried of course to assume the leadership of the rebellion, or at least to participate, but he failed. He failed at his city, where his character, beliefs and allegiances were known, and in other rebel fortresses and bases (Her VI.5,1–2); but he was accepted in Lesbos (Her VI.5,2), with territory lost repeatedly to the Athenians and then conceded to the empire by Hippias, as was the Sigium (Her V.94,1). From there he raised a buccaneer squadron of eight triremes and moved to the Bosporus, to control the exit of the straits, commandeering the vessels passing by and thus creating his own fleet (Her VI.5,3). This is a safe sign that at least the European, if not both sides of the straits were controlled by the rebels. Once Miletus had been sacked, Histiaeus sailed to and besieged Thasos (Her VI.28), hoping to get both plentiful resources from the gold mines of the islanders located on the mainland (Her VI.46), and an island refuge in case things became even worse in Ionia. These were exactly the thoughts and course of action of Aristagoras, which means that Histiaeus was the schemer who devised the contingency plan followed by the latter.

Histiaeus' presence with his fleet at Lesbos, while the epicentres of the action were Miletus and the Hellespont (Her VI.288,1), leaves some questions unanswered. Once gone rogue, he wanted to atone or to betray the revolt to Darius and be pardoned? Most probably he played double jeopardy. Though, in his effort to secure supplies, he raided the shore just opposite Lesbos, where a considerable Persian force was operating under a certain Harpagus who is not mentioned before (Her VI.28,2). The objectives of this imperial force are open to speculation. Perhaps, although the Imperials were around Miletus, this force was keeping in order the re-conquered Hellespontines and thus Harpagus may have been the successor of Hymaes (Ray 2009) who had died of disease earlier (Her V.122,2). Harpagus was victorious in the clash with Histiaeus' private army; in this case, Herodotus specifically reports that it was the cavalry, returning in the nick of time, which won the day for the Imperials charging the already engaged Greek phalanx (Her

VI.29,1). Herodotus' wording is very specific and makes a good listener or reader curious as to where this cavalry had been in the first place and whether it was under the command of Harpagus or was an independent command which operated nearby at the time and thus Harpagus' command may be understood as deprived of cavalry. Histiaeus was taken alive, but once in custody, Artaphrenes and Harpagus murdered him to make sure there would be no pardoning by Darius (Her VI.30), nor any uneasy versions of previous events presented to the monarch.

The Scythian connection

The most important issue of that time, and the least understood or known, is the whereabouts of Miltiades; in this issue, the haze of time and lack of sources is exacerbated by the bias of Herodotus. Still, there are some facts: Miltiades suggested the destruction of the bridge at the Ister and the Scythians had requested with envoys to the Ionians exactly that. It is more than probable that Miltiades had contacts with the Scythians, at least with their envoys and his proposal was actually a suggestion to conform to their plan. Even if that occasion had been their very first encounter, which is dubious, the resulting understanding and the common objectives suggest that they established a relationship. When Darius crossed to Europe, some or other Ionian would have tipped him off about Miltiades' proceedings, if for no other reason than to demonstrate his own loyalty, reliability and allegiance and reap the imperial gratitude which was always a reliable prospect (DB 63). Histiaeus would be the most probable such agent, but Miltiades considered a Parian, Lysagoras (Her VI.133,1) as the culprit, long after Histiaeus was dead.

The Scythian campaign had been an unqualified disaster (Grundy 1901) as the Persians were continuously sending expeditions or feigned expeditions to Thrace (campaign of Megabazus and Otanes shortly after 513 BC; feigned campaigns of Megabates and Aristagoras in 500 BC. The Persians would set course to Thrace, for example, and then midway turn west to take the islanders unsuspecting. It was a disaster, no matter how many new territories were added to the empire – or were claimed to have been occupied by the Empire – the objective was not realized, the Scythians remained impervious to imperial lessons, the imperial prestige was tarnished and the casualties were significant. The retirement of Darius' host induced an avalanche of defections and revolts, with the bridge over the Bosporus being destroyed – or the infrastructure for its forming compromised – by the locals, who suffered severe retribution later by Otanes, the general of the Hellespontine regions (Her V.27,2). Darius thus had to cross from the Hellespont (Her IV.143,1), squarely in Miltiades' fief. Was there an understanding? Or was it precisely at this point that Miltiades became exiled from his fiefdom, and possibly found refuge (Burn 1962) at the court of his father-in-law, King Olorus, in Thrace (Her VI.39,2)? It is a given that after the fall of Miletus Miltiades returned, or migrated, to Athens with most of his personal belongings and retainers in four triremes. Although he had some loss, starting with five triremes, which is at least 1,000 sailors and most likely many more boarders, as he had been maintaining a personal bodyguard of 500 (Her VI.39,2) says a lot for his affluence. One vessel was captured by the Phoenician navy and the captain, a son of Miltiades, was brought to the king's presence. Instead of revenge on a proxy, Darius actually turned the man into a prominent vassal, probably at the instigation of the Peisistratids, who had previously profitable understandings – and undertakings – with his father (Burn 1962). It follows that Miltiades retained considerable resources when returning to a city owning, or able to mobilize, only fifty galleys as a state fleet, whatever the definition of state fleet at the time. What happened between Miltiades' self-exile to Thrace and his escape to Athens?

After Darius' return to Asia, the Scythians returned the favour to the empire; they crossed the Ister and invaded south, all the way to the Hellespont. Herodotus narrates that Miltiades ran into exile to avoid their onslaught, and returned to his seat after they retired. Perhaps he genuinely understands it to have been so and it is not due to his bias, but it is difficult to believe this as the facts do not add up. First, how, after his expressed intention to destroy the empire and the king's person, had he been left in charge of his fief, when Megabazus and Otanes were either pacifying or conquering the region(s) anew (Her V.1–27)? Second, how exactly did the Scythians cross the Ister? Had they had the means, they would have done so to pursue the Persian host, not wait a decade or so for a punitive expedition. Third, Miltiades was the one Greek who they would NOT brutalize, nor his territory; he had the guts to play by their plan and they knew it. Failure to see it to fruition was not *his* fault; on the contrary, he suffered retributions by the Persians. And fourth, when exactly did these events unfold?

A much more logical reconstruction of events is as follows: Darius is tipped off about Miltiades' intentions and the latter escapes even before Darius crosses *back* over the Ister, or shortly afterwards. Darius cannot cross from the Bosporus back to Asia due to rebellions, possibly erupting in concert with the Scythians, which implies Miltiades had an even more focal role in the events. These rebellions, especially at Byzantium, do not allow safe embarkation of the imperial troops to the fleet and/or local vessels; thus Darius advances W-SW to the Helle's peninsula, invades Miltiades' fief, from where his fleet performs the crossing of the army uncontested and unmolested.

Miltiades of course has fled to his father-in-law, in Thrace. This implies the imperial control did not include the whole of Thrace, not even in a nominal form.

There, Miltiades remains in (self-)exile, while his territory is absorbed into the empire. Moreover, the empire stages its punitive expeditions of Megabazus in Thrace from this base, at least until securing, in conditions of utmost urgency, another staging point with facilities allowing transportation and billeting of troops, Perinthus (Her V.1). It is Miltiades who comes to an understanding with the Scythians so that as they invade the necessary means to cross the Ister might have been supplied by Miltiades' collaborators in Thrace or rebellious cities of the Black Sea region upon the explosive phase of the expansion of the Ionian Revolt, in 498 BC, after the burning of Sardis. The Scythians had overrun the Persian Thrace down to the Hellespont and were contemplating how to cross it and invade Asia. They do not find any solution, their supplies dwindle so they pack their spoils and retire. Consequently, the Persian occupation in Thrace and Europe is no more, except for some fortified positions, as is Doriscus, and Miltiades is restored, not because the Scythians had retired, but because they destroyed the Persian power base in the area and the peninsula of Helle was free of the imperial yoke once more.

This Scythian raid and attempt to invade Asia from the Hellespont, which meant utilizing Hellespontine vessels, must have been timed with the Ionian revolt, or slightly after its eruption, as Miltiades, a personal enemy of Histiaeus, most probably had no clue of the conspiracy. The Scythians needed little in terms of preparations. Thus, the rise of the Hellespont created a very flammable situation for the Persians: the Scythians were roaming through their new conquests and showing every intention of invading Asia. The Ionian fleet had appeared nearby instigating revolt and offering transport services to the Paeonians from Asia to Europe. Such transport services might become available to the Scythians in the opposite direction. This prospect is the only rational explanation for the actual prioritization and division of tasks among the three imperial task forces after saving Sardis and beating the raiders near Ephesus: two out of three were delegated to the Hellespontine region, and the third embarked on a very conservative disciplinary campaign, almost timid. The two forces in the north were attempting to seal the Hellespont against any Scythian seaborne invasion and one of them was diverted to the south due to the rebellion in Caria, which could arouse the whole southern coast of Asia Minor, possibly all the way to Phoenicia, thus cutting the strategic supply line through Cilicia and destabilizing the whole western part of the empire.

The Persians were mostly successful, as the rebellion was contained in the south and suppressed in the north. The Scythians, unable to cross, retired, but the European territories of the Empire, the *Skudra*, were no more. Miltiades returned to his fief, according to Herodotus, three years before his final expulsion (Her VI.40), meaning between 497 and 496 BC. Histiaeus, who might have attempted to assist the Scythian crossing, had no trouble sailing up the Hellespont (the Asian coast being perhaps under imperial control due to Daurices, the European under the rebels) and made camp near the Bosporus for quite some time, commandeering – or arresting/ mustering/ seizing, words are a matter of perspective – vessels coming from the Black Sea to Propontis, mostly merchantmen (Her VI.5,3). His ulterior motive must have been to prepare for another attempt to mass transport European troops to Asia; conceivably from his fief in Myrcinus, had Aristagoras not made a mess (Her V.126) of his instructions, or a new wave of Scythians. Alternatively, it might have been to be ready for a mass migration of the Ionian Greeks to Europe. In any case, the rebellion continued for some years, with Miltiades giving the example in Europe while some bases of the Empire, such as Doriscus, were holding out but without any spectacular result in re-establishing the Imperium at these lands; it was perhaps this failure and caution instead of aggressiveness which later prompted Xerxes to replace the respective commanders (Her VII.105).

Epilogue

The events narrated previously may have been developing from 499 BC (the year of the rebellion) to 497 BC at the latest, if the night ambush in Caria happened during a second campaigning season of the Persians. After this disaster, the Persians are no longer heard to operate in Caria and the Carians to partake in the rebellion (Grundy 1901). Histiaeus' capture dates perhaps in 493 BC. The battle of Lade, with the imperial fleet facing and, after initiating a mass defection, annihilating the rebel one (Her VI.14–5) is usually considered as taking place in 495 BC but more probably in 494 BC, with the siege and fall of Miletus following suit in the sixth year after the eruption of the rebellion by Aristagoras (Her VI.18). The massive mopping up which swept the rebellious islands of Lesbos and Chios and the Hellespontine region was undertaken by the victorious Imperial fleet during the next campaigning season (Her VI.31 & 33), probably during the year 493 BC, to be followed by the expedition of Mardonius in 492 BC (Her VI.43). This means at the very least a two-year *lapsus* in the Herodotean narration of the Persian operations. It may be surmised that at this time the Carians were effectively withdrawn from the operations – perhaps under a separate treaty (Grundy 1901). The same must be understood for several Ionian and Aeolian cities, including Ephesus (Burn 1962; Grundy 1901), which was unspoiled, and Kyzicus (Her VI.33,3). The Asian coast of the Hellespont and much of the Propontis were already suppressed once more into bondage (Her V.117 & 122), although Miltiades was keeping the fire of the rebellion kindled at the European coast of the Hellespont and Histiaeus was operating in the vicinity of the Bosporus.

Herodotus reads rather confidently for his timelines up to the ambush near Pedasus and is certain since the campaign of Lade. However he realises that something is amiss in between and keeps providing temporal points through the story of Miltiades (Her VI.40,1) and the total duration of the Cypriot revolt (Her V.116) as well as the duration of the insurgency from the rise to the fall of Miletus (Her VI.18). Modern scholarship deals with this very thorny issue by supposing that the chronicles of one or two missing years were lost to Herodotus, or that Herodotus' timeline, accounting for two years, is compressed and the events of the first phase should be understood to fill up to five years (Grundy 1901; Burn 1962); alternatively, that the disaster in Pedasus required another imperial army which took some time to be raised (Grundy 1901).

But reshaping and reshuffling Herodotus, especially when he *insists* he knows accurately something, is a questionable practice. It is more probable that something happened and caused that lull in the operational tempo of the empire. If the Babylonian archives mentioning Xerxes as king count his time as co-regent as regnal years, the respective events must be predated by the years of the regency, which are 11–12 and the two Babylonian revolts attested for the beginning of his reign actually took place during his regency, long before he became king, perhaps in 496 BC (Gertoux 2018). These uprisings may have been the consequences of the imperial reverses in the efforts to suppress the western uprising or direct results of the revolt *per se* as it was spreading from the far west to the Levantine areas. This conflagration at the heart of the empire accounts for a lull in the western front and the observed lack of westbound imperial armies as the flow of forces was interrupted in Mesopotamia and the available reserves were redirected to the much more vital central sector of the empire.

When the Babylonian uprising had been resolved, imperial forces were freed and promptly dispatched to the west. Up to then, the suppression must have been assigned to more or less local forces mobilized by the neighbouring satrapies (Her V.102,1) and not imperial troops as suggested by some modern scholars (Grundy 1901). This theory explains the consternation of Darius when conversing with Histiaeus (Her V.106,1) and the latter's dispatch to the western theatre. Darius, a seasoned counter-insurgency veteran sounds vexed with the events as he should not have been, had there not been some serious complications. Nor should the appearance of a few thousand mainlanders (Athenians and Eretrians) been of consequence. But the obvious Athenian tendency to export their mischievous political system was leading by default to rebellions that may have spread in the realm like a wildfire. The latter coincided with the prospect of a Spartan invasion from the west (Her VI.84,2), as a consequence of their proclamation to Cyrus (Her I.152,2–3), followed by a pact with a clause for a Scythian invasion either in Central Asia (Her VI.84,2) or through the Dardanelles (Her VI.40,1). Were all these meticulously planned and executed or spontaneously happening while a Babylonian uprising erupted? Darius had no way to tell and the sum, real or prospective, was another thing altogether, a worst repetition of the multiple fronts of 521–519 BC (DB 16–30).

Once the Persians destroyed the rebel fleet and razed the rebel base at Miletus (Her VI.18), they took a year to recapture the major islands (Her VI.31) and the Hellespontine cities (Her VI.33,1) in a brutal campaign of reprisals (Her VI.32) by their mostly Phoenician navy (Her VI.41,1); reprisals that might have been rather selective, though, in terms of class, person and/or clan (Burn 1962). Most, but by no means all, of the affected areas were at the European side, as Hymaes and Daurices had already reduced (most of) the Asian coast (Her VI.33,1). Still, Herodotus' description of the fate of Kyzicus (Her VI.33,3) implies that not all the Asiatic coast had been pacified. In any case, the Phoenicians stopped only due to their mystical terror of the Black Sea, refraining from a pursuit of the Greek fugitives into the bosom of the Euxine (Her VI.33,2).

Chapter 8

The Operations of the Ionian Revolt

The operations during the multi-year confrontation that was the Ionian Revolt – longer by far than the actual Greco-Persian wars, which were decided within two campaigning seasons at the very most – are by definition difficult to recreate. The rebellion occurred at the end of the standard campaigning season, after the fiasco at Naxos, which weakened and demoralized the Persians and had the Ionian fleet concentrated and still mobilized and fully manned. When the event came into being, the fleet was back, the imperial infantry that made up the invasion land army (Her V.32) was perhaps on its way home – or deactivated – while the naval arm was still concentrated and not demobilized (Grundy 1901). With the winter at their heels, the Imperials could do little. The rebels were able to get organized and ask for assistance. Only Athens and Eretria obliged (Her V.99,1), both instigated by sentiments of friendship, kinship (Her V.97,2), mutuality (Her V.99,1), greed (Her V.49,4 & 97,1) but conceivably by alarm as well (de Souza 2003). Aristagoras would have told them of the imperial projections against Euboea first – where Eretria was situated – and the mainland afterwards, with Athens being literally next door. The initial phase of the imperial invasion plan was the recent attack of the empire against Naxos; a failed attack it was, but a most direct display of intentions. It was a plan suggested by Aristagorus (Her V.31) and he was in charge (Her V.33,4 & 31,2), but these details must have been omitted during his eloquent requests for assistance.

The Athenians dispatched twenty vessels (Her V.99,1); they might have sent pentekonters, not triremes, to assist Aristagoras' insurrection (Haas 1985). There are many reasons for that, which may have applied exclusively or inclusively. It may have been a matter of arms acquisition; Athens might have no triremes at the time, or not enough of them, to dispatch and to risk. It might have been a matter of policy: pentekonters might have been supplied by private interests and most of the rowers/troops may have been their associates or volunteers. It might have been an issue of strategic consideration: twenty pentekonters were manned by 1,000 rowers which were doubling as soldiers, while the trireme needed four times that number, an astounding 4,000 men, thus increasing the expenses but also the exposure of Athenian human resources. Or, last but not least, it may have been a matter of objectives and ulterior motives. Pentekonters were much better for transporting considerable loads, a fitting choice for an expedition possibly instigated by greed and intended primarily to loot and plunder, as is obvious by Aristagoras' arguments to the Spartans (Her V.49,4). It is almost certain that the essence, which persuaded the Athenians, had been the same, plus some emotional arguments that the Milesians, and the Ionians in general, were colonials under Athens and thus they were entitled to ask for assistance.

The Athenians were bound to oblige. If the Athenian government at the time was against Cleisthenes and his Medizm, which must have been the case due to the dispatch of reinforcements, it is most likely that it would also have been very sensitive to the Ionian ancestry and clinched the argument. This Ionian ancestry had been feverishly attacked by Cleisthenes, by disowning the four Ionian tribes and replacing them with ten Attic ones based on residence, not bloodline (Her V.69,1). The immigrant status of his family, with its preposterously close tyrannical associations; the similarly originated wealth, which was donated by Croesus (Her VI.125), a king; and the close blood relations with Cleisthenes of Sicyon, a bookcase tyrant (Her V.69,1) meant that their democratic credentials and their patriotic ones were at the very least debatable (Grundy 1901). By attacking the roots of the natives and proposing another, alternate, Pelasgian lineage as Herodotus feels duty-bound to mention (Her I.56,2) although he disproves of it himself (Her VI.137,-2), the immigrant family became integrated into the body of the population. So it did with other immigrants and their origin was washed into residence rather than bloodline, thus allowing them to occupy privileged positions in public life thanks to their wealth.

The first rebel operation, with the opening of the sailing season of 499 BC (the most probable year) was the mass escape of the Paeonians (Her V.98); the conception of a real mastermind. The megalomaniac Achaemenid emperor, treated with extreme caution and leniency by the Greek sources for incomprehensible reasons despite slaughtering, crucifying and enslaving people due to his own (Her V.14) or his wife's whim (Her III.134,5) was not to take lightly the loss of his human property. Without risking one man, the rebels fixed a rendezvous with the fugitives, massively transported them to the safety of Chios and from there, at leisure, via Lesbos to the Thracian Aegean coast, and more specifically to Doriscus (**Map 7.1**). In this way, the fugitives were able to return home by land (Her V.98). The Persian control in this area, hammered to its ultimate extent through the wedlock of the line of Megabazus with the Argead kingdom in Macedon (Her V.21,2) which became if not subject, then either tributary or allied, was evidently a thing of the past. The fugitives were never harassed, although at Doriscus a viceroy was in place since Darius' Scythian expedition (Her VII.59,1). The Persian control was shaken off once more (Her V.103,2) in the region along the straits (Her V.27,2; Ktesias 25) and, as later developments show (the campaign of Mardonius – see below), in the whole of Europe as well. From the expedition of Darius to the campaign of Xerxes there is never a satrap of Skudra (the European imperial territories) mentioned in the narrative or the sources, nor a satrapy enumerated in the Persian Empire. It is possible that the governor Artayctes was established at Sestos (Her VII.33) most probably after the crossing of Xerxes in 480 BC and definitely not earlier than the campaign of Mardonius in 492 BC.

A Persian cavalry force, operating as always independently, was pursuing the fugitives and did so all the way to the shore; it had been mobilized too late, as it was not able to intercept them in time (Her V.98,4). This was the object of the rebel-fugitive conspiracy; to drag the imperial cavalry out of position as west as possible, opposite Chios (Her V.98,4) and have it there out of breath (**Map 7.1**). While the rebel navy were taking the revolt north, to the Hellespont, and south, to Caria and Cyprus, an amphibious task force with the token reinforcements of the mainland (Her V.99,1) entered the scene. They had one eye (or both) on pillage and loot, but their presence was prone to implicate the mainlanders definitively and unequivocally. And they made their move.

It was a most resolute decision (Grundy 1901), to attack the nest of the serpent; as the conflagration expanded in the periphery far and wide, attracting or pinning imperial garrisons or yeoman forces, the rebels emerged, as mentioned previously, off Sardis, possibly hoping to raise the Lydians into rebellion (Grundy 1901) and exterminate the Persian base of power in all respects: head, troops, infrastructure and seat. Their failure to raise the Lydians was fatal. This human buffer allowed the Persians to retire in the keep of the citadel in decent order and numbers, covered by the fire outbreak. The latter may have been an accident, a deliberate action of the rebels to cause panic so as to stun resistance and infiltrate the fortified citadel or a Persian desperate measure to intercept the invaders by a wall of flames. The rebel operation was based on surprise, swiftness and the Lydian co-operation. The third being an abject failure, the first being degraded by the compromising of the second due to the fire, the raiders must have plundered the burnt capital and left as fast and far as possible. They could not besiege the citadel and everything moving in Asia Minor, from the garrisons and the mobilized militias and reserves of the satrapies to possible imperial levies, including the cavalry found off-position, would converge to Sardis conveniently allowing more and more areas to embrace the revolt, having got rid of garrisons and occupation troops.

The just as brilliant retirement through the mountains, back-stepping on their ingress route (Her V.101,3), made things difficult for their pursuers. The raiders went through perfectly known terrain, but their pursuers had to cross the mountains themselves, a tricky business, perhaps fraught with ambushes and traps, in unknown terrain, and turning *away* from the destroyed and despoiled, highly vulnerable capital. The operation, seen as a raid, was a dream success: much loot must have been obtained, Sardis would be neutralized as a commissariat and command hub, the Persian prestige was once more tarnished with the Satrap fleeing to the citadel for his life while his capital was turning to ashes under his feet, and the raiders back at their starting point unmolested. No surprise that this event made even some less than enthusiastic cities endorse the rebellion (Her V.103,2).

But things were not all as they seemed. The seat of the Persian power was the *citadel* of Sardis, not the lower city, and the personnel needed for peaceful and wartime administration must have suffered very few casualties. The shock was great, but both the resources and hardware, which were safeguarded by the walls, were intact and allowed the development of a response. Burning the city alienated the Lydians to pure enmity towards the Greeks and they were the natural human shields of the Persians. This phase of the war had not been won and this accounted, strategically, as a defeat. The empire would be able eventually to concentrate and dispatch overwhelming force; a massive defeat would have cleared the rebel territories from imperial infringements and imperial officials with intimate local knowledge, contacts and intelligence. Furthermore, such a victory would have attracted more subjects under the banners of rebellion. The Lydians for one were perfect candidates, having seen the satrap slain and his suppression mechanism destroyed.

Three task groups had converged on Sardis, as previously mentioned. They were under Otanes, Hymaes and Daurices, all married to Darius daughters (Her V.116,1) but not necessarily residing in Persis, since members of the royal family were assigned to the most distant satrapies, as Masistes and Achaemenes (Her IX.113 & VII.7). Finding the Persians mostly alive and well, the lower city destroyed and the raiders gone, they could do little more than try to exact revenge. They doggedly followed the rebels to their lair (Her V.116). Herodotus believes they caught up with them in Ephesus (**Map 8.1**), before they had time to board their fleet and leave the way they came (Her V.102,2). This is rather strange. Had they been in Ephesus, they would have retired into the city to board at ease, making insulting gestures to the Persian field armies. The truth for the battle of Ephesus, the first imperial success, was that the rebels were most probably spontaneously inclined to fight considering the battlefield and their decent odds; they were not brought to it by the Persian pursuit.

The rebels had excellent morale, having outgeneralled the Imperials, burnt the capital and failed to exterminate the Satrap and the base of the imperial power by a very narrow margin. They had spoils aplenty. They had a fine army arrayed,

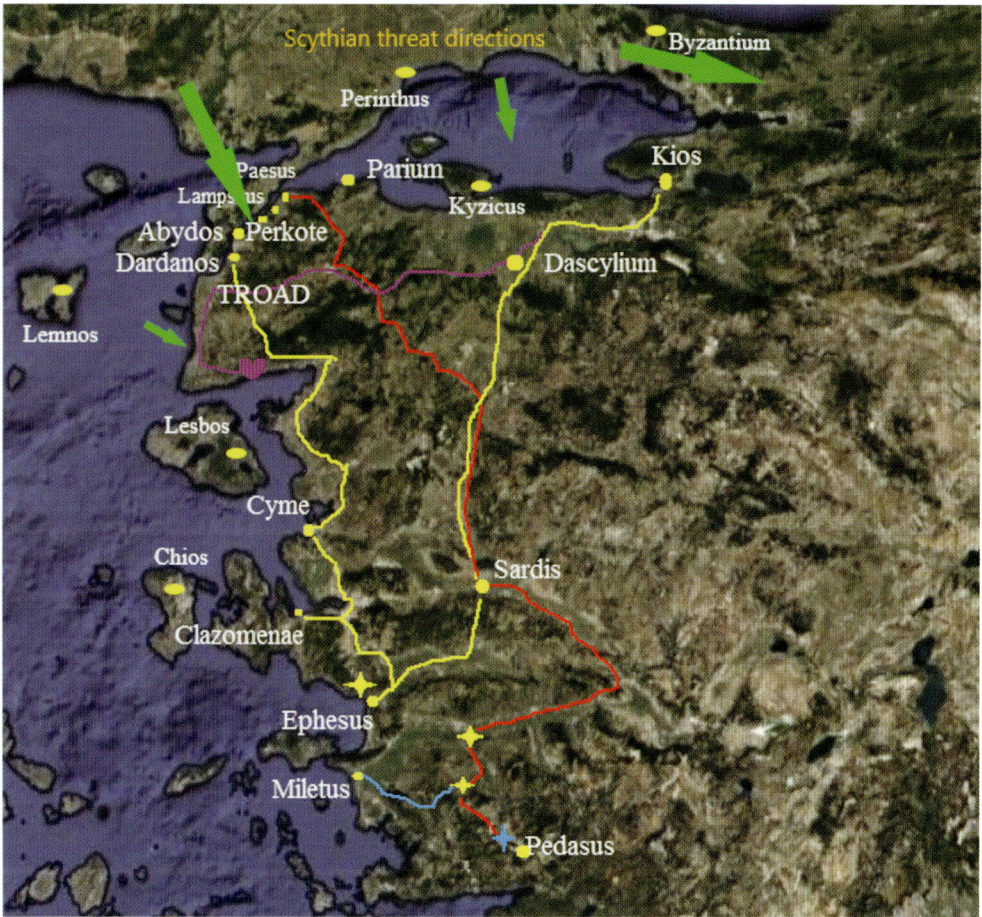

Map 8.1.
Green arrows: The possible attack routes for Scythian invasion.
Yellow lines: Initial moves of Suppression forces
Purple line: Hymaes contingency campaign in Troad
Purple heart: possible location of Hymaes' death
Red line: Daurices transition and campaign in Caria
Blue line: Milesian reinforcements for the Carians
Stars: battles. [Blue: insurgents' victory; Yellow: imperial victories]

believing that the Persians were inferior troops in an open battle as Aristagoras was claiming at Sparta, while describing the sparabara (Her V.49,3); he probably believed it himself, as it was not some lack of field prowess that brought the subjugation of Ionia to the Persians beforehand (Her I.161–76). With the Imperials taken by surprise, mobilized in a hurry and out of breath in their pursuit, while the rebels had time to regroup, rest, organize and deploy, the latter enjoyed every possible advantage. To these, one should include the security afforded by a great walled city nearby and the proximity to the sea, plus plentiful provisions. If they could beat this Imperial force they would recuperate their failure at Sardis; the Persians would have trouble assembling another such force.

They considered the options. The first was to win the battle for the rebellion with their superior Hoplites then and there. The second was to simply board their vessels and leave, exposing Ephesus to the Persian wrath, and, most importantly, to the Persian engineers and siege warfare, which had brought about the subjugation of Ionia before (Her I.162,2) and the collapse of the defence of the most formidably fortified cities in Babylonia and Egypt. They opted for the first. To be able to collect the spoils and go back, or move to another theatre, the rebels had to resolve the issue then and there, possibly while the Imperials had no cavalry, as none is reported by Herodotus. In any case, the battle was a clear defeat, shattering once and for all the morale of the rebel infantry, but – this is very important – neither their determination nor their resilience. Ephesus was not stormed, but seems to have been knocked out. Next time it emerges into the narrative (Her VI.16) it plays a dirty role in favour of the empire (Grundy 1901; Burn 1962) although its role during this early time is questionable.

The rebels and their mainlander allies were badly mauled. The Athenians, there for the plunder, understood their mandate was over, took their survivors and their part of the spoils and went home (Her V.103,1). It was a clear desertion. Whether by cowardice, recall, despair and casualties or due to the expiration of their mandate, they had come, they had plundered and they had fled. Aristagoras, who despised the Persian troops (Her V.49,3) and refused to listen to Hecataeus who proposed a naval strategy (Her V.36,2–3), opting for Hoplite decisive engagements instead (Grundy 1901) was just as astounded; he correctly understood that if the rebels could not smash Imperial forces in the field, Persian siegecraft had already spelled their doom in advance. It was rather insightfulness – albeit belated – rather than faint-heartedness (Her V.124,1) that drove his actions since, in any case, he initiated Plan B, a mass evacuation (Her V.124,2).

The three Persian generals, Otanes, Daurices and Hymaes had crushed the rebel field army and thus could move freely by land. They dispersed to operate independently, so each had a powerful army at his command, enough to take a whole theatre (**Map 8.1**). Two of them turned to the north, one (Hymaes) to southern Propontis and one (Daurices) to the Hellespont. The third, Otanes, who must have been the known general of years past (Her V.25,1) as the satrapy of Dascylium was first given to Megabazus and some years later is in the hands of Megabazus' son Oebares (Her VI.33,3), stays put. Actually, he embarks, with the home troops of Artaphrenes, into a most unimpressive campaign of suppression, resulting in two cities taken (Her V.123) with utterly unknown temporal specifics as to when, in what order and after how much delay for each. Still, these two cities, one in north

Ionia and the other in southern Aeolis (Clazomenae and Cyme respectively), sliced off the rebels of the northern theatre from Ionia proper, the cradle of the revolt and brought the Imperials once more to the Aegean coast and in possession of a major port. In any case, the Erythraean headland was holding, along with most of the nuclear part of Ionia (Burn 1962).

Actually, from Ephesus, both task groups, one of Daurices and the other under the joint command of Artaphrenes and Otanes must have moved northwards from the coastal road. The former moved to the north without losing any time in the Aegean and once in Troad, he must have entered the plateau from the western approaches of Mount Ida. Emerging in the plain he moved north to the entrance of the straits and started reducing the Asian coastal cities and sealing the Hellespont for any Scythian incursion. His success in reducing five cities in so many days (Her V.117) speaks for the (lack of) fighting spirit of the latter (Burn 1962), as the area most probably went into rebellion due to coercion by the Ionian fleet. At least one of the five cities, Lampsacus, was strong enough to have caused quite some issues to Miltiades when he lorded over the Chersonese (Her VI.37). Daurices intended, most probably, to continue to the east, to reduce the southern coast of Propontis starting with the city of Parium and including the peninsula of Kyzicus, until reaching the area of operations of Hymaes and making contact with the latter's rearguard. Hymaes, starting from Ephesus, took the inland road from Sardis to Dascylium and emerged to the SE coast of Propontis, where he reduced the city of Kios (Her V.122,1) and obviously intended to keep up in order to seal off the Bosporus, the second major access point for the Scythians. Understandably the rest of Propontis had a lower-priority vulnerability, as the Scythians would need proper, massive maritime transportation to cross, not simple ferrying services as in the Hellespont and the Bosporus. This threat was becoming less intense once the Asian part of the Hellespont was restored into Imperial control and the shipping of the rebels could not find refuge in its ports to negotiate the rather temperamental stream and weather of the Hellespont.

The last area of vulnerability to an amphibious attempt by the Scythians, improbable though possible, was the NW corner of Asia Minor, Troad and Aeolis. It was the third army, of Artaphrenes-Otanes, which was supposed to deal with it. Starting from Ephesus they moved on the same coastal road that Daurices followed, but they intended to reduce as many cities as possible, actually to subjugate Ionia anew, and then move to Aeolis and assist the garrisons left by Daurices to keep the Hellespontine cities docile. But they failed to accomplish this plan as throughout the campaign they took hold of just two cities, as already mentioned. This would make Hymaes double back before securing the Bosporus, to secure the far more vulnerable NW frontier of Asia, as will be discussed later.

And then the lightning strikes: Caria declares in its entirety – more or less – for the rebellion. Daurices, having half-finished in the Hellespont, as he had concluded the Reconquista of the Asian shoreline of the Straits and was approaching the coast of Propontis (Her V.117), was best positioned to respond, and had the best army. He surged south (Her V.117), trying a whirlwind campaign that would stunt the new rebels before they had time to organize. His 'buddy', Hymaes, takes over the vital area of the Hellespont, leaving behind the less vulnerable Propontis (Her V.122,2). The new developments with Caria made Troad vital, as the insurgents could use it as a base to undo Daurices' work in the Hellespontine area; at the same time, the force of Artaphrenes-Otanes is not available; it has to stay near Sardis should a Carian army emerge. Thus, Hymaes was the only available solution. He must have retraced his steps west to Dascylium and from there continued west, to take the eastern slopes of Mount Ida in the plain of Troad (Her V.122). After a brief time, during which he subdued all the wider area of Troad and thus brought the whole shore of NW Asia Minor under the Imperium, he died (Her V.122,2), possibly from disease, as nothing else is reported by Herodotus. This is the end of the operations of his army, which features in the narrative no longer, but might have been the one mentioned in the area some years later under Harpagus (Her VI.28,2).

The empire is not safe from the Scythians, as Hymaes' demise left his business in NW Asia Minor unfinished. At the same time, Cyprus and Caria were in full revolt, threatening to raise other, eastern areas as well. In this context the empire seems hollow; an army, probably local levies of the satrapy, is assembled and directed to Cyprus along with a fleet. Caria is on fire, Europe (Skudra) is a lost affair and the only thing that may change the scales is time for the empire to prepare and mobilize vast resources. It is at this time, at the latest, that Darius dispatches Histiaeus to the coast, given that the burning of Sardis figured in their face-to-face meeting (Her V.106).

At the same time, Daurices, with an excellent track record as he had participated in the battle of Ephesus and had reduced at least five rebellious cities in the Hellespont, almost sealing the vulnerable Asiatic coast by himself, was moving to Caria, to take the new rebels as unawares as possible. From Paesus, his last conquest, he turned SE, skirted Mount Ida from the east so as to find the Dascylium-Sardis road, which he followed SE after Sardis until he emerged in the valley of Meandrus river, where he turned west to Caria.

He failed to catch the Carians unprepared; the latter had mustered their army to an advantageous position, at the confluence of the rivers Meandrus and Marsyas. While the Carians were deliberating deployment behind Meandrus, to use it as a defensive barrier, or crossing and lining up in front of it, to make escape impossible and thus fight with superior resolve (Her V.118,2), the Persians arrived, crossed the river Meandrus and attacked (Her V.119,1), showing how superior morale and determination is prone to render tactics ineffective or even irrelevant.

There are no accounts of the battle, but it is important that the location is mentioned, the casualties also (for the battle of Ephesus nothing of the two has been recorded by Herodotus) but neither tactics nor anything else. Most importantly, there is no mention of cavalry and it is most likely that there was none. The fighting was bitter, the Persians prevailed and as they were fleeter, the pursuit must have devolved to a carnage; still, not the butchery that a cavalry pursuit would have caused. The Carians, badly beaten, with a 5:1 negative exchange rate, were able to extricate themselves and assemble at Labranda, to the south, with their morale shattered and actually considering mass migration or asking for terms (Her V.119,2). And there the Ionians, headed by the Milesians, the foremost perpetrators of the rebellion, came inland to their aid (Her V.120) – a gesture the Carians were never to repay.

The third act was something of a repeat; the Persians were triumphant, and from the rebels the Milesians, who had been foremost to assist the Carians, ended up worst (Her 120); something probably indicating their prolonged stay on the battlefield while others fled. In a short while, all three major rebel conscription areas, Ephesus, Miletus and Caria had been smashed on the battlefield by one Persian army, justifying the failing spirits of Aristagoras (Her V.124,1).

At that point, Daurices was a hero of the Persian Empire, level with Zopyrus and others. Taking a page from the book of his father-in-law he had almost single-handedly suppressed the Ionian revolt by reducing city after city and winning battle after battle. He had quelled any doubts of the efficiency of the lighter Persian line infantry against the heavy behemoths, the Hoplites, destroying the morale of the rebels. His whirlwind campaign in the Hellespont kept the Scythians out. In his wake Lydian levies were following (Her V.121), possibly ardent loyalists, but, after the burning of Sardis, just as probably a wider assortment of political and social factions. His winning two battles in a row with the Carians was somewhat standard in Darius' counter-insurgency booklet (DB 18–9; 26–8;29–30; 35–6). At this point he must have thought to capitalize; with the Carian host beaten time and again and practically decimated, it was a nice opportunity to invade and quell the rebellion before it became established – an excellent PsyOps (Psychological Operations) and propaganda deliberation. If he succeeded, which was almost certain, the revolt would have been contained to Ionia and Aeolis proper to the north, to the latitude of Cos to the south, and some kilometres deep. Cyprus and some other rebel cells in Asia Minor would be quelled fast enough and then it would be time to resolve the issues in Europe.

If this was indeed so (Ray 2009), his move southwards began just after the battle of Labranda, in the same campaigning season, with the highest morale and confidence; other scholars (Grundy 1901) believe that the invasion was initiated at the next campaigning season, with his army being reinforced by units under the other two commanders (Her V.121). But his confidence, to the point of arrogance, and the practices of his overlord and father-in-law better support the version of the immediate invasion. Confidence makes arrogance and the latter erodes caution. The multi-victorious army, knowing it had smashed the enemy field armies, advanced speedily and confidently.

The Carians, though, mustered anything they had, scraped the bottom of the barrel and lay in wait, in ambush, attacking at the dead of night. In one stroke the scales were tipped. Ray (2009) tries once more to reconstruct the battle with imaginary data, but Herodotus reports the extermination of the most successful Persian army ever taking the field against the Greeks, with all three of its commanders slain. The two others were not mentioned before but their corpses must have been collected and identified among the dead; Myrsus, the commander of the Lydian loyalists, or avengers, was also killed in action (Her V.121).

Caria was spared the invasion; but with its army decimated at Marsyas and Labranda, it could not –or would not – play any further role. The extermination of Daurices and his army had, in some hours, created a very different reality: one-third of the Persian forces had been eliminated, along with their most capable commander. Another commander had died, Hymaes (Her V.122,2) leaving his army leaderless. And the third commander, Otanes, was engaged in a rather overcautious, if not timid expeditionary tempo. This was a surprise: he had been most energetic when appointed a decade or more ago (Her V.26–8). Although the narrative of Herodotus does not reveal when he had his meagre successes by storming two cities (Her V.123), which may have been before the double disaster of the army of Daurices and the demise of Hymaes, it is possible that the caution was a directive of Artaphrenes as Sardis was in cinders and he needed a powerful army nearby to protect the rebuilding effort and discourage opportunistic and/or repetitive raids from other interested parties, such as Mysian bandits, amongst others.

In any case, Darius must have been in great consternation. His forces, battered and demoralized, were inadequate to make any further progress. Fortunately, they had incapacitated the enemy before plunging into their current plight, but the issue clearly demanded royal troops. What was even more important was that the casualties and the manoeuvering had left other satrapies practically defenceless and very vulnerable to possible insurrections. Darius knew everything about insurrections and their dynamics. Thus it is perfectly understood that the Persian offensive took quite some time to occur in Ionia. The first available forces must have been delegated to the near satrapies to stabilize them and preclude any further expansion of the revolt. Quelling the revolt in Cyprus did much to further this effort.

At the same time, the rebels were trying to find their footing. Despite their miraculous salvation thanks to the victory of Heracleides in Caria (Her V.121), it was obvious that they were no match for the Persian infantry after all. They lost all the battles, although the infantry battle at Cyprus was lost due to defection and treason (Her V.113,1). On the other hand, they were doing well at sea where they were more than holding their own. Hecataeus had been right in that they could win the war if they concentrated their efforts at sea. Their navy had flawlessly executed two massive amphibious operations, the evacuation of the Paeonians (Her V.98) and the transportation of assault forces to attack Sardis (Her V.100). They had soundly beaten the Phoenician fleet off Cyprus, in a battle where the engaging marines were Greeks and Phoenicians; the Persians were disembarked, along with their other vassals, and left the two marine nations to fight it out between themselves. The result was a signature Greek victory (Her V.112,1), which makes a bit weird any historical claims that the Greeks in later decades were particularly afraid of the Persian armadas – or of the Persian naval power and the Phoenician prowess – and considered the Imperials undefeated at sea (Plut Vit Them 7).

At this point, it is possible that Datis the Mede enters the stage (Burn 1962; Holland 2005). There is no reason to deny his origin as a Mede; the nation had provided the Empire with loyal and capable commanders (Her I.2 & I.156,2 & I.161–2). After all, Herodotus specifically considers him of Median race (Her VI.94,2) and thus the notion that he was the *Satrap* of Media (Sekunda 2002) is unsubstantiated. His sons were cavalry generals under Xerxes (Her VII.88,1), but not satraps, neither in Media, where the Satrap must have been Tigranes, a Persian and Achaemenid (Her VII.62,1.), nor anywhere else. Similarly, the same scholar's view that his army was mainly drawn from his own satrapy is not very convincing, neither for the campaign of 490 BC nor for the one of 494 BC.

Datis must have been a most prestigious and important official (Lewis 1980; Holland 2005), possibly the long arm of Darius in quelling the revolt, the role originally assigned to Histiaeus. The latter had not been dispatched to the thick of the rebellion as an advisor for the local officials there, nor as a mediator with the rebels. Before leaving Darius' presence he had promised to subdue Sardinia (Her VI.2,1) and thus he had an executive mission. He might well have been appointed *Karana*, head of all the Imperial forces and officials in-theatre (Sekunda 2002; Lewis 1980), as was later Cyrus the Younger (Xen Hell I.4,3) and Memnon the Rhodian (Arr Anab II.1,1). If so, one may speculate that this was insulting to the ego and authority of Artaphrenes, let alone pricking his jealousy. In such temper, the Achaemenid Satrap must have set up the foreigner *Karana*, thus manipulating him to escape and be branded traitor and massacred all the recipients of his letters (possibly sealed by Darius himself) who had expressed any kind of consent towards his mandate; or, by massacring said recipients, he prompted Histiaeus to defect (Grundy 1901). Subsequently, given half a chance, he murdered the Greek to cover his own tracks; the severed head sent to Darius could produce no testimony nor apology and explanations to the latter (Her VI.30,1).

As Datis carried the imperial standards to Athens later on, and Histiaeus had promised to conquer Sardinia (Her V.106), it is almost certain that Datis had replaced Histiaeus in form and function. He was a very shrewd and capable man. He may have had Darius convinced that sending in troops by land was counterproductive: they took time to approach, needed money and support to do so and were exposed to ambushes by an enemy who knew their whereabouts – especially now that the most fervent loyalists, the Lydians, had been knocked out. Datis must have been instrumental in raising an imperial, not satrapal fleet (Burn 1962), intending to accomplish three things: to transport fast considerable forces from the Middle East to the Aegean; to challenge the rebels for the control of the sea; and, once having wrested it, to be able to attack by land and sea, while at the same time safeguarding the empire from any notion of Scythian landings.

The dispatch of a massive fleet, including this time the Cilicians and the newly re-conquered Cypriots plus the Egyptians (Her VI.6), took time but it was to be the ultimate Persian campaign in the area. This fleet was massive, with the Phoenicians thirsty for revenge, plunder and extermination of the Black Sea commerce where they had never dared to venture. And it was not just *a* fleet; it was bringing an army on its decks. The levelling of Sardis was not merely a military setback and disaster for the prestige of the empire, nor simply a humanitarian crisis, it took out the best located and capacious Persian military base. Supplies could not be concentrated, stored and delegated; troops could not be mustered, stationed, billeted, outfitted and trained, as was to happen when Xerxes led his own invasion (Holland 2005; Her VII.32 & 37 & 146). Thus an armada, with its commissariat in the bellies of some vessels, was a very promising approach.

The possibility that the armada was under Datis, and Mardonius was under his command (Burn 1962), is very enticing; it is a most curious thing that Herodotus mentions not one of the Persian commanders of this final campaign, although he has mentioned quite a number of the previous ones by name – some of them quite obscure. However, the above does not apply if indeed this expedition refers to the one which called to the Dodecanese and met with a miraculous reverse at Rhodes, a fact that persuaded the Achaemenid commanding officer to consider the city of Lindos as under divine protection and leave (Burn 1962). The templar inscriptions narrating the miraculous salvation of Lindos may imply that Datis was the chief of the imperial fleet which fought at Lade (Her VI.6) and attacked Rhodes and other islands off insurgent Caria *en route* to Ionia to quench the rebellion, with Mardonius as his subordinate. Or that he did so in 490 BC, en route to Ionia and then to his appointment with the Fates, at the plain of Marathon. The last piece of information makes the older dating most probable (Burn 1962), along with the fact that Mardonius is nowhere mentioned to have attacked Rhodes in 492 BC, although he had plenty of time and he was in person with his fleet during the trip from Cilicia to Ionia (Her VI.43,2–3) where he met his designated army.

The showdown was to happen off Miletus, the lair, epicentre and refuge of the rebels, which housed the Ionian fleet, the main rebel arm after the unexpected discrediting of their infantry. The rebels concentrated their fleet, 353 triremes (**Table 8.1**), at Miletus. It is interesting that the Ionians proper, in terms of geography, that is the inhabitants of Ionia on the Asian coast, contributed very few vessels, except Miletus with 80. All the major contributions were from the islands, especially Chios, Samos and Lesbos with a total of 230 vessels amongst them. Ephesus had not been among the rebel muster, and suffered no despoiling (Burn 1962); nor had any city of Caria (Her VI.7–8).

The Greeks would fight this time against a major, or rather, imperial fleet, not a satrapal force. They were heavily outnumbered as the enemy had a round figure of 600 ships-of-the-line (Her VI.9), equal to the royal fleet at the Scythian expedition (Her IV.87,1). The fact that a border, basically counter-insurgency action requested the naval arsenal of a royal expedition says much for the magnitude of the threat this revolt had been for the crown. Notions that the Persian admirals would not revert to subversion due to their massive numerical advantage are ill-founded and rather intended to cast doubt on the Persian numerical advantage. A good general,

Table 8.1. The rebel fleet (islands in *italics*)

City	Vessels
Samos	60
Lesbos	70
Phocaea	3
Erythrae	8
Chios	100
Teos	17
Myous	3
Priene	12
Miletus	80
Total	**353**

as says Sun Tzu (Art of War IV.15) fights *after* the battle is already won. But, most importantly, royal fleets had never been tested in a sea battle, and their cohesion and ability to combine and co-operate in different languages and procedures was an issue, making the High Admiral most uncomfortable; later cases which may be ridiculed by Persian executives, knowing nothing of sea fights and sailing in seasoned mariners' vessels (Aesch Persai) may well cover a very real need for seamless vocal communication within but mainly among vessels, especially of different marine nations within the empire. Up to then, though, the imperial fleets were shadowing or carrying the land army, as in Egypt, Scythia and in many other cases. They had not fought a sea battle, at least not to our knowledge, and their morale would have been somewhat shaky as the last confrontation of an imperial detachment against the rebels had been a resounding defeat off Cyprus (Her V.112,1).

The rebels had mustered their naval squadrons in the vicinity of Miletus (Her VI.7–8) and knowing that the imperial resources far exceeded their own, they were deliberating on how to address the issue of being in a clear numerical disadvantage despite scraping the bottom of the barrel (Her VI.7), a fact sapping their cohesion. The commander of three out of 353 rebel vessels, Dionysius of Phocaea, might have been selected on merit as well as to alleviate frictions and jealousy from among the major contributors (Burn 1962). The scheme is not unheard of, as it was followed in the battle of Lepanto (Rados 1915) and very successfully. Dionysius promised victory should they allow him to train them and to teach them a manoeuvre which was perfectly suited to their present condition, but required the utmost discipline, co-ordination and cohesion; both skill and drill (Her VI.8 & 11). It was the *Diekplous*, (**Fig 8.1**) possibly of his own invention, as nobody had ever heard of something similar. The alleged ability of the imperial navy in 480 BC to execute this manoeuvre (Her VIII.9), an issue conjectured but never proven, may have passed to the Imperials through rebel captains who were captured during and after, or defected before, the battle of Lade.

The diekplous – a Greek naval term for 'infiltrating the enemy's line of battle' – was changing the scales. In those days, ramming was the standard method of engagement. Both Greek and Phoenician representations show rams in vessels since the 7th century at the latest, and despite fervent and even prejudiced attempts to explain them as cutwaters, the fact remains that using a finely constructed, extremely expensive, precisely balanced vessel of almost 200 men, some of them top professionals and one of them a millionaire, as a hauler to load it with 10–20 Hoplites and thus degrade its speed, sap its balance and leave the fate of 200 in the hands of 10 or 20 is simply unorthodox if not outright idiotic. The crew could be best exploited by being the propulsion for the ramming. This was the only valid reason for so cumbersome a vessel, in operational terms, that is seaworthiness, autonomy, capacity at such high price in human resources and their sustenance.

Ramming was intended mainly as a flank attack, perfectly applicable in small-scale encounters or against pirate vessels, but much more challenging in massive fleet actions of extended lines. The larger fleet could always take the smaller at the flank, or a fleet considerably faster could do that to one more cumbersome by extending faster (**Fig 8.2**) flank-wise (*Periplous*). Otherwise, it was a grim action of repetitive ramming, recoiling to get some distance so as to build up speed for another attempt to ram, or to evade the enemy onslaught; an action between vessels prow-to-prow, like a phalanx infantry match. The comparison between sea-fights and land encounters is followed many times but it may be somewhat speculative. Having said that, it must be remembered that the officers were the same men who commanded fleets and armies in all naval states, and the national ideology in conflict matters always carries extreme prestige and weight.

As the vessels approached, clashed and recoiled to ram again and again until battering the enemy, grappling an enemy vessel upon contact – or even upon approach – and boarding it with a marine contingent could decide the issue with minimal danger for the friendly hull, while providing prisoners (for labour or ransoming) and a decently operational vessel for the fleet. Boarding thus was, in prow-to-prow confrontations, a decisive action and the most sustainable mode of naval battle, which favoured the side with the better or bigger number of fighters; the larger and higher vessels that could load more marines and were able to withstand some battle damage due to ramming and collision; and compact formations.

The above are the methods of fighting which must have governed both Lade and the naval battle off Cyprus. The diekplous of Dionysius made all these considerations somewhat irrelevant. It was about darting *between* two enemy vessels, not *onto* them. Shearing their oarage was an added blessing; but the main purpose was to get behind them, U-turn and deliver a ram attack from the hind quarter or the flank. Similar endeavours along the enemy line could collapse it by creating gaps and thus expose its vessels to front-quarter ramming or even flanking and periplous (**Fig 8.3**). It is obvious that larger vessels, with longer oars, needing more room abreast, offered more tempting opportunities for diekplous. The beauty of this tactic was its applicability to a less numerous fleet, with vessels with or without size, endurance or durability advantage. It favoured the resolute and precisely navigated, agile warship.

The Ionian crews had had enough after some short days of really hard training (Her VI.12), and probably of remaining at the ready all day long to allow no opportunity for sneak attacks to the Imperials and to exploit any opportunity themselves – as was to happen at Aegospotami in 404 BC (Burn 1962), where the

Athenian fleet was caught off-guard and exterminated (Xen Hell II.28). It was nothing short of a mutiny, the crews refusing to undergo even standard training (Her VI.12,4). Thus the diekplous was out of the question. Some captains correctly understood the issue as a disastrous defeat in the making (Her VI.13,1); but also something just as threatening, a radicalization of the crews and respective social strata, which was prone to infect the citizenry beyond the constraints of the fleet and develop to sedition, with rioting, violence, disorder and factional cleansing. Herodotus, an ardent democrat, refers only to the former of the two as a concern of the Samian commanders, leading them to give in to the imperial subversion efforts and accept an understanding (Her VI.13,2). Having a soft spot for Samos and privileged sources of information, Herodotus acquits the Samians of treachery by advancing such reasoning (Her VI.13). He also overplays their role in the naval victory off Cyprus (Her V.112,1) and their participation in the second Ionian revolt, before and during the battle of Mycale (Her IX.103,2 & 99,2 & 91–2); he does not scold their ardent Medizm in Salamis (Her VIII.85,2) and is apologetic for their hideous actions in Sicily (Her VI.23) where they were seeking refuge after the defeat at Lade (Her VI.22).

Although Herodotus tries to implicate the Lesbians in the treachery, the fact that Lesbos suffered retributions (Her VI.31) while Samos did not (Her VI.25,1) means that the desertion was agreed only between the Samian commanders and the Imperial authorities through the tyrant Aeaces (Her VI.13,1). The Lesbians did not play the traitor but the coward, seeing the Samian squadrons at their side (Her VI.8) making sail (Her VI.14,2) and leaving their flank hanging, vulnerable to periplous.

Considerably smaller, the rebel fleet was probably jammed in the straits between Lade and the mainland to protect their flanks from such an eventuality and deny access to the Imperials through the strait between Lade and the mainland. The E/NE to W/SW orientation satisfies Herodotus' report of a roughly West-East orientation of the battle line(s) (Her VI.8,1) while allowing for the Greek squadrons which cut through the imperial line to turn either to the north (Chians) or to the south (Dionysius) to escape (Her VI.16,1 and Her VI.17, respectively). It also allows for the flight of the Samians and the Lesbians northwards, to their homelands (Her VI.14,2 and 14,3 respectively), before the initiation of the engagement (**Map 8.2**). Now the Imperials rolled the frontally engaged rebel fleet from the open sea, the position of the Samians to the West (as it was nearer Samos), towards the East, the position of the Milesians (Her VI.8), by the mainland coast and nearest to Miletus. The spontaneous nature of the flight of the exposed Lesbians (Her VI.14,3) explains why they secured no leniency (Her VI.31–2).

Dionysius, with his command, performed the diekplous, did some damage, and then escaped as he knew the rebellion was now a lost cause. After exacting

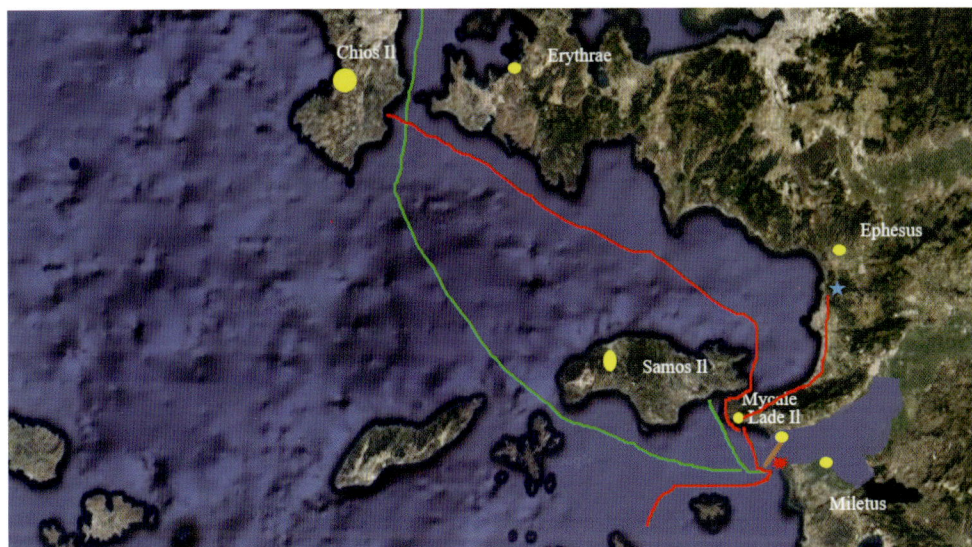

Map 8.2.
Green lines: The desertion of the Samian and Lesbian squadrons before the battle
Red lines: the escape routes of the Chians and the Phocaeans after the battle (red star)
Blue star: the slaying of shipwrecked Chian crews by the Ephesians

some revenge by sailing off Phoenicia, boarding and commandeering vessels and supplies necessary for the trip, he moved to the straits of Sicily and Italy and had a great career as a pirate (Her VI.17). Whether he or his descendants made contact with Themistocles, during the latter's initiation of the western naval policy of Athens (Green 1970), thus providing intelligence on diekplous and shipbuilding for triremes, remains conjectural. But his raid must have driven home a warning to the imperial naval staff, making them extra-cautious after the battle of Salamis in 480 BC and perhaps precipitating the recall of the Phoenician squadrons at that instance (Diod XI.27,1 & 19,4; Her IX.96,1). Similarly, the leverage to defeat a confederate Greek fleet was also duly noted, to be used further and it is the main reason for any degree of true Imperial gullibility displayed at Salamis (Her VIII.75–6; Diod XI.17,1–2).

The biggest contingent of the rebel muster was the Chian, of 100 vessels, posted at the centre of the line, more or less (Her VI.8). Having its flanks secured, it adopted an alternative strategy, as diekplous was not an option anymore. The Chians went for a boarders' fight. The naval battle was to be fought in the straits to negate flanking, thus speed and manoeuvreability for the rebels were irrelevant. It was going to be a frontal, Hoplite-like action. The Chians reinforced their boarders' units, to forty Hoplites per vessel (Her VI.15,1), a massive 4,000 Hoplite force which accounted for a significant part of their total Hoplite host, no doubt.

If the Chians had the same social percentage of Hoplites as in Athens, the 20,000 sailors were entrusted with the lives of 4,000 Hoplites, which is one fifth. At least an equal number must have been available, which means the boarders were almost half of the total Hoplite levy. This means they could not be Elites, as Herodotus clearly and emphatically considers them (Her VI.15,1); at least not in the same sense as Mardonius' guard at Plataea (Her IX.63,1), the Athenian 300 Hoplites in the same battle (Her IX.21,3) and similar units mentioned by Thucydides, with the 600 of Syracuse (Thuc VI.96,3) being the largest. The 1,000 Argives (Thuc V.67,2) were another unit type but still, they were 1,000, a mere 25 per cent of the Chian boarders. Only the Arcadian unit of the 4th century, the massive 5,000 *Epilektoi* of Arcadia (Diod XV.67,2 & XV.62,2), also known as *Eparitoi* (en Hell VII.22), has been comparable in numbers.

The massive boarding parties constituted undoubtedly a tactical innovation, at least in that day; or, rather, a backward surprise (Thuc I.49). In any case, its astounding effectiveness caused the Persians to adapt by furnishing additional marine detachments formed by competent, dependable and loyal central Asian troops in later campaigns (Her VII.184,2), a fact that changed their tactics and created vulnerabilities. It must be remembered that up to that day the naval engagements were committed with the native marine complements; throughout the campaigns of the Ionian Revolt, but also during previous ones, there is no mention of non-native boarders, only of transported troopers. At the battle of Lade, at the battle off Cyprus (Her V. 112,1) and then during the punitive naval campaign to suppress any coastal cells of the rebellion (Her VI.33,3), it is clear that the Phoenicians, not the Persians, are the causative agent. Persian forces may have landed at Chios and Lesbos (Her VI.31,2) as they are big islands, but the rest of the campaign of 493 BC is attributed to the Phoenicians (Her VI.25,1 & 34); the other three naval nations, that is Cilicians, Egyptians, Cypriots (Her VI.6) are not mentioned any further, perhaps due to insignificance, or, conceivably, but less probably, having been dismissed to save Darius some costs.

Herodotus says nothing about how the Milesians fared in battle. But the Chians, at the centre, fared decently. Their massive boarding parties surprised the Imperials and wreaked havoc, breaking through the enemy line and taking enemy vessels as prizes (Her VI.15,2). There are no numbers reported, and it is not clear whether they cut the Imperial line because they were able to capture enemy vessels, or diekplous allowed them to cut the line and subsequently, instead of ramming, they boarded and occupied the enemy vessels. The thing is that a number of their vessels (it is not reported whether high or low) were badly damaged or actually incapacitated and could not make full speed, but could sail for some time and distance to a safe coast at Mycale (Her VI.16,1), not far from Miletus (**Map 8.2**). This implies vessels damaged by front-quarter ramming and smashing, as flank ramming is fatal for the hull – a corroboration for the arguments presented before on the prevailing tactics of the time. The Chians left the Milesian territory, moving on foot. But on their way north, to get near their island and cross back there, they went through the Ephesian territory where the natives mistook them for pirates and slaughtered them, as they were exhausted and battered (Her VI.16,2). True, the morals of the day, but especially the proceedings of Histiaeus (Her VI.5,3 & VI.26 & VI.28) do indeed make the story believable. Still, the Ephesian attitude – and conduct in general throughout the events – implies something more sinister, something involving the Imperials pursuing the Chian fugitives and perhaps putting a price on their heads (Her VI.16,1).

The fall of Miletus and the extinguishing of the revolt

The Persians in 494 BC united all their armies to one and turned to Miletus, ignoring other cells of insurgents (Her VI.6). It is understandable; it was the hearth of the rebellion. Crushing it would decide the issue for the Empire then and there. But it was just then that they *could* do so, because they had seized the initiative, nullified the Scythian threat and contained the uprising. Moreover, their assets now included one army standing headless in-theatre (that is NW Asia Minor); another, rather slack army nearby under a not very inspired but very cautious dual leadership; a new commander-in-chief (C-in-C)/ *karana*, possibly endowed with additional land troops as reinforcements, but definitively with a brand new navy. The most important was that now they had a unified command over all their forces in-theatre, land and naval. (Her VI.6).

Thus, after their victory near Lade, they pursued the defeated fleet (Her VI.16,1), but engaged in earnest in besieging Miletus by land and sea (Her VI.18). Their siegecraft was once more successful, raising a question over the need for a seaward blockade. Such conditions are necessary when starving the population, not when storming the fortifications. The massacre that followed (Her VI.19,3) had a terrible effect on Greek conscience and although it fuelled much defeatism, as it was supposed to, it also stabilized resolve and grew determination, especially with the Athenians who watched the notorious play 'The fall of Miletus', only to fine the author Phrynichus and forbid it to be performed ever again (Her VI.21,2) – a democratic resolution which would have made the Inquisition proud. The imperial fleet wintered in the destroyed city (Her VI.31,1), allowing the message of abstract terror to spread, and in the first days of the next spring, they proceeded with the mopping up (Her VI.31). It is possible that since Samos was very near, they installed the Medizer tyrant Aeaces immediately (Her VI.25,1), before the winter lull. It is this winter that Histiaeus, having heard of the fall of Miletus (Herodotus says

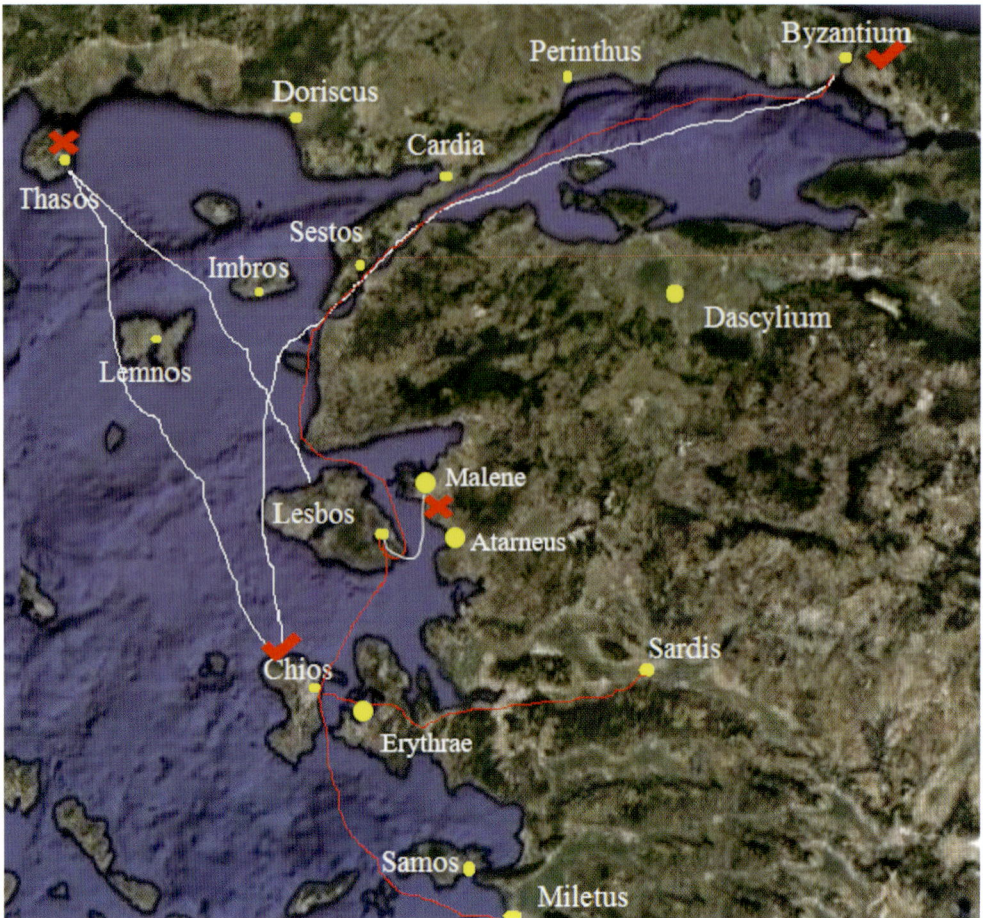

Map 8.3.
Red line: Histiaeus' escape and his venture to Byzantium
White line: Histiaeus' proceedings after the battle of Lade.
Red ticks: Histiaeus' successes
Red X: Histiaeus' failures/defeats

nothing about the duration of the siege, but it must have been short, the remaining part of the late summer and autumn after the battle of Lade) aborted his operations in the vicinity of the Bosporus (**Map 8.3**), where they were intent on building a privateer navy, and land in force to besiege Thasos (Her VI.28), the intention behind this decision being discussed later.

The imperial fleet first subdued the large islands (**Map 8.4**), Chios, Lesbos and Imbros (Her VI.31,1), the second not reaping any benefit from the desertion at Lade (Her VI.14,3), which means it was due to terror and cowardice, not treason (Burn 1962). For these operations, the relatively small boarding parties of the fleet were sufficient, 6,000–12,000 men. The crews would assist as devastators, support troops, engineer troops and light infantry, but still, it is possible, or rather probable,

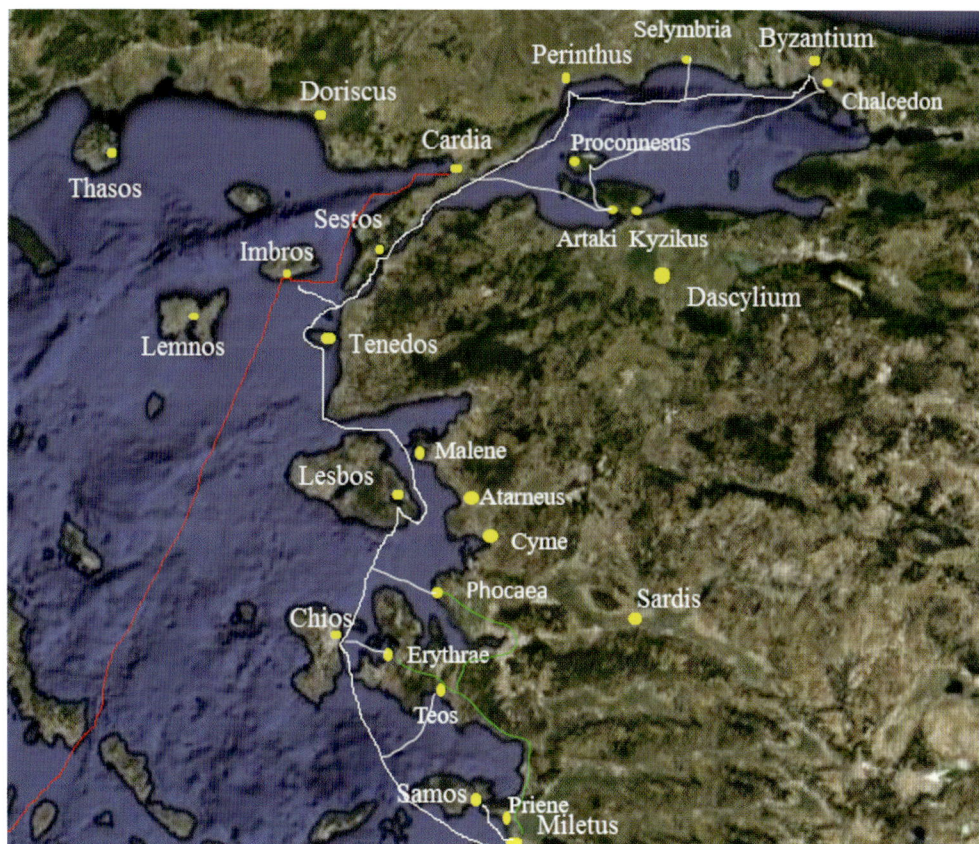

Map 8.4.
White line: the mopping up by the imperial fleet
Green line: The possible course of the imperial army for extinguishing the revolt in the mainland
Red line: The escape of Miltiades

that units of the land army were used to effect amphibious attacks and then net the population (Her VI.31,1) who obviously considered any kind of defence as vain. It is not clear whether the fleet or the combination of fleet and army were used to subdue any Aegean coastal cities of the Asiatic mainland, but the army, possibly delegated to several task groups, stormed all the remaining continental cells of the resistance (Her VI.31,2); these were the very ones they had skipped a year ago to concentrate on Miletus (Her VI.6). Amongst them were the five cities sending small naval contingents in Lade (**Table 8.1**).

This period is the latest conceivable, regarding the Persians' dealings with Caria; it is more probable that developments followed the fall of Miletus promptly (Her VI.25,2). Caria offered no further resistance and submitted by convention, although Herodotus mentions that some cities (without naming them) were besieged before surrendering or being stormed (Her VI.25,2). In effect, Caria is never heard of after the ambush off Pedasus where Daurices was slain (Her V.121). It may be that Caria had capitalized on the success of the ambush and kept neutral or had already capitulated (Grundy 1901), so that Herodotus' narrative of the ultimate Carian surrender (Her VI.25,2) may be either erroneously dated or suggestive of the official conclusion of a very closely kept understanding. The above perfectly explains why the Persians granted territories of Miletus after its razing to Carians, and most specifically to the important city of Pedasus (Her VI.20), located very near the stage of the extermination of a whole army under Daurices (Her V.121).

After finishing with the major islands and, at the same time, with Histiaeus' private army (Her VI.28–9), the imperial fleet entered the Hellespont and delivered swift vengeance to the European side (Her VI.33), which included Miltiades' fiefdom, but also to the cities of Propontis and of the Bosporus. It is important that the fleet never took any stroke of oar into the Black Sea, and that there were still cities in the Asian coast of Propontis which up to this time either capitulated more or less of their own free will with the Persian authorities (Her VI.33,3) or were still defying the *Pax Persica*. This indicates that Hymaes' campaign had stopped short of them and nobody (i.e. his successor) thought it necessary to continue along these lines; one more piece of evidence supporting the Scythian Invasion hypothesis mentioned earlier.

The next day: When the End completes the Beginning

Herodotus tries to present the story of the campaigns of Histiaeus, after his defection and his forming a privateer band, in some context (Her VI.26–30), to make it more relevant and clear. His purpose is commendable in terms of history, but in terms of operations the crucial time factor is not meticulously laid down; especially the relative timing with other events. It is obvious that his sources are wanting, and he himself, a first-generation historian, was not familiar with the Persian protocols as intimately as was Xenophon, who not only travelled and mingled with Persians, but also fought for one of them against them in their own country. Thus, Herodotus does not know the status of Histiaeus when sent to the coast, nor his exact and purported relations with Artaphrenes, the local Satrap. Most of all, he has no idea of his intentions and how the latter evolved and changed.

Histiaeus was ambitious and wanted to run, or reign over, something more than an ungrateful metropolis (Her IV.137,2). He wanted his own kingdom, his own city and subjects, but he could envision himself as an independent ruler in all probability within the sphere of the Achaemenid patronage (i.e. protection and, should the need be, imposition). What he could *not* tolerate was being the subject of some arrogant Satrap, like Artaphrenes, subject to his whim and greed (Grundy 1901). From the moment he asked for Myrcinus, a land being literally at the Far West of the Empire (Her V.11,2), not yet shaped into a satrapy, this was his plan, which was unacceptable to Persian aristocracy at its very core as shown by the intervention of Megabazus (Her V.23,2). It is not at all certain that when he first escaped to the rebels his intentions *for* the uprising were genuine; he might have intended to quell the rebellion, to be a hero and get the king's permission to rule his fiefdom in Myrcinus under the royal protection. But Artaphrenes was very glad to have him branded as a traitor (Her VI.1–2). If Histiaeus tried to replay Zopyrus (Her III.158,1), neither the Ionians were gullible enough (Her VI.2,2–5,2), nor Artaphrenes inclined to assist him. After that, Histiaeus defected for real.

The logical sequence, as already mentioned, is that when at Sardis, he contacted by the letters which might have had the royal seal, important figures among the local Persian administration, possibly to enact another policy for containing the revolt and to assume supreme leadership in-theatre. Artaphrenes executes all who declared for Histiaeus for presumed, assumed or attested treason, which means he set Histiaeus up, forcing him to escape to evade a possible murder attempt. In this way the Milesian incriminated himself. But it may be that, as Herodotus has it (Her VI.2–4), Histiaeus first escaped – or simply moved away – from Sardis as a first step. This he might have done sensing hostility if not immediate danger, or as part of his plan, whatever the latter had been. Then, from relative safety or having been where his plan dictated, he dispatched his letters, allowing by his absence Artaphrenes to taint him as a defector and thus charge the recipients with treason, execute them all and make any proof of Histiaeus' possible undercover mission disappear.

It is very probable that Histiaeus, once the Persians established their land supremacy (there is no way to know his thoughts and convictions on the subject before the verdict of battle), was set to organize a mass migration, at least of the Milesian citizenry, to his fiefdom in Myrcinus (Her V.23,1), which was then beyond the Persian reach. There he would be a benefactor to his subjects and perhaps a moderator with the Persians, having orchestrated an internal migration which was prone to further the imperial interests in Europe by creating a fortified, rich and advanced base and commercial hub, possibly the capital of a new satrapy.

As the Ionians had no intention of allowing him any leeway (Her VI.2–5), he persuaded *some* Lesbians – incidentally, of Aeolian, not Ionian, stock (Her VI.8,1) and very possibly representing private concerns – to provide triremes for a most notable plan: to control the Bosporus and commandeer a fleet out of the merchant shipping of the Ionians which emerged from the Black Sea (Her VI.5,3). This means that the Bosporus was not under the sway of the Imperials at the time; indeed, its gates, Byzantium and Chalcedon, were subdued only in 493 BC by the imperial Navy (Her VI.33). Many of the vessels would have been high-capacity merchantmen, good for mass transportation of freight, but many others would be private double-role pentekonters (Fields, 2007), with excellent freight capacity but also considerable fighting potential in both naval and amphibious contexts. They were more flexible and thus better than the triremes on many accounts. With the triremes as his core, which could pursue and overtake any type of vessel (Fields 2007), he could create a privateer navy to enact his migration schemes, as the 'official' Ionian fleet of triremes could not be replaced, outdone or overtaken. Histiaeus was not to tackle any imperial fleets at that time.

Once Miletus was levelled, Histiaeus tried to change the timetable; he had been hopelessly outrun by the facts. He went to Thasos (Her VI.28,1), to acquire loot and more ships and possibly real estate; the Thasians had a fleet (Her VI.46,1) but did not man it to defend, which means it was available for the taking should Histiaeus have been victorious. Just as important, they controlled considerable territories on the opposite mainland coast (Her VI.46,3), and this system of island–mainland was a dream for Histiaeus' migration plan, after Myrcinus became unavailable, or too restricted for a massive migration, or both. If he could subjugate Thasos within the winter, at the first sign of the spring he could realize the migration with the ships he had plus the survivors of the Ionian fleet. But there was a catch: without subduing Thasos, his plan for mass migration could not work. The establishment of the Thasians was by definition competitive to the Myrcinus project and perhaps the Thasians had a hand in the ultimate failure of the latter and the death of Aristagoras (Grundy 1901). With Myrcinus aborted for quite some years, maybe six, since the campaign of Daurices and the demise of Aristagoras, Thasos and its estates on the mainland were the only suitable receiving grounds available immediately to the prospective refugees (Grundy 1901). It must have been along these terms that he persuaded some Ionians too to join this operation (Her VI.28,1), and the latter must have been the very bellicose and desperate Chians (Grundy 1901).

The clock was ticking and once the imperial navy mobilized, next spring, to exploit its victories off Lade and at Miletus, Histiaeus' original plans were irrelevant, as he had logged no progress in Thasos (Her VI.28,1); he needed more time, but the storming of Miletus, instead of a prolonged siege effecting starvation, had wrecked his plan (Burn 1962). He also needed stronger forces, even at that point, to try to salvage something out of the wreck. He assembled as many troops as possible by conscripting fugitives (Her VI.26,2 & 28) and tried to enlist the devastated Chians (Her VI.26), beaten in the battle of Lade (Her VI.27) and slaughtered near Ephesus (Her VI.16,2). Always defiant, with their home squadron they tried to resist (Her VI.26,1). Histiaeus, already holding a grudge since they had him ejected some years ago when he first appeared as a master rebel (Her VI.2,2 & 5,2), fell upon them with his armament and allegedly obliterated the island (Her VI.26,2); not fully, as the

Imperials found something to destroy, pillage, slaughter and net (Her VI.31). But he must have caused quite some damage before recruiting some Chians.

Having acquired, bled and increased his army, he had to feed it (Her VI.28). Instead of bringing in supplies beforehand, he had used his navy counterproductively in assault missions and spent any accumulated provisions; the same was true for the rebels, who used their fleet for defence and not for collection of supplies. Now that their fleet was beaten, there could be no supplies. A brilliant plan was to seize some from the opposite, Asian coast (Her VI.28,2), which was already subdued by the Persians, or it would have been shortly after. A reasonable endeavour, to rob the enemy of supplies and increase one's own. The operation was set for the first sign of reaping next spring, perhaps in May (Burn 1962), after a sorrowful winter. But, in an exemplary failure of intelligence, a Persian army under Harpagus (a Persian and thus unrelated to the general of Cyrus who had originally subjugated Ionia) was nearby (Her VI.28,2); the Greek contingent was numerous, so as to quickly loot and fetch as many supplies as possible, and, although caught at a disadvantage it gave the imperial infantry quite a match (Her VI.29,1). It is almost directly stated that the imperial army was infantry only (Her VI.29,1), probably being the army of late Hymaes (Ray 2009), last seen in the Hellespontine area (Her V.122,2), now under a new commander. Most likely it had moved south, towards Miletus during the converging last year's attack (Her VI.6), and now it was returning north under the mandate to conclude the suppression and perhaps assist the fleet against the coastal cities and islands (Her VI.31). Histiaeus must have supposed it was still south, out of position, a fatal mistake as its commander must have learnt some lessons from previous rebel practices which had succeeded in defeating in essence, although not in fact, the satrapal forces by rendering them irrelevant in space and time, like the imperial cavalry during the raid at Sardis (Her V.98,4 & 100).

The result of the battle and the conclusions on the Persian use and low availability of cavalry have been discussed previously, as has the fate of Histiaeus and the reasons for such proceedings, which thoroughly displeased the King of Kings (Her VI.30,2). What must be discussed here is the immediate intentions of Histiaeus had he been successful in obtaining supplies for his forces. It remains purely conjectural, but he must have intended to attack the Imperial navy while the latter was preparing for the campaign but before it started from Miletus (preferably), or as early as possible afterwards, before it gained momentum. Finding the enemy fleet ashore, either dragged to the beach or resting at anchor, the small navy of Histiaeus would aim for a surprise attack. Ramming anchored vessels would be like spearing fish in a barrel; boarding, taking and towing them would be just as easy. For beached vessels, home-made incendiaries could be used to destroy or at least incapacitate them. Home-made incendiaries, based on rags, brushwood and fat or oil and primed by stone or torch could be placed in multiple sites of a vessel by two-man teams to spread fast, while the raiders would move quickly from ship to ship and prevent the stunned crews from reaching the sea to try to quench the flames.

Five two-man teams could work per trireme simultaneously and be done in 2–4 minutes; then approach another and a third. This is the limit in terms of time (15–20 mins) before resistance gets organized, and in terms of weight and volume of incendiaries carried while retaining a decent fleetness of foot. A pentekonter, without any boarders, could dispatch three such squads of 5 pairs and keep 20 rowers in position, for the ship to be ready to depart. A trireme could dispatch 10 such squads, for 100 oarsmen, while 50 remain at the ready. The merchantmen could bring along the incendiary supplies and marines, who would assist in the torching and also tackle enemy crews and/or security details. By these, purely conjectural, estimations, if the eight triremes of Histiaeus were intact and fully manned, in under half an hour they could destroy 8x3x10=240 enemy vessels, one-third of the enemy fleet; the complement of each pentekonter could disable 3x3=9 ships. All these are conjectural, but might have been the only realistic, although far-fetched, plan of Histiaeus, a known opportunist and risk-taker, to stop the disaster from concluding into the devastation it was to become.

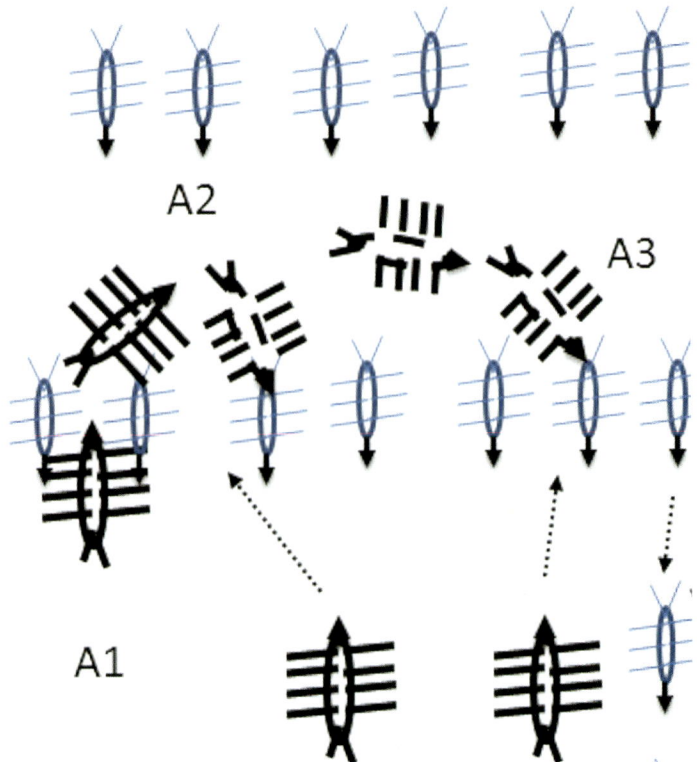

Fig. 8.1.

Envelopment by
A: fastest vessels
B: Larger fleet

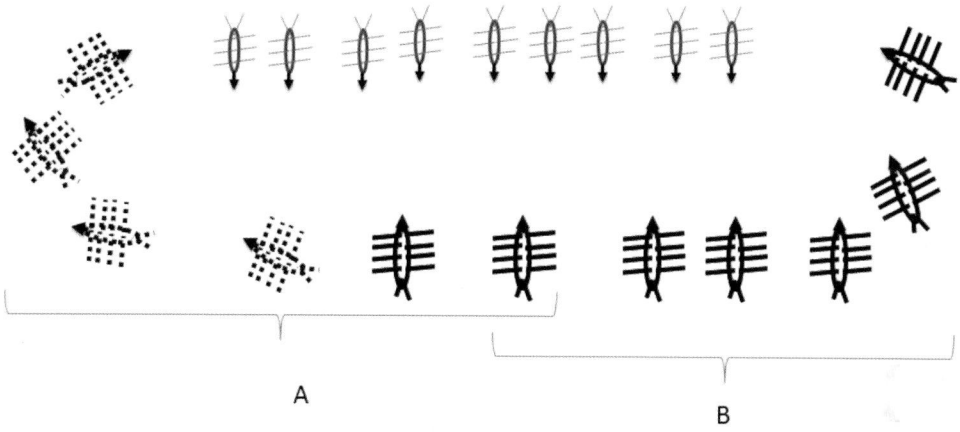

A

B

Fig. 8.2.

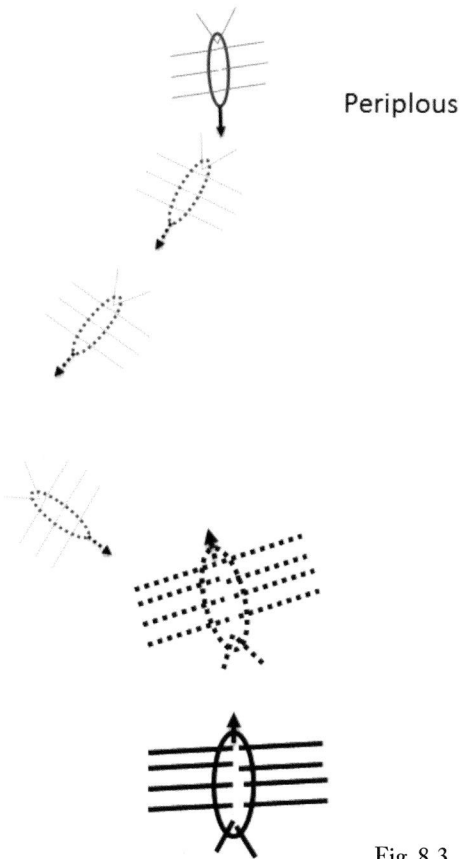

Periplous

Fig. 8.3.

Chapter 9

The First Onslaught:
The Campaign of Mardonius

O nce the suppressive campaign was over, the victorious army and navy of the empire, loaded with glory and loot, was probably disbanded. Their personnel had been campaigning for at least two years or rather two expeditionary periods and the intervening winter (Her VI.31). Some of the crews and subject troops had to return to their farms, stores and professions to keep the royal taxes incoming, while the slaves had to be brought to the sovereign's presence to hear their sentence. Thus, Herodotus' statement that the leadership of this victorious army was suspended and replaced by another team (Her V.43,1) is somewhat odd. Once the army was disbanded, the leaders were also demobilized and assumed their peacetime offices.

In any case, the next year another task force emerged, army and navy. It is likely that the fleet mobilized and crewed was the same, as their access route took a month at worst; the army must have consisted of other mobilized classes, since the access time was measured in months and thus the veterans could not be further spent on the road, even on the king's one. The Marshal (*Karana* or *Spadapatis*?) of the next year's campaign was Mardonius, a young aristocrat, nephew of Darius and married to one of his daughters in true Darius nepotistic style (Her VI.43,1). He may have been included in the previous year's expeditionary force (Lewis 1980; Burn 1962) and the stellar performance of that army had him promoted on the spot; Datis, the commander-in-chief of that immensely successful Persian army was superseded and must have been green with jealousy (Burn 1962), which possibly accounts for Herodotus' enigmatic reference to a change in leadership. Obviously, the previous commander would have loved to see his commitment through with another year in charge, as his successes would have been a most powerful argument. And this is especially so if he had indeed been Datis the Mede, a man capable enough to succeed where the bridegrooms of the king's daughters had ultimately failed. A man who had been able to access the hard core not only of the Persian nation, but of the familial cadre of royal *bandaka*/subordinates, viceroys and commanders or generals; a man destined to gain prominence in history for his checkered performance in the battle of Marathon in 490 BC.

Starting from Susa or Persepolis, and following the King's Road, Mardonius, who had returned to the capital to be decorated and promoted, initiated his campaign; he brought his army in Cilicia and left it to his deputies to bring it to Ionia (Her VI.43,2), most probably Sardis, the western endpoint of the King's Road (Her V.53). From there to the Hellespont the army probably followed the itinerary Xerxes was to follow a dozen years later (Her VII.42–4); or the opposite of that of Daurices (**Map 8.1**). Although the raising of a new army is the most probable course of action, it may have been that he led massive reinforcements and actually took charge of the army on the spot (Grundy 1901), since Persian armies could remain afield for many years, as was the case with Cambyses' army in Egypt. In any case, Mardonius joined his assigned fleet, mustered at Cilicia as well, and sailed to the Aegean (Her V.43,3); a very logical decision if indeed he had served the previous year under Datis in the fleet (Burn 1962; Lewis 1980) and thus had developed contacts and relations.

Having plenty of time at his disposal while waiting for the army, he is said to have revised the regimes in the Ionian cities of the mainland towards a democratic or at least representative constitution and in any case abolishing the tyrannies, the up-to-then operative *motto* of the Persian occupation (Her VI.25,1 & V.27,2 & V.96,2 & V.11,2 & III.147). It is true that on this particular occasion, the Persians had the luxury of relaxing the constitutional rules in these cities, in which the island states, Caria and the Dorian cities of the south were not included (Burn 1962). This was so because the most radical elements (individuals, political parties and whole social groups) had been eliminated during the rebellion or in the wake of its suppression, with mass-murdering and massive deportations in the form of chattel slaves, eunuchs and harem members. Additionally, the financial reforms initiated by Artaphrenes (Her VI.42) removed the extra-heavy taxation (Grundy 1901; Burn 1962); a fact that Herodotus does not recognize as he specifically says that the amount was more or less the same as before (Her V.42,2). This is not consistent with the great energy spent on the fixation of new sums (Her V.42,2). Probably the new way to estimate the taxation kept more or less the same yield but changed the distribution of the burdens by using more objective criteria based on land, and thus on land income, meaning the higher classes; consequently, some burden was lifted from the commerce and the commoners (Burn 1962).

The combination of financial bleeding and a most oppressive, obsolete and exploratory form of government had proved toxic for the realm and even Artaphrenes was able to grasp this truth. Easing taxation would boost the economy, produce more income for the state and less incentive for future rebellions, as people having a good livelihood have little propensity to revolt and endure physical hardship and dangers. Some fifteen years after their contact with Cleisthenic Athens, the

Persians had correctly assessed the issues involved and found democracy not a bit less gullible or more definitively hostile to their interests, rule and authority than more authoritarian forms of (self)-government. Democracies, additionally, with the chaos they entail by definition, make very difficult a clandestine state-backed plotting for rebellion, a delicate issue as proven by Aristagoras' proceedings. Having addressed the issues of domestic oppression and taxation, the Asiatic Greeks, or rather the surviving ones, were not overly set to their national and racial ideals; some of them fought valiantly *against* them in Salamis, a dozen years later.

Mardonius had a clear mandate, to round off the suppression of the Ionian Revolt by winning the peace and by delivering submission and, where needed, punishment beyond the borders of the Empire. The revolt proper had been quelled and the instigators and the participants were crushed and subdued with savagery. The extra cruelty shown to flourishing Miletus, the foremost city in Ionia at the time, which was not to recover and be of any consequence under Persian authority, was to be expected due to its focal role but also to its privileged status as a voluntary ally of Cyrus, something striking a nerve – or, rather, two – with Darius and perhaps leading to the original alienation between the sovereign and the citizen body, which brought about the revolt with such fervour. In all, the Ionian cities of the coast, between the invasion of Harpagus and the suppression by Datis, were ultimately reduced to insignificance. One need only compare the only 100 triremes supplied to Xerxes' armada (Her VII.94) with the Ionian contributions to the fleet at Lade (Her VI.8) to reach such a conclusion.

Still, there had been assistance from their mainland brethren, who had the audacity to invade and pillage imperial lands and assault subjects. Darius knew that, if unanswered, this outrage would find imitators and would also sap his prestige and paternal image; a repetition of the events with the Scythians. He intended to invade Greece anyhow (Her III.134,6), but now he had the pretext, additional causes and, most importantly, the momentum. Mardonius had as an objective to deliver punishment to Athens and Eretria, the former being not just aggressors, but also oath-breakers and insurgents. They were not one bit less culpable than their Asiatic Ionian brethren; on the contrary, they were much worse offenders, since they had, of their own accord and spontaneously, asked, received and accepted the imperial protection (Her V.73).

The main phase of the campaign was to start from Sardis and the fleet would ferry the army across the Hellespont; no bridges and such luxuries were projected this time. From there on, they would re-assert the imperial control in Europe, where it had never been firm, but had slackened to insignificance as a result of the severing of communications with the body of the empire due to the rebellion. There is no need to assume Mardonius was tasked with limited objectives, as maintained by some scholars (Lazenby 1993; Holland 2005; Shepherd 2010). Once the formalities with former subjects who had proven lacking in terms of faith and loyalty were concluded a full-blown invasion south would round things up in terms of the revolt and secure the western border (Grundy 1901; Green 1970). The ambitious invasion of Europe-at-large, a set intent of Darius (Her III.134 & V.31 & VI.2) would follow in successive steps. Having seen what he had, Darius and his staff doubted any ability, not to mention propensity, of the mainland Greeks to resist effectively.

The first part of the plan worked smoothly. Thrace was brought under control once more and communication was re-established with the isolated Persian outposts. The fate of King Olorus, the father-in-law and host of Miltiades is not mentioned. Thasos, the prosperous island with its mainland wealth was reduced to servitude just for the sake – and profit – of it (Her VI.44 & 46,3); not even its resistance against Histiaeus (Her VI.28,1), without which the Persian operations to mop up resistance might have been seriously hindered, was to matter before the conquering hunger of the King of Kings and his apostle.

But while being in Macedonian territory, or, most probably, in its eastern vicinity, and set to bring the astute Alexander I of Macedon in line, disaster struck Mardonius; and it struck twice in quick succession. It is very strange that Herodotus, a most pious man, always seeking the divine intervention in and interpretation of events unfolding (Her IX.100,2 & IX.65,2 & VIII.20,2), fails repeatedly to identify any heavenly retaliation against Darius and his staff, as he did with Cambyses and then with Xerxes, sometimes clearly crossing the limits of exaggeration. Or how he failed to connect the eerie series of disasters falling upon the Chians, which he does acknowledge as of divine will (Her VI.27), with their attitude towards the Lydian rebel Pactyes who was seeking refuge from the wrath of Cyrus the Great (Her I.160). As if the democratic Athenians kept some reverence for the alien monarch who had offered them his protection in their time of need, back in the early 500s BC.

The first disaster that befell the expedition was a massive wreckage of the Persian fleet off Mount Athos (Her VI.44). It made painfully obvious that the celebrated Phoenician mariners of the imperial fleet had little experience of the weather and other particularities near the Greek shores, which makes doubtful the assertion of Herodotus regarding Phoenician presence in the Archipelago, and Thasos in particular in ages past (Her VI.47). The fleet must have been the one of the previous year with any casualties made good, which means 600 vessels (Her VI.9,1) plus a relatively small number of merchantmen for provisions and support of both fleet and army, an arrangement allowing fast movement of the latter, without encumbrances from the heavy transportation trains and local shortages. There is no mention of any Ionian conscripts or quota, which is understandable as the area had just been pacified and conscription was not organized as the available manpower was striving to integrate once more into the imperial normality. They were neither trusted, nor in a position to participate. They were still vanquished foes, not yet fully accepted as subjects ready to atone for their misdeeds.

On these grounds, the loss reported by Herodotus is no exaggeration; massive naval losses are attested for the classical period around Mount Athos (all 50 triremes of a fleet and only 12 surviving crew members) and even worse ones in different locations in the Mediterranean (Rados 1915). Three hundred vessels were reported destroyed (VI.44,3). The 20,000 casualties (Her VI.44,3) were a logical 33 per cent of the shipwrecked sailors, a total of 60,000 as produced by 200 men per trireme (Her VIII.184,1) for 300 triremes (Her VI.44,3), had all the shipwrecked vessels been triremes. Herodotus never implies, in this case, that the destroyed vessels were all triremes, and thus counted against the battle fleet; still, triremes were notoriously vulnerable to poor weather, especially compared to merchantmen and pentekonters. The fleet was badly mauled, the condition of the rest of the vessels might have been compromised and the same was true for the crews and, understandably, for their morale. The losses should not have led to the abortion of the naval campaign; twelve years later, a massive loss in two successive storms (Her VIII.7 & 13 & VII.190) of slightly less than half the number of triremes of the royal Grand Fleet (Her VII.89,1 & 184,1) plus transports and support ships (Her VII.191,1) did not fully compromise its operational ability, although it did degrade it considerably (Her VII.236,2).

But, almost concurrently, a man-made disaster struck the Persian army. A nearby tribe, the Brygi, made a night attack, infiltrated the imperial advanced lines and wrought havoc, killing quite a number, wounding Mardonius and causing chaos (Her VI.45). It is a recurring issue; another successful general, after a re-subjugation campaign running most successfully, had been too cocky, too confident, and was ambushed – not assaulted in his camp, as in this case – at night, ending very dead and his army exterminated (Her V.121). He too was the husband of a daughter of Darius. His name was Daurices (Her V.116). To maintain that the Brygi had been made privy to the Persian ineptitude is not impossible, but is overreaching. The European tribesmen had always employed night attacks as an equaliser tactic, along with ambuscades in broken ground. In any case, Mardonius somehow had failed to learn any lessons from the sorry end of his relative. He survived, he did not lose his entire army, and in fact, he was able to subdue and conquer the culprits (Her VI.45,1), showing great persistence and resilience. Surprisingly, he did not annihilate them to a man, or at least he is not reported to have done so, although this little adventure was sure to cost him his career.

An intact army might have been able to continue with the remains of the fleet, at least up to a point. An intact fleet might have been able to toss the army some more distance, to Thessaly, which was shimmering after losing her grasp over Phocis and Boeotia, perhaps just a generation ago (Buck 1972). But with both arms beaten, and the Karana wounded, further advance was inadvisable. Mardonius might have made contact with the Thessalian tyrants (or princes) of the Clan of Aleuas around that very time, possibly within the territory of Alexander I. This presupposes that he advanced far more to the west than usually suggested, past Mygdonia, and near to the Gulf of Therma – a good distance from the longitude of the disaster of his fleet (**Map 10.1**).

The uncelebrated return of a victor

But he prudently decided that with both arms crippled he had to return (Her VI.45,2) and be satisfied himself – and his liege – with the re-establishment of the Persian rule all the way to Macedon and, most probably, with the fixation of the border of the empire proper to Strymon river (Boteva 2011), at the middle of the longitudinal width of the Haemus Peninsula. This is implied by the fact that when Xerxes retreated and Mardonius had been exterminated, the westernmost of the Persian garrisons that remained in the northern Aegean coast was Eion (Lazenby 1993); additionally, the ceremonies performed by the Persian Magi to cross this river (Her VII.113–4) and not the much larger ones like Nestos and Hebrus, indicate a different kind of passage, not merely geographical but to another, foreign land. Beyond Strymon, in Macedon, there were tributaries, not subjects. But the Skudra was re-established and was probably attached to Dascylium, or it potentially formed a new satrapy, with Sestos as capital (Her IX.115–6).

Darius must have been furious and considering both events, especially the massive shipwreck off Athos, as gross incompetence; his view of the Brygi night attack would have been even more severe, especially after the checkered records of Daurices and Hymaes. Mardonius had obviously taken no heed of Daurices' blunder leading to the night ambush. It must be noted that the Persians were quick to take in lessons and adapt in sectors where they were defective; both their next campaigns to Greece were meticulously planned to evade issues with Athos, the Accursed Mountain (Grundy 1901), either cutting a canal behind it, for the invasion of Xerxes (Her VII.22,1), or avoiding it altogether under Datis and Artaphrenes (Her VI.95,2). In other cases, though, they seem less responsive. Nocturnal action was an established weakness. After the blunders of Daurices and Mardonius, it is no strange thing that Leonidas tried the same against Xerxes (Diod XI.9,4); the latter though may have indeed learned something and thus survived the attempt. In the days of Xenophon, the lesson had been learned and the Persians encamped very far away from their Greek mercenary opponents (Xen Anab III.4,34) while in the days of Alexander the Great, at Gaugamela Darius III kept his host in position, awake, all night long in explicit fear of a nocturnal attack (Plut Vit Alex 31,4).

Darius I was a bit slow in learning lessons but was learning them well. The young haughty, aggressive and arrogant aristocrats he collected for his daughters were meant to be a personal defence against impostors. But in terms of leadership, they were not proving a sustainable solution, as their defeats outweighed their victories in every case. Mardonius had wrecked a perfectly good army, which had to be disbanded and replaced by raising a new one; that meant it would be some time before the empire would be able to resume the offensive. This was a really bad development, as the momentum built by the previous victories was to decay and the prospective and future enemies had much more time to prepare; and a most definite warning. With the fleet it was even worse; a victorious fleet had been wrecked and their morale was lower than grass. Replacing the casualties alone would strain the treasury, which meant the vassals would start bellyaching. Terror was a perfect means to inhibit revolt, but although it was cheap, indeed, it was not proving very successful. The lull, however, was a nice opportunity for diplomacy and Darius, while the message of terror from Miletus was being driven home, sent heralds to demand tokens of submission, earth and water, from the cities of the Greek mainland (Her VI.48,1) and perhaps from the western Greek colonies of Sicily and Italy as well, not bothering to conceal his true intentions any further. It was an ultimatum, tantamount to a declaration of war. As a careful reader may notice, Darius reverted to diplomacy *after* his invasion plan, based on surprise, shock and awe, was ruined; not before. Diplomacy was the conduct (not continuation) of war with other means, especially when the main ones seem inadequate, and this is particularly evident in this case.

For the new endeavour, Darius turned again to a seasoned general, who had led a most successful campaign and had been overridden for the sake of in-family. He was Datis the Mede (Her VI.94,2), Datis who delivered, Datis, his royal inspector in Sardis just before the final campaign (Holland 2005; Lewis 1980). Datis, who had revolutionary operational ideas (Burn 1962; Bradford 1980); too revolutionary for a Persian, as he was a Mede. Moreover, he was a most capable, proven commander and seasoned administrator, able to deal with Artaphrenes, the maverick Satrap of Sardis. Darius might not have held the revolt against his brother, as he was himself quite used to such events. But the near loss of his capital, Sardis, and the six years needed for the quelling along with royal reinforcements (a whole fleet) were somewhat disappointing, despite the obvious responsibilities of the relief generals, who were all choices of the sovereign and his relatives by wedlock. Last, but not least, Darius must have entertained many and disquieting thoughts after Artaphrenes' cold-blooded murder of Histiaeus (Her VI.30,1), a move never sanctioned by the king who must have had many questions over the issue of how his trusted and beloved henchman turned traitor only to endorse a cause lost from the very beginning in the long term. Thus, Datis' ability to 'co-operate' with Artaphrenes during his inspection tour of 495 BC, but also during the campaign of 494–3 BC, was much appreciated.

Datis had known Artaphrenes and worked with him successfully. Both had a hidden disgust or simply beef with Mardonius. Mardonius was appointed general to invade Thrace and Greece, in 492 BC, after being a subordinate to Datis for two short seasons in 494–3 BC; which means that Datis was superseded and bypassed, if not overlooked. This was very hard for the Mede to swallow (Burn 1962). Artaphrenes was also frustrated to the extreme, as his long-due intervention to lower or transform the taxation on the Ionians and to establish institutions for resolving their differences (Her VI.42,2) – possibly without the interference of the satrap or any imperial official, insinuating limited autonomy – was, to a degree, credited to Mardonius (Bradford 2001). The latter came to Ionia for the second time in his life, actually as a passer-by, and declared the abolishment of tyrannies and the establishment of more representative forms of government in Ionia (Her VI.43,3), both taking credit for such a move and sapping the authority of Artaphrenes who had been keen on setting tyrannies (Her VI.25,1 & V.27,2 & V.96,2), as per standard Persian policy (Her III.147 & V.11,2). A royal nephew coming in his yard and making major concessions sanctioned by the king (Grundy 1901), concessions that were mirror opposites of his own constitutional policy, was an undermining of his authority and a massive loss of prestige he could not have taken lightly. Thus, somehow, from the whole of Ionia, not one pilot or mariner warned Mardonius about the temperamental nature of Mount Athos.

It was a given that an expedition sanctioned by Darius would include at least one family member sharing the leadership. Aristagoras against Naxos had Megabates (Her V.32), Datis against Miletus had Mardonius (Lewis 1980), who was the son of Darius' sister and of Gobryas, one of the seven conspirators, chamberlain to the king and second most powerful man in the empire (Hyland 2018; Fields 2007; Waters 2004; Sekunda 2002), or rather fourth (after the regal Trinity was re-established and Xerxes became co-regent and heir apparent). Now, once more Datis would have to put up with a young scion of Achaemenid lineage. This time it was to be another nephew of the king; Artaphrenes the Younger, son of Artaphrenes the Elder (Her VI.94,2), a good choice and a guarantee that the satrap would not undermine the expedition. Actually, the concept of dual leadership in expeditionary forces seems to apply whenever a stranger was heading them, a very safe indication that Aristagoras might well have been in charge of the failed campaign against Naxos in 500 BC and, at the same time, that Megabates had exceptional powers, especially to inspect, audit and report on him, exactly as inferred from the narrative of Herodotus.

The forces (i) of Artybius in Cyprus, (ii) of the three sons-in-law of Darius in the Ionian Revolt, (iii) of Mardonius in 492 BC, (iv) of Megabazus and (v) then Otanes in Thrace and (vi) of the generals/proxies of Darius mentioned in the Behistun inscription during 521–519 BC operations were headed by a single commander each. Cases (i), (ii) and (v) used local expeditionary forces and this must be the case for (vi). Cases (iii) and (iv) were imperial projects and a royal expeditionary force, similar to the one Mardonius undertook in 479 BC in Greece, had been assigned in each case. And, finally, cases (i), (iii) and (v) included naval assets. This suggests another possibility for dual leadership: the participation of royal units from the heartland along with satrapal/local musters, to beef up the latter; the use of a naval component *per se* is not important as a factor for dual leadership.

Part III

Marathon: The Plain of Freedom

Chapter 10

Hoplite Supreme

The campaign that culminated in the famous battle is one of the events described least competently in the works of Herodotus. This must be due to the animosity of Pericles to the family of Miltiades. For this reason, one has to make as much as possible of accurately narrated events.

Herodotus describes the army dispatched in 490 BC as numerous and well-furnished (Her VI.95,1), under the joint command of Datis the Mede and Artaphrenes son of Artaphrenes, Satrap at Sardis (Her VI.94,2). These two might have met and co-operated during the final stage of the suppression of the Ionian Revolt. This new army emerges in Cilicia, where it meets with the assigned fleet (VI.95,1); this meeting point implies a royal army, not (only) satrapal levies. A mixed army most probably, with a royal contribution under Datis enhanced by satrapal levies, which must have been mobilized under Artaphrenes the Younger. Importantly, it *is* a new army, as the previous one, of Mardonius, had been badly mauled and probably decommissioned after its inglorious return, with the commander in disgrace (Her VI.94,2). Trying to fix the mistakes – not only those of Mardonius – Datis must have suggested that this time the Accursed Mountain, Athos (Grundy 1901), was to be avoided altogether by an approach through the central Aegean (Her VI.95,2).

It was the first time the Persians would embark on a massive, amphibious-only, operation. They had moved armies by ships to invade Samos (Her III.139,1), the islands of northern Aegean (Her V.26), Naxos (Her V.32) and Cyprus after its revolt (Her V.108). They had also used fleets to shadow and support land invasion forces, as in Egypt (Her III.19,2 & 44.2). In the latter campaign, the stage had been set for the imperial navy to flank enemy holding forces so as to unlock the advance of the army (Holland 2005), a routine most feared by the Greeks. Not only in Marathon, in the form of amphibious outmanoeuvring of the Athenian army (Her VI.115), but also during the invasion of Xerxes. In the latter campaign the risk was identifiable during the preparatory phases of the battle of Salamis (Her VIII.60) and, in a less orthodox manner, before Plataea, as described by Chileus the Tegean in Sparta (Her IX .9,2).

In 490 BC the previous idea was evolved: a major offensive would be seaborne, with the assault troopers carried on the decks of the war galleys (Her VI.95,2) while the rest of the vessels carried supplies and support personnel plus spare space for the plunder and the slaves. Also, for the first time, there were horse transports (Her VI.95,1) a striking novelty (Burn 1962; Lazenby 1993) intended to afford the amphibious task force an invaluable mounted arm, most indispensable for a land campaign in some depth. Being shipborne, the army is by definition limited and thus elite. The prospects of a small, flexible task force of elite troops instead of a massive invasion army like the one assembled and led by Xerxes must have been discussed by the Persian leadership of the time quite extensively. And it has been argued hotly among scholars throughout the ages who occasionally fail to remember that the card of the small, elite task force was played in the campaign which cumulated in the battle of Marathon (Delbruck 1920; Burn 1962). And it did not play well.

Once aboard, troops in the triremes and horses in the horse transports (Her VI.95,1), the task force sailed to the west, skirting Asia Minor. Herodotus does not describe the early phases of the campaign, but it is possible that the fleet called to different islands off SW Asia Minor to subjugate them, if the attempt of Datis to storm Lindos (Burn 1962) refers to this campaign and not to the one four years earlier, just before the battle of Lade as mentioned previously. Up to this point, it is like mopping up areas that were overlooked due to urgency in the naval campaigns of 494 and 492 BC, although this may be inaccurate and the sailing might have been uneventful. This last proposal is corroborated by simple logic; Mardonius would surely have settled similar issues with his navy before launching to Europe, especially as he was aboard for the trip from Cilicia to Ionia. As the fleet moved northwards, with obvious (or declared?) destination the Hellespontine area and Thrace (Her VI.95,2), one may surmise that despite repeated expeditions, the area had not been totally and utterly pacified.

But reaching the latitude of Samos, the imperial fleet turned due west (Her VI.95,2) to initiate an aggressive island hopping of conquest (**Map 10.1**). The first target was Naxos, which was taken by surprise, as it must have been a day's warning or less from the turn of the fleet westwards to troops landing on its beaches. There was no time for preparations to withstand a siege, and the Naxian host, which in the days of glory some ten years earlier was 8,000 Hoplites (Her V.30,4), had no expertise nor stomach for a pitched battle, especially with a force vastly superior and – what a prodigy – supported by a seaborne cavalry arm! The city was taken summarily and all the inhabitants caught by the imperial patrols and raiding parties were enchained and enslaved (Her VI.96).

Naxos had never harmed or insulted the Empire; attacking it twice in ten years was simply an act of cruel imperialism. The news and the smoke from Naxos made the successive landings more of a cruise than a campaign. A second pillar of smoke completed the carrot and stick policy (Holland 2005): Datis landed at Delos and

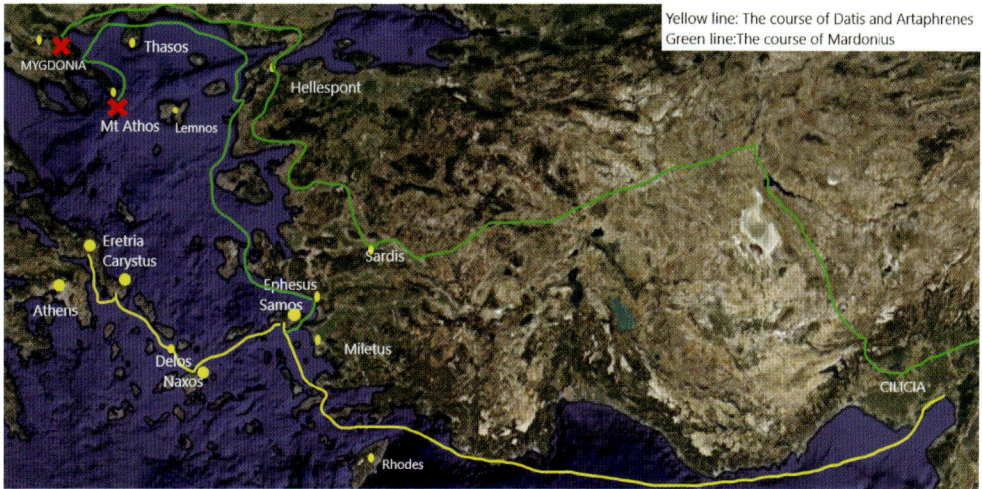

Map. 10.1.

called back the terrified islanders who had been evacuated to the nearby islands, declaring his most solemn purposes and intentions towards Apollo, the God of the island, by his own account and by royal decree (Her VI.97). After the religious atrocities in Ionia some four years before (Her VI.19,3), especially against Apollo, this show of tolerance towards the same God sent positive waves to Delphi and appeased the previously and currently subjugated Ionians (Holland 2005), who had joined the armada late (Her VI.98,1) and were not only a source of intelligence and linguistics but also hostages and proof of the goodwill of their recently subjugated-anew-cities (Ray 2009).

This tolerant, albeit highly political, gesture tends to be inflated, to prove the alleged Medizm of the Apollonian priesthood (Burn 1962) due to the stunning divination of the Oracle of Delphi to Cnidians back in the days of Cyrus I (Her I.174). This may have been true at that time, under Cyrus, but *not* under Darius. The reputable oracle and Temple of Apollo situated at Didyma near Miletus was thoroughly plundered and levelled after the suppression of the Ionian revolt (Her VI.19,3), thus showing a state of perpetual war between Ahura-mazda and his servants on the one hand and the followers of Apollo on the other; a state of war underlined by Xerxes' torching of the apollonian oracle at Abae and his attempted plunder of Delphi (Her VIII.33 & 35 respectively).

In any case, the policy of Datis was an unqualified success. Everybody in the islands surrendered and duly produced hostages and naval contributions to participate in the campaign (Her VI.99,1). Only Carystus initially declined but it surrendered after a brief siege and some pretence of devastation (Her VI.99,2) and followed suit. Carystus was a most strategic site: it was the entrance to the Southern Euboean Gulf and its territory formed with the island of Andros a sea channel from which fleets descending from the north had to pass through to enter the Saronic Gulf (**Map 10.1**). The invaders needed a friendly local state of affairs there, as it was a stepping stone but could be used also as a base (**Map 10.2**). When the Imperials were in Carystus, the next targets, Athenians and Eretrians, would be kept in uncertainty of the highest order: the next Persian attack may be either just across the channel, Attica, or along the coast, to Eretria (Bradford 2001). The defenders would not know where to concentrate, even if they were up to concerted action.

The next target, a capital one this time, was to be Eretria, a state that had indeed hurt the empire by assisting the Ionian revolt with a meagre five triremes (Her V.99,1) and was thus one of the two major objectives. It had been marked for total destruction and its population for deportation (Her VI.94,2). This serial pursuit of major targets allowed the militarily very sane concentration of force on one objective at a time while keeping the enemy divided, and cannot be considered an indication of mediocre numerical strength as Burn (1962) proposes. The Imperials started from the easiest and smallest target and proceeded gradually, knowing that each step was to build their morale, sap that of the enemy and compromise the bigger target, both in terms of morale and in terms of possible reinforcements for a decisive fight. To concentrate so as to achieve crushing superiority is both ancient and contemporary wisdom in Shock and Awe; Xenophon stated that winning overwhelmingly is not a problem, but a blessing (Xen Hipp 8,11).

The sacking of Eretria

Approaching Eretria, the Imperials, excellently informed of the assets of the city, overshot it while inspecting the shorelines. Hippias, the Medizer Peisistratid who instigated the campaign and served as a political liaison, negotiator and military advisor knew the area, but the commanding officers scanned for troops. The city might have been able to field 3,000 Hoplites and 600 cavalry (Bradford 2001). The latter was a very dangerous proposal if it could intervene with the landing, and this must be one of the reasons for assigning cavalry to the expedition. Then, seeing none, the Imperials disembark at three coasts, near the city but far enough away so as to hit the beach unimpeded (Her VI.94,2), *especially by the cavalry*. In such uncontested landings, the Imperials seem to use a new, aggressive operating procedure: they disembark cavalry first (Her VI.101,1) to secure the mounts and allow them to stretch after the voyage. This allowed their cavalry to raid the area in depth, provide reconnaissance and loot and terrorize the locals (Demosth Or 59,94; Plut Mor 305) with little warning, and possibly to intercept or delay enemy forces sent to contest the landing or attack the bridgehead; *especially* enemy cavalry.

The Eretrians had decided not to risk a battle, but to trust their walls; they had requested reinforcements from Athens, which they received just in time; an impressive 4,000 Hoplites from the Athenian military colony at Chalcis to their NW, established some 15–17 years earlier (Her VI.100,1), after the victory of the infant Democracy against the Chalcidians (Her V.77). They were true, they were many, they were near, they were fast and they were not weakening the Athenian metropolitan host by one man; the Athenians were not to leave Attica defenceless or compromise its defence by crossing the channel while the enemy had naval superiority, or rather dominance, and could easily outmanoeuvre them or cut them off (Burn 1962). A sensible decision, exactly to the tune of the decisions of the allied general headquarters ten years later, which left Attica to the torch.

But since the Eretrians were terrified, deliberating whether to imitate the Naxians and flee to the mountains or to undergo a siege, the Athenian reinforcements, once tipped off (Her VI.100,3), had no intention of being trapped in a besieged city and thus retired to the opposite side of the Gulf, to Oropus (Her VI.101,1), in the NE corner of Attica (**Map 10.2**), leaving the Eretrian allies alone. It was actually an act of mass desertion (Grundy 1901). Still, the position of the Eretrians was far from hopeless. Naxos had admirably withstood a siege ten years earlier and Eretria was a stronger city. Unfortunately, the enemy was infinitely more powerful than before with triple the vessels and much better prepared, with an advisor very capable in machinations and well-networked locally. Hippias' father, Peisistratus, had resided in Eretria for some years and from there started his ascent to power in Athens, followed by his sons (Her I.61–2).

For some days the defence was successful, but in less than a week, two aristocrats opened a gate (Her VI.101,2), thus allowing a total and complete Imperial victory,

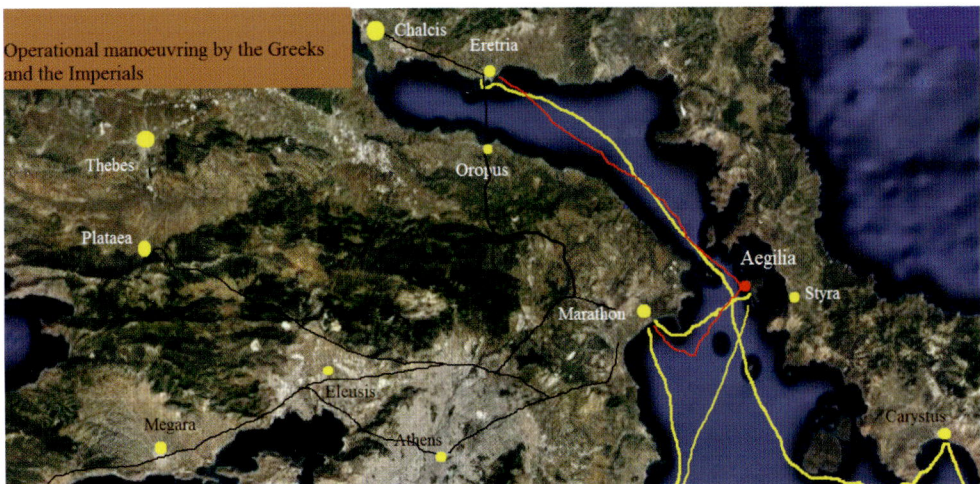

Map. 10.2.

resulting in the expected atrocities. The city was razed and burnt to avenge the burning of Sardis (Her VI.101,3). The population was arrested, enchained, enslaved (ibid) and moved to a nearby island for safekeeping (Her VI.107,2), along with the loot, expecting to be joined shortly by the oncoming harvest (captives and spoils) from Athens, as the task force moved from Eretria some miles down-channel, to the beach of Marathon (Her VI.107,1).

It was a place well-known to Hippias, where his family had strong ties and affiliations that allowed him to hope for a repetition of his father's ascent to prominence: from Eretria he crossed to Marathon with allies and mercenaries where he assembled his supporters. Then he moved through Pallene, where he brushed aside by surprise his mustered and overconfident but undisciplined enemies, to the Acropolis of Athens (Her I.61–3). Marathon was a spot well-watered, near to Eretria, suitable for cavalry action and grazing and offering a perfect and safe anchorage (Burn 1962). Hippias had every reason to assume that his supporters and followers would muster under his standard and the somewhat intimidating assurance of the Persian spears (Burn 1962; Lazenby 1993). The reason this never happened, and both the medizing democrats of Cleisthenes and the followers of the Peisistratids did very little to promote the Persian cause, might have been the result of the cruelty shown in Eretria. Instead of paralysis through terror, Datis effected a wake-up call for the medizing Athenian riff-raff, who, if not actively assisting, proved neutral or supportive to the upper-class Hoplite campaign (Grundy 1901).

Attica invaded

The fall of Eretria took some days to happen (Her VI.11,2) and afterwards the imperial army took some more days to move to Attica (Her VI.102). Some Athenians, as were the 4,000 reinforcements who retired ignominiously (Her VI.101, 1), had witnessed at least some of the action and brought valuable intelligence back to Athens. If their retirement was indeed an issue of cowardice (Grundy 1901), such intelligence might have been instrumental for not pressing any charges against them, although their sheer numbers, which practically doubled the Athenian Hoplite army (Ray 2009), would have been enough to steer them out of any trouble or even reproach.

More preliminary intelligence must have come during the Persian island hopping (Her VI.99,1), which was the definite early warning that a menacing armada was incoming. Thus, the Athenians had some time to deliberate. The deliberation was to fight on land; not to attempt any naval defence (Burn 1962; Grant 2012). With their fifty or so vessels, one per *naucraria* (Haas 1985; Tarn 1908), the latter would have been suicidal; the same could be said for their cavalry (Ray 2009), 100 horsemen, two per naucraria (Spence 1993; Haas 1985). Most importantly, the

Athenians deliberated that the invader should be met as far from the city as possible (Her VI.103,1), to deny (i) any opportunity to the imperial sappers and engineers to decide the issue, as in Miletus and Cyprus; (ii) an effective isolation and interdiction of their army to meet and make contact with the expected Spartan – and perhaps other – reinforcements (Burn 1962); (iii) any chance for the collaborators and agents to interfere, as had happened in Eretria (Bradford 1980) and (iv) a free ride to devastate Attica.

There was a finite number of suitable landing places, and the Board of Generals must have identified them, along with the most convenient itineraries to reach them in force and the best positions from where to deploy. Especially after the fall of Eretria and the deportation of the inhabitants (maybe not all of them, but quite a proportion of the population), even moderate Athenians would have been much more determined and the defeatists much less prominent and outspoken. Thus, as the magnificent Persian organization neatly took in and stored loot and prisoners on the island of Aegilia and re-embarked materiel and troops (**Map 10.2**), the Athenians had a day or two to deliberate, even then, that the enemy would be met away from the city walls, to deny him contact with the traitors within and, most importantly, access to opportunities engineered by said traitors. The two most prominent choices for the Persians, and their guide, Hippias, were Phaleron and Marathon (**Map 10.4**); not the only ones, but the most prominent. The former was the main port and base of the Athenian fleet and allowed a fast dash to the city. The latter was an area with political and natural advantages. The former

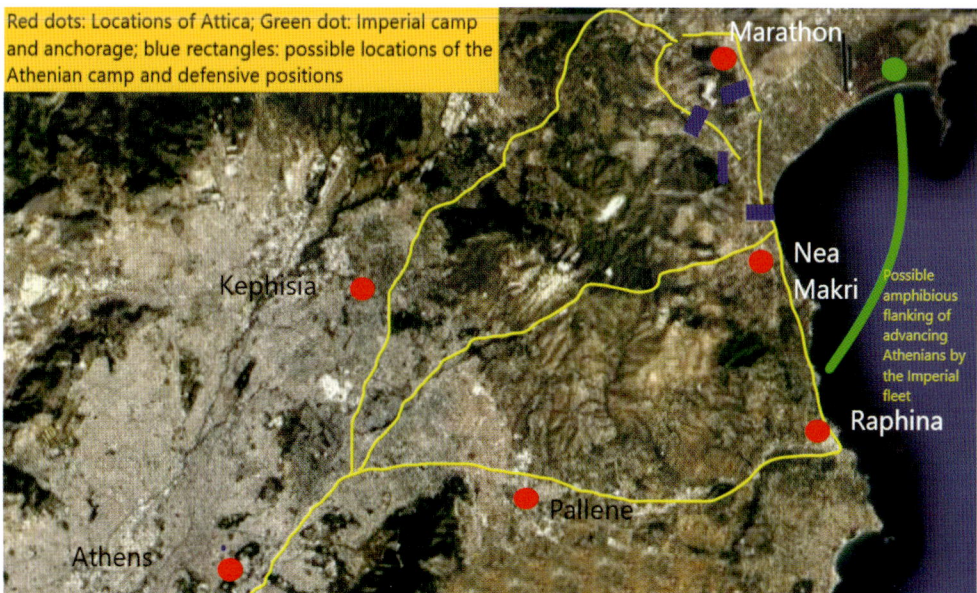

Map. 10.3.

included the strong support of the locals for the Peisistratids – or at least this was what Hippias (would have) counted on. The latter included good cavalry ground, a decent anchorage, fodder and water, a short distance from Eretria and the prisoner of war camp established for the Eretrian loot and slaves on the island of Aegilia (Her VI.107,2), a usefully long distance from Athens and several egress routes that created uncertainties to the defender (**Map 10.3**) and allowed a campaign of devastation from a central position, so as to entice the Athenians out of their walled city (Sekunda 2002).

Both areas, and possibly some more, must have been identified, reconnoitered and inspected beforehand and the same must have happened for the routes and tracks connecting them to Athens (Her VI.116). Once watchers (or beacons) reported that the target of the enemy fleet was Marathon (Burn 1962), the Athenian army moved forward, having been mobilized beforehand and kept on high alert, while at the same time dispatchers were sent to possible sources of reinforcements; definitely to Sparta and Plataea – the latter being their subject pure and simple (Badian 1993), no ally or friend (Her VI.108,1) – but possibly elsewhere as well. The expedited march to Marathon was something like eight or ten hours. Given that after landing the Persians had to raid the area so as to secure their immediate surroundings (Plut Vit Aris 5,1), feed and rest their horses, establish camp and organize their bridgehead (Bradford 1980; Burn 1962), the Athenians had a day, at the very least, to move to intercept. They needed 8–12 hours. But even if the Persian army had been able to bypass them and move towards Athens, they could return, if tipped off by observers, or continue; the Persian army would be facing a walled city and the Athenian army would have been in front of an exposed fleet, having just cast anchor and begging to be captured. There is no way, no matter what Green (1970) felt, that the Persians would have started a 40-km expedition through passes without having established a camp to protect their fleet.

The main Athenian asset was the Hoplite army. If at 10,000 Hoplites or so (Paus IV.25,5 & X.20,2), it was just a third of the free citizens (Her V.97,2); the other two thirds were prospective Medizers and the slave attendants of the Hoplites were deemed more dependable than such free folk and were raised to follow their masters in the campaign and eventually to the field (Paus I.32,3). Thus, this army was the prime concern of the Athenian leadership. This means one thing only: that the army took the road from Kephisia to Marathon (Hammond 1968; Grundy 1901), or the road to Nea Makri, but *not* the nice long road through Pallene (Green 1970). Both choices are shorter than the approach through Pallene; they are also fully negotiable by infantry, but not so by horses *en masse*. Some scholars who deny such a prospect by judging its suitability for a Second World War-type infantry division (Burn 1962) simply miss the point: the quintessence of the campaign was the Decree of Miltiades (Arist Rhetor 1411a; Demosth 19303), probably prepared, voted and put into effect before the fall of Eretria.

The deliberation was 'take food and march' (Burn 1962); it is Napoleon's verdict, 'where two soldiers can pass, an army can pass' (Bonaparte 1830); especially a Hoplite army, with Hoplites and attendants, and possibly draught animals but, most probably, no carts. An army which might have got moving at night (Clement Stromat 162,2), through partly non-existent roads and paths, as was the Kephisia road (Burn 1962; Berthold 1976) but also the one through Nea Makri. Had they taken the coastal road through Pallene, the Persian fleet could launch a landing behind them (Berthold 1976), the way it might have happened in Egypt under Cambyses and in the same manner as envisaged for Thermopylae and the Isthmus of Corinth in 480–79 BC. By *not* taking a road running along a coastline, the defenders were not subject to outflanking by the enemy navy and amphibious forces. It must be noted that the Nea Makri road, ending in the whereabouts of the Vrexiza marsh, at the south entrance of the Marathon plain, but much shorter than the angular itinerary via Pallene, might have been the return itinerary of choice and should be given consideration for the Athenian arrival at Marathon as well, as it shuts the southern exit without taking the Hoplites into an area suitable for cavalry operations as does the route through Pallene. Its rough, overland character meant that an amphibious manoeuvre further south, as in Raphina, would not cut off the Athenian army at Marathon (**Map 10.3**).

Thus, if the Persians intended to make a surprise dash to Athens or to any other place in Attica (a limited, cavalry-only raid as the infantry would be making camp), they had to take the road through Pallene and thus would not run into the Athenian army on the march (Hammond 1968; Grundy, 1901). Such an occasion would have been catastrophic for the natives (Berthold 1976). The southern, main road through Pallene, spacious and level, allowed precisely this: a fast Persian column dashing into the Athenian Hoplite army as the latter would be squarely in a window of vulnerability; in marching order to Marathon, at break-neck speed, which means lax in discipline, low in readiness and out of formation – and possibly of breath as well. One such disaster had befallen the Athenians before, during Peisistratus' quest for power (Her I.63) and the current Board of Generals had no intention of inviting a replay. Thus, contrary to what some scholars consider a gift to the Persians, that is an open road to Athens (Green 1970; Sekunda 2002; Berthold 1976), the Imperials would have had the opportunity for only limited raiding with their cavalry while setting camp. In truth, they would do nothing of the kind before getting everything they needed for the security of their bridgehead in place, disembarked or unloaded *and* becoming absolutely positive about the whereabouts of the Athenian army. The imperial operational tempo was too slow to have an opportunity to intercept the Athenians *en route* (Burn 1962). Although the Athenians could not bet on it, they could count on it. But in any case, the Athenian army had a safe approach to Marathon. The imperial task force was unable to easily negotiate the roads through Kephisia or Nea Makri, which offered the defending Athenians opportunities for an ambush.

The Persian commanders had selected Marathon for many reasons, among which was that they had no intention of walking to Athens; at least not immediately. They raided nearby to catalyze the movement of the Athenian army to their whereabouts, obligingly leaving all ingress routes accessible (Grundy 1901; Burn 1962) – if one believes the Imperials had time, intention and resources to occupy, control and guard them. Once the Athenian army reached Marathon, the Imperial command could assess its size and thus the size of their prospective fifth column, but also keep the army as far away as possible from the city, from the approaching Spartans and the Plataeans. Both reinforcement bodies would then have had to walk 40 more kilometres to engage and their supply trains just the same to deliver. Furthermore, the Imperials wanted the reactionaries (the Hoplites) away from the city, to allow more enlightened and co-operative Athenians, their collaborators, freedom of action. The final appeal of Datis for a conditional surrender (Diod X.27), if it happened, was an opportunity to acquire some first-hand intelligence and establish contact with sympathisers. The idea must have been that the Athenian traitors would make the move and the Imperials would force it home, suppress any resistance and carry away the reactionaries to Asia, allowing Hippias to control the less radical social groups (Burn 1962) – which must have been the actual interpretation of the events in Eretria.

To accomplish the above, the Imperials did not need to fight. They had to keep the enemy fighting element away from the city and the looming events (Sekunda 2002) and provide credible support for such developments. Fighting was to be avoided and pursued only with enough tactical advantages secured. Still, one should remember that Datis had no reason to doubt a victory if an engagement occurred, and that the standard of Achaemenid counter-insurgency as effected by Darius and his proxies dictated one or two decisive field victories before proceeding to siegecraft (DB 18–9; 26–7; 29–30), thus having the opponent with shattered morale and seriously depleted, possibly unable to fully man the fortifications. This approach made easier and much faster the final step, the storming of the fortified position.

Since the invasion was amphibious, there were few support troops, thus actual siegecraft was also a last resort, a fact corroborating the previous argument. Erecting mounds and sapping circuit walls demands a considerable workforce (fleet rowers might have been destined for such duties), time and commissariat. Time was all-important: if the operations dragged on, other Greeks might grow sinew – or conscience – and assist the Athenians. Surprise, as in Naxos, and encouragement of some locals to co-operate, as in Eretria, were far more advisable; fighting an open battle in advantageous terrain with high morale and a comfortable numerical superiority was the third-best option (Burn 1962). Interestingly, it seemed to be the most compatible with the Athenian war mentality, as demonstrated by their recent string of field victories against invaders, a fact that may have something to do with a possible unsatisfactory condition of their walls; although the causality of the two facts remains debatable (Lazenby 1993).

Miltiades knew the Persian *modus operandi* and understood that they would advance their infantry from Marathon to Athens through Pallene while devastating Attica with their cavalry and meet their fleet at Phaleron. Thus they would isolate the Athenians from any help, especially the Spartans, (Grundy 1901; Burn 1962) while establishing easy contact with their agents within the circuit – a repeated motive in Persian siege warfare (Her VIII.128,1 & VI.101,2 & III.158). The Athenian army was positioned to cover all possible ingress routes available to the Imperials, a fact allowing it to manoeuvre at the operational level with impunity, should the need be (Grundy 1901). The Vrana valley offered such luxuries. Athenian operational manoeuvring was likely to be unimpeded by Persian interventions as the Hoplite host and their subordinate light infantry (their retainers) could hold the high ground of the passes with token forces against the Persian army. On high ground they were safe from imperial cavalry onslaughts; additionally, the imperial archers were also at a disadvantage to advance and fire. The inclination marred aiming and reduced range, while the selected or prepared positions offered the defenders some protection from incoming missiles. Herodotus – of course – says nothing, but fieldworks are insinuated (Nepos Milt 5), most probably palisades (Delbruck 1920; Ray 2009; Hammond 1968) to cover either prospective deployments and/or the position(s) already held.

Palisades do not only repulse cavalry action; they also infringe with infantry assaults, and Miltiades must have been introduced to such practices defending the Chersonese against marauders, both light infantry and horse, from nearby Thracian territories. Alternatively, the Athenians might have been taught the trick by Cleomenes I (Ray 2009; Front Strat II.2,9) when he invaded Attica to oust Hippias (Her V.64,2) and repulsed with casualties the Thessalian cavalry under Cineas who were supporting the latter (Her V.63,3). The very silence of Herodotus on the subject bolsters the proposition that Miltiades was responsible for such works, at least in executive if not intellectual terms.

And what about the main, (partly) coastal road to Athens to the south, through Pallene or Nea Makri? How were the Athenians able to shut that too? They were not. And they did not. To egress from Marathon it was a narrow strip between seashore and mountain foot, if the marshland had been dry in early autumn or non-existent at the time (i.e. Lazenby 1993). If it were not, it would be even narrower, a nightmare to cross under attack. The Athenians shut the one road that was important to them, the double, bifurcated pass to Kephisia and Oinoe and by just being there, hemmed in and threatening, they denied the second, southern access to the Persians. If they were to try to follow the second road, to Pallene or Nea Makri (the latter not a very appealing option) the Athenians would take their flank or rear (Grundy 1901) or any rearguard the Imperials might have deployed (Delbruck 1920). Still, there is not *one* example during the Persian Wars of armies advancing under threat while covered by rearguards.

Contrary to some scholars (i.e. Lazenby 1993), the Athenian priority was the security of their army, *not* the shutting of any approach to Athens. The army being lost, no passage could have ever been denied. The Athenians could not block all exits from Marathon, nor apply modern strategy and defend a range from behind. So they did it the Hoplite way, defend it from before, so as to deny the enemy access to the various egress points, although wisely kept on ground most unfavourable for their opponent.

The aforementioned concept of a Persian advance under a rearguard, to any of the available passes, was a good way to precipitate an engagement, had the Imperials wished to do so. They did nothing of the kind, staying put and watching. Thus they did not wish for a fight even on their terms. Empires are not built on bravado, but on war economics. Psychology, influence, diversion are more appropriate means; Periclean Athens, Macedon, Rome and every other empire ever since (and possibly before) understood this simple and plain truth.

Well, these means have their limitations, too. The Persians were excellent manipulators and had a perfect understanding of the temporal parameter. They used it to their advantage admirably. They took their time from Eretria to Athens, to allow the message of terror to strike home, while making all the proper arrangements with the spoils of war. The bitter fruits of resistance, the desolation, the destruction, coupled to the menacing cold-blooded efficiency of their bureaucracy in handling and processing the product of such devastation, as if an everyday amenity, would break any warlike spirit. Thus, once in Marathon, they knew that the more they kept the Athenian army away from the city, the more its resources would be strained and also the more likely would be a *coup d'état*.

But they also knew that they could not keep fooling around indefinitely themselves. It was, up to a point, a matter of provisions, exacerbated by the fact that they had to care for their prisoners as well. Issues of supplies could be partially managed by straining their new subjects, Carystus and the islands. The main problem for the

Imperials was in the plain of Marathon. As the days passed, the Spartan arrival was getting closer and the Imperial staff had no idea as to how many they would be. The Spartans were genuinely pious (Green 1970) and this piousness was to cost them a king and 300 elites some ten years later. This means they would launch an expedition immediately after the full moon at the latest. 'Immediately' would be a matter of hours, as the troops would have been notified, prepared and kept at the ready; and this was the best-case scenario for the Imperials. Moreover, keeping their host stationary against the Athenians was counter-productive for the Imperials; not only for their troops' morale, which would be dropping due to inactivity and lack of progress after an almost stellar campaign, but especially for their enemies', who would grow accustomed to the Imperial presence and perhaps demystify it. This would erase any direct psychological advantage the razing of Eretria would have produced.

There is no concrete evidence that the actual battle was fought with the Imperial cavalry absent; there is such a report, but it is not a definite conclusion. Even if this was the case, it might have been that the cavalry was caught off position or operating independently (Hammond 1968), as they customarily did (Her VI.29 & IX.49,1 & IX.32), out-of-area and too far to intervene during the battle. But it is more plausible that the whole point was exactly the independent, deep cavalry action. When the opportune moment arose, the conspirators would signal to the Persians and they would board their cavalry and send it to Phaleron (**Map 10.4**). Cavalry only, no boarding of infantry whatsoever, contrary to Green's views (1970). From there the horsemen would gallop to Athens, finding the gates open and

Map. 10.4.

perhaps a coup in development. Cavalry surging through open gates, no matter how few, would achieve a formidable surprise (Burn 1962) and send a panic tsunami throughout Athens; nobody would count, nobody would ever observe there was no infantry. In the chaos and murder, the psychological impact would have decided the issue for the Imperials; the collaborators were their infantry and their amplifier, making the panic widespread and paralysing everything. With families and fortunes in Persian hands, the Hoplites could capitulate or roam, as guerillas, the wilderness of Attica, since the Persian infantry and the fleet (probably all the fleet but for the horse transports) would prevent them from swimming to Euboea... The prospect of the Persian infantry being transported to Athens and after its occupation moving to Marathon to trap and destroy the Athenian field army (Green 1970) is overcomplicated and unnecessary.

The opposing armies

There are some interesting issues about this particular Persian army. First, it is under two commanders. It is the first time this comes into the attention of the reader of Herodotus. Previous cases concerned commanders of separate forces operating, or moving, simultaneously, with the possible exception of the army annihilated off Pedasus (Her V.121) and the campaign against Naxos (Her V.33). Whether the two commanders in Marathon are equal or one is second-in-command, or simply the Master of Horse of the host, one cannot tell. But if there is a seniority issue, Datis the Mede is the leading candidate (Plat. Menex. 240a) for Spadapathis; Artaphrenes is a young aristocrat, son of Artaphrenes, Satrap of Ionia (Her VI.94,2) and contrary to Datis, never mentioned in a way suggesting a commander as in making proclamations (Her VI.97,1), executing operations (Plut Vit Aris 5,1) or inspecting the ships searching for specific items of plunder (Her VI.118,1) among other things. After the blunder of Mardonius, Darius, nepotistic *par excellence*, stopped assigning supreme commands to sons-in-law (Her V.116 & VI.43,1), cousins or nephews (Her V.32) etc. and used a seasoned commander, Datis, who might have been instrumental in the suppression of the Ionian revolt (Holland 2005; Burn 1962) and perhaps the author of the idea of an amphibious-only campaign. The family man was delegated to a second and perhaps subordinate role. Still, there is another possibility: that the dual command was a solution whenever a satrapal force was augmented with a royal one for a specific campaign. This explains why the campaigns against Naxos of 500 BC and 490 BC had dual command schemes, contrary to all others, pursued by either satrapal or imperial forces but not both.

Rather than considering suspicious the recurrent number of 600 war galleys for Persian fleets (Her VI.9,1 & VI.95,2) as do some scholars (Shepherd 2012; Ray 2009; Burn 1962), the recurrence implies rather a standardised Achaemenid naval echelon (Sekunda 2002), possibly two basic fleets or rather naval districts of 300 vessels (Sekunda 1989) and thus it should be accepted without any fuss as accurate and representative of the Achaemenid Standard Operating Procedures. Infantry and cavalry are another issue altogether. The horse transports limit the number of cavalry to the order of thousands, and few at that; 1,000 horse is the absolute minimum operational unit, a mounted hazarabam. The number and capacity of the Persian horse transports are unknown. The later Athenian ones, which were retrofits of older triremes and thus in no way more capacious, took 30 mounts and their grooms and riders. A 40-strong horse-transports squadron would allow slightly excess capacity (1200 mounts), for the mounts of high officials, liaison officers and commanders – and this only if the imperial vessels, built from the start as such, were limited to the capacity of the Athenian retrofits. If not, fewer vessels would suffice.

Furthermore, if 30 infantrymen were delegated to each fighting vessel, on top of the native marines, a practice dictated by the 40-strong rebel Chian boarding parties (Her VI.15,1) and repeated by Xerxes' navy (Her VII.184,2) the boarded infantry was at the very least 30x600=18,000 and, supplemented by at least 10 native boarders, 24,000 fighting troops, cavalrymen excluded. Support troops were on the transports, which ferried supplies and secretariat and were expected to load the plunder and the captives; thus, denying the existence of such vessels (but for the horse transports) as proposed by some scholars (Sekunda 2002) seems incompatible with the whole idea of a seaborne campaign. On the other hand, taking the figures of Menexenus of Plato (240a) to suppose a fleet of just 300 triremes but rejecting all the other figures and even vessel types in this particular work (Ray 2009) – which is notoriously inaccurate and meant to bolster the Athenian spirit and morale – is simply a quest to trim Imperial numbers near to or less than these of the Athenians. Indeed the Imperials could not pursue simultaneously both main targets, Athens and Eretria, by dividing forces (Burn 1962) as they had done during the Ionian revolt (Her V.116); perhaps they did not want to, as the previous example had led to a strategic stalemate after just one reverse, the ambush in Caria. Perhaps they declined to act similarly even to subjugate the islands of the Cyclades (Her VI.96 & 99) and selected a strictly sequential rather than a simultaneous expeditionary plan. Nothing informative here, the principle of concentration was known to the ancients; they were ancients, not ignorant.

But still, the Imperials were well-informed on their objectives by Hippias. Thus, keeping in mind that both cities were walled (and Naxos as well), which means that all their available manpower was prone to be brought to account, plus the fact that the fortifications are force multipliers for the defenders if they can man them properly, the Imperial host must have planned accordingly. Expected casualties during the successive operations should have been factored in, and resulted in a force size superior to the possible united field armies of their enemies by quite a margin. As the Achaemenid army organization was based on the 10,000-strong division, the baivarabam, the invading army is much more probably to have included three baivaraba, that is 30,000 infantry, probably including the native marines. This implies 50 troops on the deck of each of the 600 triremes.

This is not something unheard of. Without even contemplating the Athenian threat of loading all people and possessions to their triremes to mass migrate ten years later, a threat considered credible, if not imminent, by their contemporaries (Her VIII.62–3) there is a very solid proof that over 40 marines could be transported if the triremes of the era were not to engage in a sea-fight. In the Tempe campaign, ten years later, an army of 10,000 Hoplites, obviously each accompanied by one attendant, was ferried by the Greek fleet to the Thessalian shore of Alus (Her VII.173,1–2). The Greek fleet in that instance was of unknown strength, but cannot have been more numerous than its full capacity version deployed at Artemisium some months later, which was 320–330 vessels (Her VIII.2,1 & 14,1). This produces 60 individuals, Hoplites or/and attendants, ferried by each trireme. The existence of some pentekonters may slightly trim the number 60, but not much as their presence in Artemisium, some months later, was quite insignificant, at less than 10 vessels of the type (Her VIII.1,2). As a result, ferrying 30,000 troops was entirely doable for the 600 imperial warships of the 490 BC campaign, and the support vessels were for hauling freight and support personnel.

In these 30,000 Imperials, one should locate the core troops, Persians and Saka (Her VI.113,1) which together should be a third of the total, more or less. Sekunda (2002) proposes some hazaraba of Persians and Saka, although the operational unit is the baivarabam and thus figures divisable by 10,000 should be sought, augmented by 10 per cent or 20 per cent for the cavalry. A similar idea is followed by Ray (2009). Whether mixed baivaraba existed in the Achaemenid army remains controversial, and there are no clues in the sources allowing for the identification of any other ethnicity in the army (Her VI.113,1); in the navy, Ionians and Phoenicians are mentioned (Her VI.98,1 and VI.118,1 respectively); as there was no clash of Ionian infantry against Athenians (a pernicious proposal to start with) the native boarders might have been withheld from the infantry line to secondary duties, i.e. to guard the camp.

Concerning other sources and traditions which raise the number of the invaders to six digits (Plat. Menex. 240a, Nepos Milt 5), before starting trimming, one must remember that the total number of troops and sailors was more than 100,000.

The 600 triremes had 200-man crews (Her VII.184,1), including or excluding the boarding parties; thus, an impressive 120,000 minimum is reached, without any support personnel and the crews of the merchantmen (including, but not restricted to, horse-transports).

The Athenian army has been traditionally estimated at 10,000 Hoplites, either including or excluding the 1,000 Plataeans (Paus IV.25,5 & X.20,2; Nepos Milt 5,1), whom some scholars (Shepherd 2012) trim to 600 by reverse-factoring their number in the 479 BC campaign (Her IX.28,6). It is clear that it consists of 10 *taxeis*, one for each Athenian tribe, as reorganized by Cleisthenes, commanded by one general elected by the tribesmen (Arist Ath Pol 22,2–3); the ten generals form the Board of Generals that deliberates by voting. The Polemarch (Arist Ath Pol 22,3–5) – elected by the whole electorate – presides over the board and has a vote in the event of an impasse; still, supreme command lies with one of the generals, rotating daily (Her VI.110) most probably by the official enumeration of their respective tribes. For both Athenians and Plataeans it was a full levy, not an expeditionary one with mobilization quota. The danger was existential and both Athens and their ally (or subject) Plataea would be annihilated in case of defeat.

Herodotus mentions no figures, and for good reasons – there are significant issues. There were 4,000 Athenian Hoplites, the Cleruchs from Chalcis, in Oropus long before the Persians landed. What happened to these? They moved to Athens, to join the main army? Were they staying put at Oropus to guard the Persian crossing there, and subsequently dispatched to Marathon, as the force nearest to the area, to occupy the position selected for the deployment of the army? This would deny any opportunity to the Persians to interdict the approach of the Athenian army to the plain of Marathon. To do that, they had to arrive there before the Persians took control of the plain, as the ingress point of the Athenian army was practically on the other side of the Persian bridgehead. Additionally, should these 4,000 be included in the 10,000 Athenian Hoplites or be added to them? Pausanias (IV.25,5 & X.20,2) leaves little doubt that the latter was not the case. Then, the core Athenian host was just 6,000 Hoplites, a really minuscule number, but compatible with the army of the era of Solon, not that long ago as may be estimated with a restrictive interpretation of some excerpts of the Athenian Constitution of Aristotle (Sekunda 2002), which brings the total to 3,600 shields; Naxos had some 8,000 (Her V.30,4). The Naxian Hoplites might have never been intended for a set-piece battle but, as in most islands, for naval action as boarders and marines. Still, it is a weird comparison. Lacedaimon, having incorporated Messene, was double the size of Attica and was fielding some 8,000 Peers and at least as many Perioikoi (Her VII.234,2); Thebes though, a city more to the measure of Athens of 490 BC, before the great expansion of the army brought by the vigorous trading with the west, fielded a similar number (Bonner

1910). It is no surprise that in 479 BC the Athenians have some 10,000 Hoplites including the expeditionary force of 8,000 at Plataea (Her IX.28,6), the boarders in the fleet under Xanthippus and probably a garrison at Salamis.

In any case, should the total be inclusive of the 4,000 Cleruchs, they would have been incorporated into the 10 *Taxeis*-brigades based on their origin before being dispatched to Chalcis, as these brigades were far from territorial: each taxis brigaded troops from different communities located in all three residential zones of Attica. On this account, Sekunda (2002) proposes a 9,000 total levy. This agrees with the restrictive interpretation of the Athenian Constitution by Aristotle, whence the four Ionian tribal brigades of the Athenian army (of 3600 shields) were formed up by three *trittyes* of 300 men, one for each residential zone; each *trittys* had ten *triakades*, the smaller organisational and conscription unit of 30 men each. If the organization of the new Cleisthenic tribes remained similar, with three 300-strong trittyes accounting for 900 shields for each of the now ten new tribal brigades (Taxeis), a 9,000 army is reached. The incorporation of some émigrés in this context was not a problem. For all the days of the waiting game, they were training with their native peers so as to develop cohesion and be able to apply the tactics of Miltiades.

Intentions and dispositions

Miltiades must have been known to Datis and *vice versa*; maybe not in person, but they were on opposite sides during the Ionian revolt, if indeed Datis had been instrumental in its suppression (Holland 2005). Moreover, many of the commanders, if not sailors also, of the Ionian fleet were his old friends and comrades-in-arms; some of them must have known him personally during the operations of the Hellespontine rebellion and the campaign of Histiaeus at the straits (Her VI.5,2–3), if not from the days of the Persian ebb from Scythia and the Thracian rebellion. Thus, Miltiades knew much about Datis. He knew that the waiting game had a reason and an expiration date. The reason was Datis' anticipation of developments in Athens, which would allow him a nice campaign similar to the ones of Cambyses and Darius in Egypt and Babylon respectively where traitors won the battle for him before the engagement was on; Sun Tzu's prerogative, to fight when the battle is already won, as had been at Lade, four years earlier.

The wide, operational manoeuvre of the imperial fleet to outmanoeuvre the whole Athenian army must have been taken from the book of Cambyses and his fleet of the invasion of Egypt (Holland 2005). The opening of the gates by agents within was already tried in Eretria (Her VI.101,2) and also effected in Babylon by Zopyrus (Her III.158). Thus, Datis, before sending his cavalry alone to a dash from

Phaleron, was waiting for his collaborators to act. Despite the early tradition of dividing his infantry forces in half (Nepos Milt 5), any infantry would be a liability in this dash due to the slow pace of advance, but also any such dispatch would weaken the field army in Marathon, which was pinning down the Athenians. Miltiades knew that Datis needed only his cavalry to conquer Athens; his Athenian collaborators would provide the infantry.

But *keeping* Athens was another matter; there Datis needed his infantry and/ or to disable the Hoplite army of Marathon. Assault was out of the question due to the position and the characteristics of the troop types. But the imperial army in Marathon could opt for an advance by the coastal road; then the Athenians would have to engage at the level against superior numbers and archers or retire, possibly under a rearguard which would make pursuit impossible for the Imperials. In the latter case, though, the retreating Athenians could not intercept the Persian infantry. All such events would develop with Athens occupied and the families of the Hoplites at the mercy of the enemy...

Thus Datis was probably lining up his infantry for battle every day to taunt the Athenians (Burn 1962); had they accepted the challenge, he would face them on his own terms, in cavalry ground with his force full and ready. Had they denied, as they did, his troops would have higher morale ('the enemy do not dare to face us'), his collaborators in Athens an even higher one, understanding that they had bet wisely. The moderates in Athens would start questioning the sagacity of resistance as an option and the Athenian troops would have suffered a plunge of their own morale, denying the challenge day after day. The repeated, everyday challenge and the psychological pressure might lure one of the Athenian generals, on his command day, to accept the challenge, especially if the Imperial formation was cutting the Athenian army off the coastal road southwards. It was a well-judged psychological move. Should the Athenians find themselves needing to retire, the Persians would have secured the use of the easy Pallene road, so they could outmarch the Athenians and catch them near Athens without risking exposure to traps and ambushes as would be the case if trailing them along the Kephisia itinerary.

On the other hand, Miltiades and his fellows were expecting the Spartans, while remaining vigilant for an opportunity to engage (Burn 1962). In the meantime they were using the stand-off time productively to observe and time the Persian battle arrangements, which, should the Athenians accomplish surprise, would be automatically executed by the Imperial troops; the operative idea behind their training and drilling. This explains how it was eventually possible for the Athenians to start their advance early in the morning before the Imperials were set into their regular positions, and still have a deployment adapted to the enemy one. This apparent antithesis makes many a modern scholar draw erroneous temporal conclusions, that the Athenian charge started *after* the Imperial line was properly formed (Holoka 1999). Moreover, the Athenians would have become accustomed to the spectacle of the enemy line-up and demystified the opponent. If the prospect of the arrival of Spartan assistance is factored in, the Athenians had no motive to accept the challenge and engage without a good reason. Might this be an opportunity or an adverse development, as would have been an attempt against their defenceless city. (Burn 1962; Grundy 1901).

But all these had an expiration date. Once the Spartans were in Athens (*Athens, not Marathon*) the prospect of treason would be less than zero (Grundy 1901). Thus Datis had to act before; if his agents did their job, so much the better, but in case they could not deliver, he had to make a move (Burn 1962). He could take the coastal road and risk a fight in questionable terms or worse; the Athenians might simply retire near Athens overland, to facilitate the impending Spartan approach. Or, Datis could execute the amphibious manoeuvre anyway, hoping that once his cavalry was seen approaching, shock and collaborators could result in an open door. That meant Datis had at most two days after the full moon that ended the taboo of the Karneia; the Spartans would start at the earliest after the full moon (Her VI.106,3) and the 200 km from Athens would take them at least four days to arrive as an army ready to engage. Thus, the next day of the full moon Datis would have to make his move to allow for any unforeseen delays or eventuality.

Miltiades knew well the limitations and motives for Datis' policy. He knew that, eventually, the Athenians would have to fight alone, without the Spartans, because Datis had the initiative and would not grant them the chance to wait for such help. Miltiades must have concluded, along with his fellow generals that even if a coup, aided by Persian cavalry, was to take over Athens, should the Persian infantry be decisively beaten the situation was conceivably susceptible to remedy upon the arrival of the Spartans. It would be preferable not to lose the city, but in any case, there was some leeway. Having witnessed the daily drill and procedure of the Persian field army without showing anything of theirs, the Athenians could achieve surprise. Callimachus, the ceremonial Commander-in-Chief (*Polemarch*), was persuaded (Her VI.110) and turned the vote for Miltiades. At least the other four generals who agreed, passed their designated days of Supreme Command to him (Plut Vit Aris 5,2; Her VI.110), probably so as to be able to execute his plan (Plut Vit Aris 5,2) upon any opportunity. The plan was made known to all and, contrary to the view of Lazenby (1993), once the battle was decided, it was a matter of timing. Miltiades, and nobody else, knew the right moment; could assess time and estimate distance and the applicable tolerances in terms of space, time, manpower (Delbruck 1920). Herodotus said Miltiades accepted the pass but waited for his designated day (Her VI.110). He was waiting for an opportunity, not for his designated day of supreme command.

And his contacts on the Imperial side did not fail him. Either because the Athenian lines, by their defensive outworks, had approached the Persians, or through the no-man's-land due to lax Imperial security, the Ionians in the Persian camp notified Miltiades the moment the cavalry was gone (Suda ~1000 AD). Where to, we can only assume, and Phaleron is a valid assumption; but Miltiades, who would have assumed similarly as a worst-case scenario, raised his colleagues and the army and after days spent to make the proper arrangements without being seen by the Persians, mobilized his units to gain every second as the sandglass had been turned.

Deployment and the running charge

The fastest way to deploy before daybreak would indeed have been by two lines emerging from the camp, going at opposite directions and forming there, in a Y pattern, with the centre forming up last (Burn 1962; Humble 1980). This is by no means difficult, as some modern scholars suggest (Lazenby 1993), especially if rehearsed. The renowned formation (**Figure 10.1**) of the deep wings and shallow centre (Her VI.111,3), a 2 to 1 ratio, possibly 8 against 4 lines deep (Burn 1962; Lazenby 1993; Ray 2009) to a battle line matching that of the enemy (Her VI.111,3) was preconceived, prearranged and perhaps tacitly practised and drilled before daybreak or after dusk, to keep the Persians in the dark and familiarise the Hoplites with performing it in low ambient light.

The argument that the wings were deeper than the centre by accident, as the Athenians tried to match the width of the Imperials (Lazenby 1993) is not simply erroneous; it borders on malice. If the Athenians had to reduce locally their phalanx depth to match the front of Imperials, they would have done so at the *wings*, not at the *centre*, to extend them – or, if they had deployed right first, they would have extended the left wing. They would have no way, and, more importantly, no reason to thin their centre where the best enemy troops were posted. Even if Miltiades

Fig. 10.1. The deployment of the Imperials (red) and of the Athenians (blue) just before the battle. The black line is the first rank of the Athenian hoplites.

had no particular knowledge of the Persian practices first-hand (Lazenby 1993), he must have discoursed with many Imperials during the Scythian campaign and with many rebels during the Ionian revolt to know that the best troops were at the centre, to effect central penetration and collapse of the whole enemy deployment. Thus, to match the line *and* to take pains, against any automatism, to keep the wings deep and weaken the centre instead, means that the centre was *destined* to give way. If this rationale makes Hannibal seem less original or brilliant (Lazenby 1993), so be it. Such concerns cannot be used as an argument against its plausibility.

The Athenian line, under the orders of Miltiades, deployed at dawn, making as little fuss and noise as possible. The tribes kept their set order – which might be standard or rotating by the day – with one exception. The *Polemarch* Callimachus was leading the right wing as per tradition for the commander (Rey 2011; Hanson 1991) and his tribe must have been behind him as a post of honour, despite the actual order which was followed by the other ones (Lazenby 1993). The Plataean allies/ subjects were posted at the far left (Her VI.111,1). Once deployed, the Athenians charged. They may have charged from an uphill position as the tradition suggests (Her VI.112,1). Or they may have closed their distance from the Persians gradually over days by advancing their defensive works and lines (Hammond 1968). Which course of action they followed, cannot be deduced. But the former is supported by the repeated efforts of the allied Greeks to position themselves similarly at Plataea in 479 BC: first at the Asopus' ridge, then at some hilly ground. But charge they did, and at a run; or at a jog (Her VI.112,1).

It is possible that the Persians, once more intending to deploy to taunt the Athenians – and this time keeping their routine for an added reason, to conceal the departure of their vessels and thus their moves – were just starting their move when the Athenians charged. Their camp is never mentioned as fortified, and it is not known whether such proceedings, being standard by 480 BC (Her IX.15,2 & 97) were standing Achaemenid Standard Operating Procedures or came into effect after Mardonius' blunder of 492 BC (Her VI.45,1), or even later than that. Actually, there was no good reason to fortify their camp and doing so would have afforded the Athenians more time to advance from Athens to Marathon and solidify their position. In any case, Miltiades would like to have the Persians out in the open and not hiding or taking cover somewhere, as the idea was ultimately to use the strengths of the phalanx to win decisively. Thus, while the Persians were once more labouring to get into position for no obvious (to the rank and file) reason, bored and half-asleep, they saw the Athenians charging through the morning mist (de Souza 2003). The morale effect of the surprise was devastating. Still, they fell into position in time, although amazed at the running charge. They met it, but it is questionable whether they had any time to shoot volleys; and if they did, the long-range shots would have been wasted, as nobody had run a charge while protected by Hoplite shields before, so they were not accustomed to correct their shooting accordingly, nor to revert to more effective alternatives. One or two arrows in direct mode per archer, inside of the 50 metres might have been fired as well, squarely onto the shields as there was no time to aim obliquely, between the shields of distant files, nor low, beneath the rim of the shield, to the shins, where greaves cannot stave off shots from close range.

Before describing the impact, one has to take a moment. The Athenian Hoplites ran. *For how long* is the usual question. *How many of them* is the correct question. Herodotus gives the distance of the two foes at 8 stades (Her VI.112,1), some 1.3 km, with ~160m per stade (Engels 1985); but this may refer to the original positions. Especially if the Greeks had advanced their positions gradually (Hammond 1968) this figure should have been lowered; the Persian deployment might have shrunk it further. In any case, is it possible that the Athenian Hoplites ran the whole distance? Experimenting with college athletes (Emanuel 2012) or asking the opinion of the Chief Medical Officer of the Imperial German Army (Delbruck 1920) are not valid approaches. They are, in a positive function; should they confirm such ability, it would be definite. But in a negative sense, they are useless. Different body indices, different training, different lifestyle. If Zulus could run, or jog 10 km to reach the battlefield and then were able to engage in hand-to-hand, gruesome combat (Morris 1965), there is no reason for the Athenians not to have been able to do so. The Race-in-Armour (*hoplitodromos*) had been an official event since 520s BC, at the 65th Olympiad (Emanuel 2012; Sekunda 1986; 1998; 2000). Sparta had been in a state of war with Persia since Cyrus II and might have promoted the inclusion of Hoplitodromos in Greek athletic festivals since 520 BC, which were officially considered preparation for envisaged war eventualities (Paus V.8,10), if not a simulation and griefless warfare.

The Race-in-Armour featured mostly distances of one and two stades (approx. 160 and 320 metres, respectively) which was the projected drastic range of the bow of the day. But there was also an event of much longer range, possibly 15 stades (Emanuel 2012), most likely intended to prepare participants for both operational and tactical moves at the run in full gear. It is not known when the latter event started being practised; still, in 490 BC even the 50-year-old draftees had been practising the basic spinoffs of the race-in-arms since their twenties. Such practice was widespread in the gyms, and some might have competed during the Panhellenic religious festivals or tried to qualify for such events. Thus, almost the whole Hoplite body had the knowledge and the training.

Moreover, any notion that the Athenian Hoplites did not take their full gear with them and left their cuirasses behind (Sekunda 2002), should be rejected out of hand, as the cuirass was the key component that most orientals – the bulk of the troops raised by the Imperials – were lacking, and of paramount importance in hand-to-hand fighting. But one should remember that no matter how well and exhaustively trained and drilled they were – and the Athenians were no Spartans – at their 40 or 50 years of age, neither lung nor knee nor waist are the same. Thus, the question becomes 'Who and how many among the Athenians could actually have run?'

The answer is straightforward: the 20–30 age-class, which was to become known thanks to Xenophon much later. Xenophon gives the specifics (Hell IV.5,14); there is no need to doubt that the practice was identical before his days and adopted throughout the Greek world, wherever there were Hoplites. It was based on biological and bioergonomic realities, to which the date, 390 or 490 BC, makes no difference. Thus, the first ranks of the Athenian infantry closed at a run; the Persians, and the Ionians who watched and relayed events and opinions and gossip to Herodotus, could not have noticed that the first two lines at best were incoming, and the rest of the phalanx was following at a trot (**Figure 10.2**). Their field of view being seriously limited, in terms of depth, the Orientals would concentrate on this obvious but elusive target, not being able to see the less elusive ranks following at a trot. Having their bodies slightly tilted with the left side projected and the right denied, and with their shields canted upwards, but still firmly resting on the left shoulder and projected up and front when a volley was incoming, the runners had no top speed at the moment of impact. But their spears, levelled and crouched under their right armpit like the medieval lances, the underarm technique

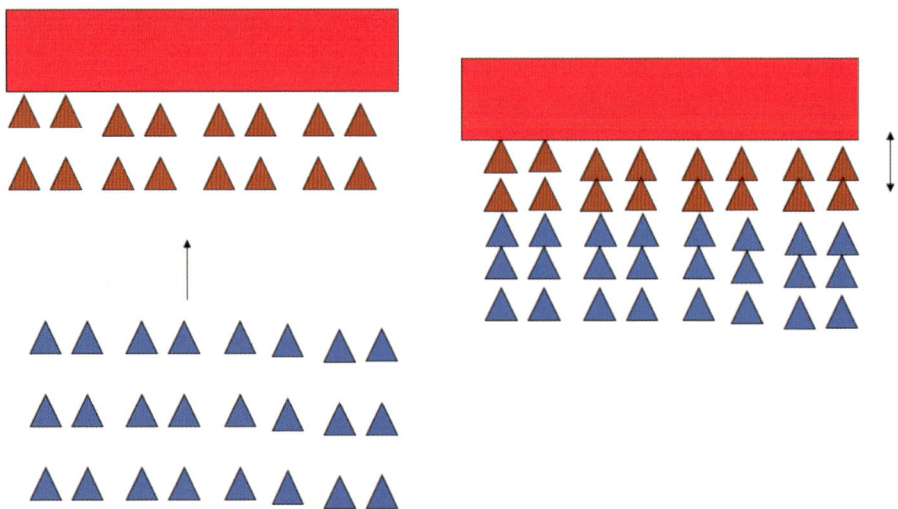

Fig. 10.2. The running charge: Left, the first Athenian ranks crash on the Imperial line and spear it vigorously; the rest close at a jog. Right: the rear ranks join in, to support and steady the engaged front ranks and to add weight to the shoving match.

(Matthew 2012), accumulated all the kinetic energy of a running Hoplite in a very small area. This produced more than enough momentum to pierce any oriental shield (*taka* or *spara*) and then either the skull or the jerkin/cuirass and the torso of the shield-bearer and throw him back, onto the man behind him with force enough to beat him out of balance.

Alternatively, a charge with spears levelled low (Sekunda 2002) is just as possible, as the ergonomics of the running and of presenting the shield are more favourable in this case. It delivers the sum of the stamina onto the impact plus the momentum of the hand thrust proper; it allows a degree of lateral correction to aim better and aim low, at the unarmoured thigh or groin (Anderson 1991; Goldsworthy 1997), where massive bleeding is deadly; even the Hoplite shield is less effective.

Crashing on the Persians, spears extended, the running Hoplites would have exacted quite a toll: the imperial first rankers, the best troops in every army in every locality and era would have ended up impaled. Smashing at the second line, or at the survivors of the crumbling first line, the charging Hoplites would have caused immense chaos and disorganization (Anderson 1970; Luginbill 1994). The Hoplites were out of breath, indeed (Sekunda 2002) but this original thrust and impact would have afforded them a respite of seconds to get a breath. They had to shove and thrust for some time until the rest of the ranks of the phalanx could reach them and steady their backs (**Figures 10.2 & 10.3**), adding their cumulative weight for a possible shoving match (Krentz 1985; Goldsworthy 1997)

They seem to have done well, judging by the results. Eventually, the Orientals, in a deeper formation, perhaps the standard 10-deep if they were Sparabari (Sekunda 2002), somehow did recover from the mental and physical shock and resist (Plut Vit Aris 5,3). That they did not panic to immediate flight once their weapons proved inefficient against an army of lunatics, who subsequently skewered many of them

Fig. 10.3. The first Athenian rank(s) charge at a run and crash on the Imperial line while the rest of the Athenian phalanx close at a jog.

and crushed some more with their outsized shields, is a testimony of the discipline and courage of the Imperial units. They came around and they began to fight back, but possibly not quite effectively for some time, affording the Athenian hind rankers time enough, as they approached trotting or running – but for much less, perhaps the last hundred metres – to arrive and take position, steadying and bolstering their engaged front rankers (**Figure 10.4**). And that must be the solution to the issue of the running charge. Possibly all Hoplite armies could run the last 150–300 metres (Sekunda 2002), but this action was called *Epidromi*, not *Ephodos*. In Greek, what is known in English as the running charge, the-charge-at-a-run or charge-at-the-double (emphasis on 'charge') is mentioned by the historians as *Dromaia Ephodos*. The first word means 'running', but the second, *Ephodos*, describes the advance, *not* the charge (Sekunda 1986). A Hoplite army, once set, advances against the enemy – *Ephodos* (Sekunda 1986) – and when very near charges, or, actually, *may* charge at a run – *Epidromi* (Sekunda 1986). By calling the Marathon event as they did, the Greeks implied that the Athenians, or *some* Athenians, ran the whole distance. And this was the novelty; to run during the entire advance, not merely for the final charge as supposed (Sekunda 2002; Emanuel 2012).

After the shocked and faltering Imperials steadied themselves due to their depth and skill, the two lines started exchanging blows. It is possible, or even probable, that the Athenians, after the first clash, refused extra-close, shoving contact. Rightly so; the Imperials were formed in a deeper line and carried shorter offensive arms. If kept at spearing distance, the Hoplites had all the advantages, with longer and probably stouter spears, larger and definitely stouter shields and better armour; thus the casualty exchange ratio was extremely lopsided. At close range, the Imperial short spears could exact some toll if handled well and with some luck. In such conditions, should the spearing be kept on for some time, it would function as a grinder and could disintegrate the Imperial line, or at least soften it enough for some determined Hoplite shoving to do the trick. Something along these lines happened in both Imperial wings, where lesser and less motivated troops faced

Fig. 10.4. As the rest of the ranks join the first rankers with minimal loss, they form up to nominal depth. A pushing, shoving and thrusting match develops.

a storm of spears and they simply broke and fled, with the Athenian wings in limited, not hot, pursuit (**Figure 10.5**). Once the flight became irreversible, the pursuers were recalled (**Figure 10.6**). How, with what kind of signal, by whom, we cannot deduce with any certainty. Trumpet would be an option, provided that the Athenians had adopted already open or semi-open helmets, like the Chalcidian and the Attic models (Connolly 1981; Snodgrass 1967).

The turning point

At the same time, the crack Persian and Saka troops at the centre of the imperial line, once stabilised, they formed and dressed their line and tried to pay back the Hoplites with their own medicine. The spearing had them at a disadvantage. Thus, they advanced violently to close the distance, bring their shorter spears and sidearms into play and perhaps shove the flimsy enemy line, of just four men – easily countable before their eyes – into breaking and fleeing (**Figure 10.5**).

However, the Hoplites of the flimsy Athenian centre had been well schooled not to let this happen. They speared feverishly, to intercept, if not to slay, the Imperials and back-stepped, to avoid entanglement. Four ranks deep, such back-stepping was achievable without devolving to disorganisation, confusion, stumbling and flight. There is no way the nimble sparabari – or takabari – would have pursued broken Hoplites as supposedly happened (Her VI.113,1) without effecting a carnage; and no such mishap occurred to the Athenian centre in Marathon. Most of the 192 dead Hoplites fell after the victory was secured, near the imperial ships (Her VI.114),

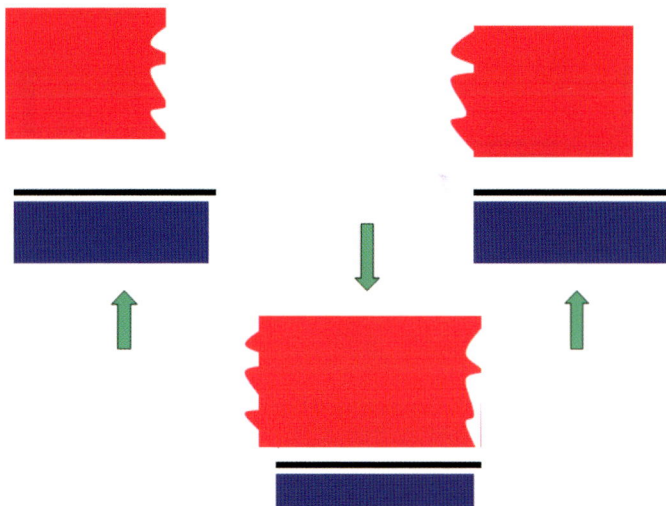

Fig. 10.5. The Imperial centre pushes the slim Athenian one far inland, but the deep Athenian wings put the Imperial ones to flight and give brief chase.

thus proving the sagacity of the limited, fully organised and disciplined Spartan pursuits (Plut Vit Lyc 22,5).

The Athenians of the centre never broke, nor fled; they were back-stepping under pressure. Thus, it was not that the Imperial centre had beaten the Athenian centre and was pursuing it inland, this is important (Her VI.113,1), it was that the Athenian centre was performing a fighting retreat (Grundy 1901; Ray 2009) to achieve two goals: to deny the Imperials the opportunity to deliver a decisive blow by pressure or impact and to lure them as far from their ships and camp as possible. Should the Athenian positions have been advanced the previous days (Hammond 1968), they may have been retreating towards these positions, flanked by palisades, to get some flank protection. As the Imperial centre detached the Athenian one, Greeks and Persians bypassed each other (**Figure 10.5**).

The Greeks had their orders and did nothing; the Persians, why did they not strike the Greek wings from the flanks? They had no orders. They may have exchanged opportunistic blows and chance thrusts as they bypassed each other, but the Imperials were frontally engaged after a most unpleasant surprise and were now sensing victory. No way would they take the initiative to leave their position and main effort so as to slap some Greeks going the other way.

Once the Greek wings had gone the other way for quite some distance, so as to disperse the Imperial wings beyond any thought of rallying and thus out of any

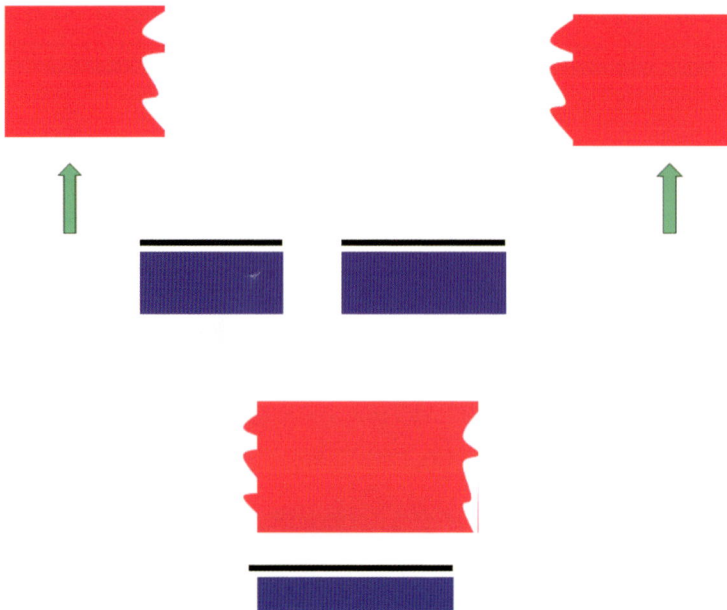

Fig. 10.6. The Athenian wings pause the pursuit and draw together, forming at the rear of the Persian centre and cutting its retreat.

further involvement, they stopped cold and regrouped. They probably formed their ranks as they were before, and drew the two wings together to form the original phalanx minus the centre (**Figure 10.6**). A Greek phalanx was thus formed at the rear of the Persian centre. Then, either the troops about-faced, or they countermarched to change front, and then charged back at the rear ranks of the Imperial centre (**Figure 10.7**). The first option would engage the rear-ranking Hoplites, fresh as up to this point they had done precious little; moreover, countermarches (**Figure 10.8**) were complicated manoeuvres and possibly Spartan specialty and privilege (Xen Lac Pol 11,8) *but* they allowed engagement with the best troops, the fittest ones and with the most relevant and recent training and drilling before the days of the campaign.

Irrespective of which method the Athenians used, about-facing or countermarching, they took the Imperial centre from behind, possibly before they were seen to be incoming. And then, the slaughter started. The Imperial centre taken from front and rear was smashed. The troops were trapped, in panic and skewered by long lances which by now and after effective shoving, must have been able to reach at least two thirds of the ranks, had the Imperials been 10 deep. Hemmed in, they had escape points at their flanks, but to rush there meant turning their own flanks to the Athenian spears. Still, many were leaking but they found themselves, as they had been lured inland, to be far from their vessels and with the great marsh of Marathon square in their way. Maddened from shock and fear, many perished in the marsh, and the others, who skirted it, were this time hotly pursued and speared in the back.

Two things must be straightened out. No matter how much one (dis)likes, (dis) believes, accepts etc. the possibility that the Athenian wings took the Persian rear, this is what Herodotus states (VI.113,2), clearly and unequivocally. He says nothing about attacking their flank(s). Consequently, interpretations of how the Athenian wings came to be in flanking position without the proper drill, either by spontaneously turning inwards as a matter of the inherent mechanics of the Hoplite phalanx (Lazendy 1989 & 1993) or by the wings detaching from the centre to execute a converging attack (Burn 1962), simply complicate a straightforward chain of events.

Other, more imaginative interpretations, which completely revise Herodotus' account and suggest that the victorious wings ran back, all the way, to the main battle and instead of taking the flanks or rear of the Persians, bypassed them and reformed *behind* the Greek centre to reinforce it (Green, 1970) blatantly mock Occam's Razor. The notion of the latter scholar that if the Athenians attacked the enemy rear, the Imperials would have been pushed *forward* and thus would have crushed the Athenian centre as it was frontally engaged with them is absurd, at the

Fig. 10.7. Either by about-facing or by countermarching to reverse their front, the joined Athenian wings attack the Imperial centre from the back and slaughter ensues. Survivors leak from the flanks towards the beach.

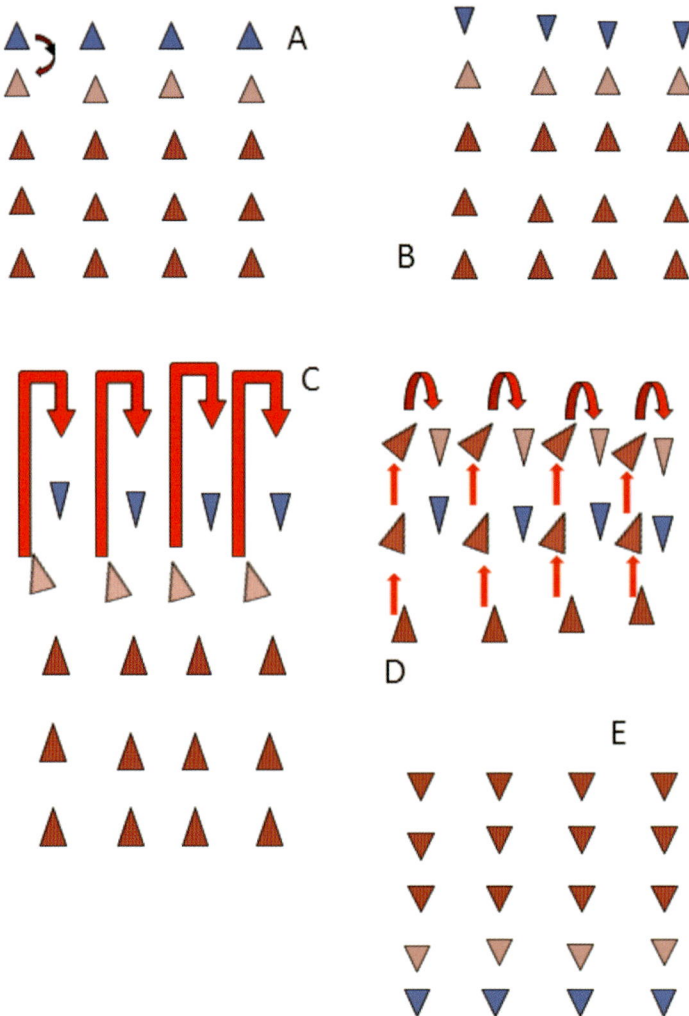

Fig. 10.8. Countermarch.

very least. Nothing of the kind happened in the battle of Cannae (App VII.4,23), nor in the battle of Bagradas (Polyb I.34) and this is so for excellent reasons: when hit from the back, a body of troops does not intensify, it weakens its pressure frontally (App VII.4,23), if not due to the unnerving and demoralizing effects of shock and terror, then because some of the troops have to turn to face the new danger and thus do not press forward any longer.

In line with the above, the second issue is the exact site of the battle. Marathon is one of the battles of the Persian wars that were fought with the orientation and the exact location still unknown to us; the problems posed by Salamis, Artemisium are comparatively minor but also refer to sea-fights; our blind spots on the events at Plataea are comparatively minor. It is hard to tell where the different phases of the battle took place, but there are some indications on the site: first, the tumulus, the monumental burying mound for the Athenian dead has nothing to do with any phase of the battle. The troops were buried in the battlefield probably for very practical reasons, such as the possibility of rotting during their transportation after the come-and-go of the army between Marathon and Phaleron. Thus, the tumulus is no sign, and moving some 200 corpses within the plain for whatever reason required minimal energy and resources; maybe ten wagons of standard, agricultural model. The trophy, on the other hand, has a very specific function in the context of the Hoplite battles regarding its exact location. It is set where the enemy phalanx/battle line first breaks and gives way (Krentz 2002). Marathon was a most unorthodox battle in every respect, even in its after-battle rituals (i.e. the state funeral of the victors *in situ*). If strict orthodoxy *was* pursued in this particular case, then at the location of the erected trophy one of the two imperial wings must have presented signs of collapse and retreat, possibly before evolving to flight.

But in this *particular* battle, the turning point for gaining the victory was the collapse of the Persian centre and it might well be that the monument marks the site where the Persians and Saka of the centre were attacked from the rear and collapsed. The key factor though to understand where and how the battle was fought is the clear reference that many fugitives of the Imperial centre perished in the Great Marsh during the flight (Paus I.32,7). Contrary to some scholars' views (i.e. Lazenby 1993), one must notice that if the Athenian wings were reorganized at the rear of the Imperial centre and attacked from behind, as proposed herein, the free right flank of the Imperials would be leaking straight to the marsh, especially if the battle had been fought with the battle lines roughly parallel to the coast and away from any notion of the Athenians defending the southern road (**Map 10.5**).

This means that their flight path, left unobstructed by the Athenian manoeuvre, was taking them to the marsh on their way towards their base and their ships. Efforts to skirt or avoid the marsh were resulting in a longer distance to cover, a

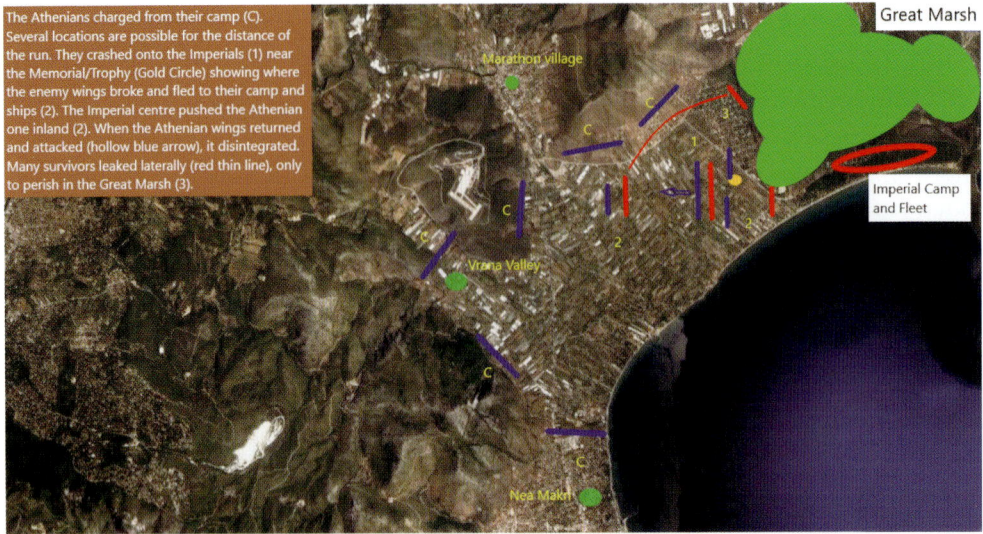

The Athenians charged from their camp (C). Several locations are possible for the distance of the run. They crashed onto the Imperials (1) near the Memorial/Trophy (Gold Circle) showing where the enemy wings broke and fled to their camp and ships (2). The Imperial centre pushed the Athenian one inland (2). When the Athenian wings returned and attacked (hollow blue arrow), it disintegrated. Many survivors leaked laterally (red thin line), only to perish in the Great Marsh (3).

Great Marsh

Marathon village

Imperial Camp and Fleet

Vrana Valley

Nea Makri

Map. 10.5.

very unwelcoming prospect for terrorised troops hotly pursued. This detail, along with the absence of any reference that any Imperial or Athenian flank rested at the beach, a very poor choice as the shallow water would allow flanking by mobile infantry, argue against all suggestions that the battle was fought *near*, and even less *along* the shore, with the battle lines perpendicular to the shoreline (Sekunda (2002) and thus with a view to the control of the coastal road.

Now the Athenians had conquered and were keeping no order. The Imperial centre being disintegrated, they were pursuing hotly – but they were pursuing lighter opponents, who had been less hard-pressed and thus had more breath and were incentivised by terror. Having reached the enemy vessels, a success unimaginable some hours ago when they were contemplating how they would bruise the Imperial army, they were now nearly destroying it. But they could not carry or spark fire to burn the fleet (Her VI.113,2). They did however capture seven triremes (Her VI.115), a mere one per cent, but a most important source of intelligence for Themistocles' future shipbuilding programme, as they were to reveal the secrets of the enemy shipwrights. These seven triremes were manned by something like 1,000–1,400 mariners, (boarders excluded as they were at the fight). What happened to them? Did they embark on other triremes and leave? Were they butchered when their vessels were taken? Or were they taken prisoners? Most probably the second. This final act of pursuit, with no order and system, against a desperate and massive enemy, resulted in many Athenian casualties for no apparent reason. It was telltale for their lack of true discipline and an excellent justification of the limited and measured pursuit practised by the Spartans (Plut Vit Lyc 22,5).

Moreover, these casualties were well-known individuals (Her VI.114); not because the well-known ones died preferentially in battle, but because this was the army of the elite of the society and did not include the lower social groups and classes. In Marathon the bourgeois were fighting, leaving the riff-raff of Democracy, maybe 20,000, at the city, as untrustworthy; they placed more trust in their slaves, who followed as attendants and perhaps were enticed to fight, than to the poor. They neither armed nor even mobilize the *Thetes* as retainers and stewards of the Hoplites (Delbruck 1920).

The poor, the basis of Democracy and suspected for Medizm (Grundy 1901) were following their two patrons. The faction of Hippias, having been an unconditional blessing for the Athenian populace under Peisistratus (Grundy 1901), allegedly became pro-Persian, once their leader invited the Median bows; that of Cleisthenes had always been so and had offered Earth and Water (Her V.73,2–3). Hippias must have pitched himself to Artaphrenes (Her V.96,) as a more reliable puppet than the volatile Alcmaeonids, as he had a blood feud to settle (Her V.55) and not simple ambition. And, much more important, his re-establishment at Athens, which would nullify the revolution, would not only stop the exporting of such practices and mentalities, but was an excellent acid test for the Athenian compliance to the imperium and an opportunity to show their good faith by honouring their commitment to the empire (Her V.96,2).

After a battle won – winning the war

The imperial host evacuated the bridgehead. Hippias, almost 80, would have been difficult to evacuate in such conditions; but Herodotus makes no mention, which means he must have been with the advance force, with the cavalry, to enact any communication between the invaders and the collaborators. This was one more reason for the spent Athenians to dash to their city, or, rather, to their other intercepting position, meant initially for the case the Persians would have tried to land on the beaches of the western coast, after leaving Eretria. All Athenian Hoplites had run or trotted in attack, engaged, some of them had run again in brief pursuit and prompt return, then engaged some more with the trapped Imperial centre, pursued it to the shore and engaged once again. It was the second engagement for the centre and the third for the wings (Burn 1962). It was fast, but gruesome. The two tribal brigades of the centre, having taken the brunt of the fight, were spent. They stayed on the spot (Plut Vit Aris 5,5) to secure the battlefield; not so much from looters from the surrounding communities, but from possible, though improbable, Imperial aggressive return.

Being there, they collected the prizes and roamed the battlefield. This roaming of the battlefield, collection of spoils and later study of the dead (by the Spartans) and their transportation for mass burial supports the figure of 6,400 Imperials KIA (Her VI.117,1). Even if the Greeks were not performing body counts – which they did; the corpses and their possession were paramount issues in the outcome of a battle and defined winner and loser in unclear outcomes (Xen Ages 2,15–6; Krentz 2002) – in this particular battle a body count was performed and thus any suggestion to review the number 6,400, especially by long shots based on yearly sepulchral practices (Sekunda 2002) sounds unsubstantiated at the very least.

The rest of the Athenian army, first of all, dispatched a runner to notify the city of the great victory (Plut De Gloria 347c), which meant, in simple parlance, that even if a coup was attempted and Persian support arrived, the city would not remain occupied. With the Persian army shattered on the battlefield and a Spartan army incoming, Persians and traitors would have been in a terrible position. This piece of news cemented everyone's resolve and sapped the confidence of collaborators who now understood they had bet on the wrong horse. No negotiations, no open doors.

Well, better safe than sorry. Despite the above, the Athenian army dashed off for Athens and deployed outside of the city circuit, at Cynosarges, to intercept an invader approaching from Phaleron, in a classical application of manoeuvring along interior lines. Both they and their runner would have climbed once more the shorter, Kephisia road, or the Nea Makri road; but not the Pallene road (**Map 10.4**). Herodotus, after all, would have mentioned Pallene if the Athenian army had taken the coastal road to either ingress or egress the plain of Marathon. This argument lacks in actual validity, as Herodotus is not at his best; he might have never visited the place, but this is no excuse. The event was wildly celebrated for decades and vital events, such as the orientation of the battle lines and the ingress and egress itineraries of the Athenian army would have been easy to ask about, if not veterans, definitely their sons and nephews.

The coastal road, easier for spent troops, was longer, a very bad choice when troops *are* spent and cannot pick up the pace, while time becomes of essence. Remarks that the Kephisia road is unsuitable for large armies (Green 1970) are off the mark. This army was not marching in formation, in ranks of four or eight under the drum and singing anthems to keep pace. They were stumbling, Hoplites and their attendants who must have taken up shield, spear and helmet at the very least, trying to make fast. And they did. They approached the city from the east, in full sight of the Persian squadrons bringing in the cavalry and took their interceptive position, not knowing the number and intent of the enemy fleet.

Seeing the Hoplites there, the commander of the task force knew things were going sour. There was no point in landing his force; the city would not succumb to some cavalry after a field victory and with its unscathed Hoplite army nearby. Thus, the Imperial vessels remained off shore, at anchor (Her VI.116) as they expected news and preferably the rest of the fleet, to determine the wisdom of a forced landing *en masse* and a direct confrontation.

The squadrons of the Imperial fleet evacuating the task force from Marathon, instead of going as fast as possible to Phaleron, to attempt a landing, collected the Eretrian PoWs (Her VI.115) from the detention camp on the isolated islet Aegilia, off Styra, (Her VI.107,2) halfway between Eretria and Athens (**Map 10.2**) and then resumed their course to Phaleron. It sounds idiotic since these captives could not escape and the Athenians had no fleet, or at least not at their eastern seaboard; their naval base was the port of Phaleron.

This attitude means the commander of the pinning force had no illusions; the whole force would do nothing, when reunited, except return home. Not only had he suffered a crushing defeat, with a large, disproportionate number of casualties of the most reliable and battle-worthy troops, the Persians and Saka of the centre

---

Box 10.1

A legacy in tactics

Themistocles, aged 38 at Marathon, Archon in the year 493 BC (Carmichael 2009; Sekunda 2002) had already initiated the fortifications of the Piraeus due to his western vision, which built upon the previous one of Solon that had been interrupted due to the policy of Peisistratus, to turn to the Euxine. As the Persian Empire cancelled all such efforts and prospects, the West was the only source of grain, but heavy competition was expected by the Dorians who controlled the western trade. Thus, naval preparations were indispensable, and the Imperial threat made things easy, as the Achaemenid proceedings against Miletus, a show of cruelty and terror, had stricken awe and fear into the hearts and minds of the hapless Athenians, on top of their guilt for breaking their commitment to Artaphrenes.

At the same time, Miltiades arrived in Athens, having escaped the Phoenician pursuit. Themistocles readily befriended and supported him when he was prosecuted by the Democrats. Having heard his thoughts and reports and being a front-line fighter at Marathon, Themistocles acquired an understanding of the Persian psyche and first-hand experience of the stunning effect of violent Hoplite charges upon the Orientals, but also of the inflicted psychological fluctuations: if the Orientals repulsed the Hoplite charge, they were becoming overconfident, arrogant, engaged and careless, very prone to tricks and entrapments like the flanking in Marathon and repeated events in Salamis, Thermopylae, Plataea, Mycale. Given that the Spartans inspected the battlefield at Marathon and conversed with the Athenians, it might be surmised that the feigned flights at Thermopylae, Plataea and Salamis had a common denominator and inspiration, the – most probably fighting – retreat of the Athenian centre at Marathon, which became ingrained in future Spartan operational doctrines against the Orientals.

Box 10.2

The Achaemenid concept of jointness

There is a one-sided view of ancient warfare concerning the infantry-cavalry co-operation and the merit of combined operations. Whether the Achaemenids during the early 5th century were *able* to do so could be the wrong question, although it is a hotly contested one; in any case, the arguments negating such an approach are indeed more convincing (Hammond 1968). But the correct question would be whether they *intended* to do so. The answer is not so clear-cut.

Historians seem perfectly convinced that the proper way and the most evolved doctrine was similar to this of Epaminondas or, even better, of Philip II and Alexander III the Great. But career military personnel are less unanimous: the close co-operation between two arms of different mobility seems a waste of resources. Examples are aplenty: the use of the tank to escort infantry, the quintessential reason for its development, was tested, has been vindicated over time in many cases, but at least operationally it is considered a foul practice, exposing it to direct fire, depriving it of its mobility and limiting it to infantry escort. Doctrines for independent armour action behind enemy lines are considered the proper way to use a tool that can bring results in operational, not tactical, terms if used independently and daringly and, most importantly, with the proper mass on suitable ground. The German Panzerwaffe is an excellent historic parallel, much better than the knightly European armies, as in early 490s the Persian infantry was the king of battle, as has always been the Prussian or German infantry; later on, in the late 5th and during 4th century, the Achaemenid infantry declined to the status of medieval infantry in knightly armies.

The same can be said for the air forces. Their initial use was to assist the land army and the navy, originally without providing interception or strike. Reconnaissance was all-important. As technology progressed, independent air branches were established; both in Britain and in Greece, with its minuscule but pioneer air force engaged in combat since 1912 in both land and sea missions, the Air Force became a separate branch. The US followed after four decades, seeing that the strategic potential the USAAC showed in the Second World War, being amplified by the nuclear bomb, was wasted within the context of an army requiring overhead support and protection in deep, but limited battlespaces compared to the intercontinental reach of the new breed of aircraft. The close tying of the German Luftwaffe to tactical and operational missions to support both army and navy, without a properly formed strategic constituent is considered a major flaw leading in part to its defeat, especially in the Battle of Britain.

Thus, it is no wonder that the Achaemenid cavalry was not closely co-operating with their infantry, but selectively and rather as an exception. They could achieve different objectives and the proximity in temporal but also in spatial terms could cause friction rather than incubate synergies. The infantry was the arm to decide battles for the Imperials; had done so repeatedly during the Ionic Revolt and there was not one reason to doubt its ability to repeat such stellar performance in 490 BC, without any need for cavalry support.

(Her VI.113,1). Not only were these Hoplites pitted against him better drilled, better trained and much more determined than the ones at Ionia (or at Eretria). It was that they had discovered a way that neutralized the imperial chief weapon, the bow; these Hoplites had smashed into them with practically no casualties, as their running tactics shortened the available time for an effective barrage, while also denying proper aiming. This had been witnessed by troops and commanders alike and had destroyed their confidence; it would have done so even if the Persians had taken their leave of Marathon with no casualties. Coupled to the fact that the foes they were seeing in front of them had suddenly appeared, almost if by magic, not behind them in a general term but squarely at their back and slaughtered them by the thousands, the morale was hitting nadir. The Imperial infantry had no stomach for anything further.

Box 10.3

Takabara vs Sparabara

It is usually assumed, for no really good reason, that the main oriental troops in the campaign of 490 BC were sparabari (plural of Sparabara). They could have been, but they might, just might, have not. In Marathon, the Imperial troops are considered to have been sparabara, the standard type (Sekunda 2002; Sekunda and Chew 1992).

It is not necessarily so. Some indications point to the possibility that takabara fought in Marathon for the Empire. First, Herodotus nowhere mentions the spara wall as he does in Plataea and Mycale. He may simply not mention it – Marathon is not his best story. Or, the Imperials may have had no time to plant it due to the Athenian surprise attack, although planting a spara takes half a minute at the most. Additionally, the kinetics of the battle, with the advances and retreats perpendicular to the direction of the original frontline, preclude such an obstacle, even erected in the most rudimentary manner. Furthermore, Herodotus' notion is that the Imperials *had* archers, while their opponents had none. *Not* that they *were* archers, as was the case with the sparabara. This implies archer units, probably the Saka, within the army, not an army of archers; a condition satisfied with the deployment of both sparabara and takabara. Directly corroborating with the previous issue, is the famous fresco of Polygnotus, Panaenus and Micon found at the Poikile (Painted) Stoa (Colonnade) of ancient Athens. If the brilliant reconstitution by Schenck has anything to do with the original, the imperial shock infantry at Marathon is the takabara, with troops armed either with taka and spear or with the bow (obviously the Saka) and no spara or sparabara anywhere to be found.

Last, but not least, is the concept of mixed troop types. The takabara is thought to have been a satrapal levy troop type (Sekunda and Chew 1992), although this might be incorrect and the takabara might have been regulars, of the Persian national reserve (Xen Cyrop I.2,13), met more frequently on the battlefield once the Greeks started offensive operations, where local Persian musters had to be mobilised to respond. Whatever of the above might have been the case, in Marathon a mixed task force of sparabari and takabari might had taken the field, with royal and satrapal regiments containing either but not both. Alternatively, a combined force might have been the case, as they were both expeditionary troops and would have provided a combined Persian nucleus, with archer-spearman and CQB (Close Quarters Combat) elements within each unit, imperial or satrapal.

One may even venture to factor this asymmetry to the renowned order of battle prescribed by Miltiades, which would have taken the respective weaknesses and liabilities into consideration. The main phases of the battle are described, or rather examined elsewhere, but, briefly, following this account the amassed Hoplites would brush the takabara aside with very little fuss, while the thin Hoplite front at the centre would make the arrow storm launched by the massed sparabari less effective. The shoving event, due to the great size of the spara, would also have been less risky for the individual Hoplites in terms of opportunities afforded to the overbearing Imperials for stabbing around, or over the spara. In truth, the Imperials with the best equipment for CQB, i.e. stabbing fight, the takabari, would not be able to perform, being pushed back by the weight of the Hoplite charge augmented by the running effect. The heavier sparabari would have caused little impression with their arrows and the weight and size of their shield would have slowed down their advance, making a breakthrough less probable, while allowing little opportunity for effectively stabbing their solid but recoiling enemies. As a result, they remained concentrated in a compact body, to be sacked and netted once the wings were disintegrated.

Chapter 11

Intermission: After Marathon and Before the Invasion of Xerxes

When the two squadrons of the imperial fleet made contact off the SW shore of Attica, in the vicinity of Phaleron, their commanders met, discussed, perhaps exchanged blames and curses. Old Hippias knew he would never see Attica again, much less rule it and decided to go home, and not try an all-out landing for a rematch. While retiring east, they were letting the word out throughout the Aegean, as they decommissioned their fresh subjects to their islands, that the expedition had punished one of the two target cities and was bringing its inhabitants in fetters to the mercy of the king. As far as anyone was concerned, but the few eyewitnesses, there was no such thing as a defeat in the plain of Marathon. A small, clearly inconsequential reverse at most (Lazenby 1993), obviously due to low-quality vassals who compromised the victorious master-race that had advanced victoriously some distance further than it should, being overenthusiastic due to their success.

The Empire Repulsed

It is certain that the fleet, going back, released the new draftees of the islands and Carystus to their homes. But where did this fleet go? Somewhere in Ionia, or Cilicia? Or both, meaning that the satrapal troops were disembarked in Ionia and the rest to Cilicia? The latter is more probable, to save the army some months of walking and thus save the Crown expenses in provisions. The Ionian vessels probably had to go all the way, to assist with the transportation of the captives and the loot, although the heavy casualties might have made their presence – and thus all related expenses – redundant. Once on land, the royal part of the army must have followed the King's Road to get straight to Susa, where the king demobilized it and debriefed the commanders. He planted the deported Eretrians in royal estates nearby. This clemency is very unlike Darius, who crucified insurgents by the thousands even in Herodotus' too lenient account (Her III.159,1). It is more than possible that the pact between the two Eretrian traitors and the imperial generals – or rather Datis – provided for no further atrocities except for deportation and he fully respected it, both as a monarch sustained by the God of Truth and as a very dexterous diplomat. A subsequent round with the mainland Greeks was imminent and humane treatment would encourage surrender rather than stiffen resistance.

On this subject, one may wonder whether the deportation of the Eretrians was total, or focused on the party opposing the traitors' own, allegedly the Aristocrats. Given the traitors' social status (Her VI.101,2) and Persian social preferences, the deportation must have been focused against the popular party and affected a hefty proportion of the commoners. It was, after all, standard Persian policy to familiarise with the rich and terrorise the commoners (Holland 2005). The very fact that 10 years later there is still Eretria (fighting for the Greek Alliance) may have been a clumsy and gross intervention of Herodotus, intended to glorify one more traditional ally of Athens. Otherwise, it cannot be explained if a total depopulation is assumed: the Eretrians sought refuge massively behind their walls and did not scatter to the country to escape. The concept of selective and limited deportation, possibly by lists handed by the Medizers, explains this prodigy and also accounts for the issue of deck space in the invasion fleet reserved for the deportees from both Athens and Eretria, who would amount to tens of thousands (Sekunda 2002). For example, Athens had 30,000 voters (Her V.97,2) and just as many women and at least as many slaves and underage of both sexes for a total of more than 100,000, which means at least 150 prisoners for each one of the 600 triremes of the fleet (or less if transport vessels are taken into account) in a total deportation scenario which would have left Hippias lording over empty and deserted ruins.

The Athenians victorious

The Athenians celebrated their victory most reverently, which was of existential scale. They proceeded to no purges of the Medizers, defeatists and so on, although these were undoubtedly well-known. The victorious aristocrats wanted nothing more than to hammer their victory and reap the fruits. And respect was the ultimate fruit of victory. Purges were not initiated even against the medizing-remnants of Eretria, nor against Carystus, which had ultimately turned to the Empire as it surrendered after some rounds of devastation (Her VI.99,2). It is this magnanimity – or reluctance – that made Miltiades ask for an expeditionary force without saying where he was intending to go (Her VI.132); nobody in Athens had any stomach for further meddling with the Imperials, after having taught them a very good lesson. Thus, Miltiades was able to secure his campaign on grounds of profit and loot (ibid), not on strategy, security and good sense. The role of his target, Paros, to the medizing of the Cyclades is obscure; Naxos, nearby, was razed (Her VI.96) and Paros was no match. Many islands had medized and took part in the expedition of Datis, not entirely voluntarily. None suffered consequences and 10 years later they were faithful subjects of Xerxes, sending their vessel quota (Her VIII.46,3) but for a few exceptions (Her VIII.46,3 & 82,1). Thus, it must be true that it was a personal score of Miltiades, as Lysagoras, a distinguished Parian of unknown involvement but definitely Medizer, had slandered him to Hydarnes, one of the seven conspirators, and a very devoted subject and friend of Darius (Her VI.133,1). Lysagoras must have been the man who had informed the close circle of the King of Miltiades' proposal to cut the bridges at Ister (Burn 1962), thus making the Athenian a lifelong fugitive and turning him into a hero against the Persian campaign to reconquer Ionia after the revolt.

The Athenians honoured their 192 Hoplites killed in action (Her VI117,1). They buried them on the spot, as moving them to the city under the sun would have taken a massive effort with unwanted risks for the decency of the deceased. They erected a tumulus and were offering yearly funerary rites and sacrifices (Paus I.32,4; Burn 1962) while the Plataeans were buried with the Athenian slaves killed in action, indicating that the Athenians thought of the gallant Boeotians as subjects and not as allies or fellow citizens (Paus I.32,3; Badian 1993). And this, even though they could have shirked their duty, remembering that the Athenian protection/overlordship had been extended to them not by the Democracy but by Hippias, who was riding with the Imperials (Burn 1962).

Next, the Athenians campaigned against Paros under the instigation of Miltiades as already noted and met with an epic fiasco (Her VI.135,1) that proved fatal for Miltiades due to a festered non-combat wound (Her VI.136,3), discredited him and almost had him executed (Her VI.136,1). Even if the account of Herodotus is even more hostile than usual and the expedition of Miltiades was partially successful as it probably targeted more islands than just Paros so as to cut the bridge of island-hopping to the empire (Burn 1962), as the allied Admiralty did in the wake of the battle of Salamis ten years later (Her VIII.111–112), the ultimate objective, Paros and its wealth escaped him. This fact poses a very troubling question on the ability of the Athenians to storm fortified places, as celebrated by Herodotus for their descendants in 479 BC (Her IX.70,2). One wonders what happened in these ten years so that the inept Athenians of 489 BC, who failed at Paros (Her VI.135,1), became the experts in storming fortifications that Herodotus has them to be, and, after all, did breach the Persian fort near Plataea (Her IX.70,2).

The latecomers. A matter of policy or politics?

The Spartans were to come to save Athens. Why? Democratic Athens had humiliated Cleomenes once (Her V.73,1) and he had tried in person to impose Isagoras (Her V.74,1) in order to get even. This was to no avail because of Demaratus and the attitude of the Corinthians (Her V.75). Cleomenes was probably the reigning king of Sparta at the time of the battle of Marathon; even if he had been already deposed, humiliating a Spartan king was never taken lightly by the Spartans – although for *this* king there might have been some peculiarities, as a war for power between him and the Ephorate was perhaps raging (Dickins 1912). A campaign at the time would have taken the fabled Spartan army away after a recent Helot war (Plato Laws 698E). Why (risk and) save Athens? After all, the Athenians were patently ungrateful, as maintained by Cleomenes, who witnessed no real gratitude for ridding them of the tyranny (Her V.90,1), no matter how mixed such blessing had been for the lower social class (Grundy 1901).

Sparta had already been at war with Persia. Even if the mission to Cyrus with the arrogant message to let the Greek colonies be at peace (Her I.152,3) had not been considered an act of war, which it had, the execution, or rather murder, of the herald of Darius, asking for Earth and Water (Her VII.133,1) in 491 BC meant that Sparta was at the crosshairs of the sovereign and would face him sooner or later, rather sooner. The ferocity and absurdity of this act implies the direct involvement of Cleomenes and no other Spartan, reverent by nurture if not by nature.

Medizm had been discouraged in Greece heavy-handedly by Sparta, as Aegina was to find out (Her VI.73). Athens had medized due to the threat of Cleomenes since the early 500s (Her V 73,3). But that was another Athens. The current Athenian government, possibly including Themistocles (Green 1970; Burn 1962; Sekunda 2002), had welcomed Miltiades, the most wanted man in the list of Darius, and had him acquitted of all democratic charges and counts of ruling Chersonese as a tyrant (Her VI.104,2) – which he did, in the name of Athens (Her VI.140,1), similar to his predecessors (Her VI.36,1). Had the Athenians really murdered the Persian herald demanding Earth and Water from them (Her VII.133,1), Miltiades (Paus III.12,7) is a more probable culprit than Themistocles (Plut Vit Them 6,2). With this action he was making irreparable the animosity between Athens and Persia, something very important for his own survival; else he could be delivered in fetters to Darius as a token of apology and penance by the Athenian medizers. Of course, it may have been that Miltiades had the herald executed and Themistocles passed the vote for the interpreter. If Miltiades was indeed responsible for the murder of an imperial herald, the hatred of many Athenians, especially the Alcmeonids for ruining any further prospect of a friendly settlement with the empire for the issues of insubordination and the assistance to the Ionian rebels can be better appreciated and understood. He shoved them off the central stage, exposed them to peril by making them play the card of the traitor during the campaign and thus forced their hand for the virulent proposal of public execution, one of the worst disgraces of the Democracy.

Still, the Athenians probably had not committed such an atrocity (Bradford 1980). They are never mentioned to be bearing such a burden (Her VII.133,2) and probably they had never had a chance: a rebellious subject (Lazenby 1993) was not entitled to official proposals for voluntary surrender. This behaviour was deceitful, a lie according to the views expressed in Behistun (actually it was a lie, one surrendering spontaneously and then reconsidering); there would be punishment, swift and severe. Even if they had not performed such a heinous act, and retrospectively made such a claim only to match the Spartan action (Her VII.133,1) it is certain that the city provided clear signs of its determination to resist the invasion and this tradition, historic or not, is just that; a token of determination and commitment. The Athenians did everything to turn the Spartans against Aegina which had medized (Her VI.49) and then to assist them at their disciplinary actions (Her VI.73,2). Athens might have been the actual reason for Aegina's deliberation to medize and bringing the proceedings of the island state to the attention of Spartans was probably caused by ulterior motives.

But at the time things were clear. This version of Athens was not medizing, helped against Medizers, had committed itself to defence and had the support of Sparta. One can put two and two together and conclude that this was a party opposite to Cleisthenes' Medizers and Peisistratids' new Medizers. Given that it is supported by the Hoplite corps, it must have been the rebooted aristocratic party, the one controlled by Isagoras and unsuccessfully counteracting Cleisthenes after the expulsion of Hippias (Her V.66,1). Isagoras might have been a dead weight due to his failure and many of his supporters were murdered by the Democratic party, after Cleomenes' ignominious flight from Athens, when trying to expel the Alcmaeonids and Cleisthenes. But the basis of Isagoras' party, the citizens of some substance, was there and was very reliable in Spartan eyes. The former, the ardent Democrats, had offered Earth and Water; despite chastising the representatives who did this (Her V.73,3), they never renounced the tokens (Holland 2005) thus maintaining an impression of Imperial protection, until ordered to accept once more the rule of Hippias (Her V.96,2). Their nuclear clan, the Alcmaeonids, had been no democrats by any measure: they had been best friends with the filthy-rich-and expansionist King Croesus of Lydia, who provided their wealth; they were close relatives of the tyrant of Sicyon, Cleisthenes and, not to be forgotten, had dealings with Peisistratus, for the division of autocratic power, which became null due to failure of a dynastic marriage (Grundy 1901).

The Spartan assistance arrived the next day, just after the battle (Plato Laws 698E), underlining the wisdom of Datis who had moved with some temporal leeway, as he could not have been certain of the swiftness of the Spartan expedition. The 2,000 Hoplites (Her VI.120), esquired by their helots, accomplished a feat of mobility across broken ground, and were most probably of the 20–30 age class, the flower of the Lacedaimonian army, sent to assist against an existential threat. The Spartans knew full well that their city was high on the list of the Persian monarch and could not afford to lose Athens (Bradford 1980; Burn 1962). They sent few troops to make as fast as possible; these troops, one should notice, were few but still enough to double the Athenian racers and move promptly, with speed and stamina, wherever the campaign would have them needed. They may have actually run the distance, or at least jogged it, as their time implies something like 100 km per day. In any case, they were the young age-classes, the standing army in full alert, but most importantly, of top endurance and speed. Time was of the essence as their arrival at Athens, not at Marathon, would safeguard the city from the traitors. The (prospect of) belated though prompt Spartan intervention made both the Persians and the Athenian traitors hurry their operations and thus fail. It is very probable that another installment, similarly to the campaign of Plataea eleven years later, would follow suit at a normal pace and once the news of the outcome at Marathon reached them by means of a runner, while they were probably on the move, they about-faced and returned to Lacedaimon without ever crossing the Isthmus (Burn 1962).

The first installment of Spartan reinforcements was late for the battle. But since they were already in Attica, they asked for permission to visit the battlefield (Her VI.120), a show of proper proceedings in a foreign territory. The Athenians, in their bragging mode and mood, happily obliged. Interviewing the Athenian veterans with the repulsive smirk, they could recreate the battle fairly accurately and could scrutinize the Imperial casualties. Not only outfit, weapons and clothing (Bradford 1980; Burn 1962), but the actual impact of Hoplite arms on their kit and bodies. The Spartans took a most valuable lesson, at no cost and they learnt it very well as Thermopylae and Plataea were to prove.

This Spartan inspection, coming on top of the Athenian roaming of the battlefield for spoils and then to collect and bury the Imperial dead, makes the number 6,400, as a round figure of course, uncontestable (Bradford 1980; Burn 1962). True, it includes not only line troopers, but possibly sailors of the captured vessels and support troops or non-combatants of the Persian camp. But it is also *lower* than the true total, not higher. Any Imperials, no matter what their status, killed in the shallows might have drifted not ashore but to the open water, and thus remained uncounted. The same goes for the fugitives who were drowned in the marsh (Paus I.32,7). Usually, such victims disappear altogether and thus were not counted.

The last issue is the attitude of Athens' neighbours. In this campaign, the Boeotians are never mentioned to medize, and are not taking part, neither themselves nor their territory, in the proceedings of the campaign. Due to the attested dislike Herodotus felt for them, one may suppose that had they medized, Herodotus would have been quick and glad to mention it. Aegina, on the other hand, strategically placed just next to the front door of Athens, played no role. The Imperials could have landed there and used it as a base to thoroughly outdo the Athenians and cut them off from the Isthmus and the Peloponnesian reinforcements. After the battle, they could have done something similar, to cause at least some damage to their land and property. But they never landed there, obviously considering the island enemy territory, a tribute to the proactive and harsh policy of Cleomenes (Her VI.50,1) and proof of his good terms with the then Athenian government, possibly including Themistocles, the character, spirit, genius and unscrupulousness of whom Cleomenes would have approved of, appreciated and liked. It is possible that an understanding between Cleomenes and Themistocles led to whatever concerted action was to be between the two states and survived after the former's demise to the kingship of his heir and brother Leonidas – a man so different from Themistocles, but able to combine and co-operate with the great Athenian scoundrel.

Epilogue: Normality resumed

After Marathon, the Athenians went back to their everyday routine and tried to solve their differences with Aegina (Her VI.88; Plut Vit Them 4,1), but to no avail. They ultimately failed embarrassingly and miserably (Her VI.93) and this enticed them to use the new revenue of silver in the southern tip of Attica, in Laurium, to build a fleet for this sole purpose (Her VII.144,1). The Spartans discovered that Cleomenes had manipulated the Oracle of Delphi to get rid of Demaratus, his co-king and Nemesis and were furious, deposing him (Her VI.74,1–75,1) and almost delivering Leotychidas, who had chastised and replaced him as an animal to the Aeginiteans (Her VI.85,1). The latter, instead of exacting vengeance for their hostage plight, they befriended to enlist his help in order to recover their hostages kept by the Athenians (Her VI.85,3). The Athenians refused to comply (Her VI.86–87), and Sparta and Aegina drew closer as a result; it is of interest, though, that the island state was since then firmly on the patriotic side, meaning that Cleomenes' high-handedness uprooted the Medizers from the executive and influence bodies, at least in a functional sense. The very similar manipulation of the Alcmaeonids, to make the Spartans unseat the Peisistratids, which was the reason for the intervention of Cleomenes (Her V.90,1), a failed one due to undermining by Demaratus, was not taken into consideration by the Spartans at any point, indicating rather a fierce infight between the Kings and the Ephorate (Dickins 1912) hidden under issues of reverence.

Somehow, since 487 BC the Athenian constitution changed towards more militant formats (Burn 1962), as the radical naval party started, under Themistocles, gaining power. The naval party became prominent and Piraeus (re)started being built. The new, fortified port was supposed to be secure from enemy incursions, like the embarrassing Aeginitean raid in Phaleron circa 505 BC (Burn 1962), which predated the silver bonanza. It was showing that Athens turned to the sea to feed her population and it was her turn to the West, the only corn-producing area free from the Persian yoke, a move vividly enforced by Themistocles, which was slowly bringing her into conflict with the former ally Corinth. The increasing commerce increased the Hoplite class and the millionaires, who were to command, condition and care for the new-built triremes (Arist Ath Pol 22,7; Polyaen I.30,6). This approach is similar to the later concept of Trierarchs, in the age of Thucydides and may well have been the first step in that direction.

The *naucraries* were responsible for raising one vessel each for the Athenian navy and this vessel must have been supplied by one of the ship-owners belonging to the naucraria, or by money paid by the naucraria to such an owner from public funds (Arist Ath Pol 8; Haas 1985), possibly raised from the higher property class of Solon (Ridley 1979). Thus there was always a link between filthy-rich private individuals and naval vessels. Once, though, a trireme is required, which is ill-suited for anything but war, and especially for trade as it requires a massive crew and has very limited cargo capacity and sailing autonomy, the vessel had to come from the state, which became possible thanks to the silver mined from Laurium. But the outfit of the vessel and the maintenance of the crew must have been delegated to the rich Athenians, of the top property class. Thus, Herodotus mentions Cleinias, the father of Alcibiades as commanding his own trireme and the same for the Crotoniate Phayllus (Her VIII.17 & 47 respectively), but he might have been so specific just to please Periclean and Alcmaeonid ears. Still, there is some evidence that all the trierarchs were expected to cater for their crews; Architeles, the trierarch of the sacred state vessel was trying to effect a general withdrawal from Artemisium for lack of funds to pay his crew (Plut Vit Them 7,5).

Darius decided to take more drastic measures, perhaps to lead in person for one last time a royal army and thus initiated unprecedented preparations (Her VII.1). Innovations like fully amphibious campaigns, probably proposed by Datis (Burn 1962), were swept aside; however, some of the technological spin-offs, such as the horse transports, were retained. But death came for him in the mid-480s. He had picked Xerxes, one of his sons, born by Atossa, the daughter of Cyrus the Great, for his successor (Her VII.3,4) early on and had him in training as viceroy in Babylon (Green 1970). He appears as heir-apparent in sculptures and paintings. Herodotus mentions that Demaratus, the exiled king of Sparta proposed to Darius the institutional means needed to select Xerxes as his heir, who was not his firstborn. Darius' ulterior motive was that this selection made the fusion of his bloodline with that of Cyrus secure (Llewellyn-Jones 2017).

Additionally, Darius must have taken into consideration other, more sinister aspects as he was himself a master conspirator. His friend Gobryas, with laurels against the insurgency in Elam in 520 BC (DB 71) was Chief of Artsibara, which is most probably an office equivalent to Royal Chamberlain, and thus he had been the number two in the realm after Darius (Fields 2007; Waters 2004; Sekunda 2002). Should his nephew, the prince Artobazanes (Her VII.2,2) Darius' firstborn from Gobryas' sister had become heir-apparent by right of the firstborn, instead of Xerxes, Darius might have found himself in peril and the line of Gobryas would evolve from 'One of the Seven' to *the* most prominent amongst the Six (Hyland 2018), almost of equal standing to Darius' own. Any member of this bloodline might develop an appetite for further aggrandisement and consequent actions, like coups, murders etc. If the line of Cyrus, meaning Xerxes or any of Xerxes' full brothers, was pushed to succession, Darius would be safer as this line was bereft of male members who might aspire to the throne. Darius had already favoured Xerxes, but the tradition pertaining to the firstborns had him entangled; Cambyses had been Cyrus' firstborn (Her VII.2,3) and thus appointed viceroy at Babylon, although Smerdis was by far the better man. In this problem, Demaratus introduced to the Achaemenids the concept of 'Born in Purple' (Her VII.3,2–3), which gave Darius the solution he needed and Xerxes the status of heir-apparent and the seat at Babylon which implies a comfortable time before the death of Darius, probably circa 496 BC (Gertoux 2018). The above resulted in the new monarch being deeply indebted to the Spartan exile.

Still another issue is the temporal parameter. Herodotus' account creates the notion that the issue of succession was settled shortly before the king's death (Her VII.2), but Demaratus had been at Susa most certainly after Cleomenes' failed campaign in Attica (Her V.73–5) but definitely before the Ionian Revolt, meaning somewhere between 510 and 500 BC. Demaratus' presence in the royal court was a good reason for Cleomenes' initial deliberation on and final abortion of the invasion of Asia suggested by Aristagoras (Her V.50). This suggests a date near 505 BC for Demaratus' arrival at Susa and the issue of selecting the successor of Darius might have arisen at that time, long before Marathon, after Xerxes had served his tour of duty as an Arstibara. This timing would allow a proper breeding and some appropriate instruction as viceroy in Babylon (Holland 2005).

While Darius was making unprecedented preparations (Her VII.1,2) the Egyptians had had enough (Her VII.1,3). Their clergy had been on the best of terms with the impostor, as he had nullified the social policies of Cambyses, who was obviously copying his benevolent father (Holland 2005; Burn 1962). The original Satrap, Aryandes, sanctioned by Cambyses (Her IV.166,1), seemed to have been on perfect terms with the natives, suffering just one minor revolt, and that during the ascendance of Darius to the throne (Klotz 2015; Mumford 2019). Darius had him marked and found a stupid pretext to exterminate him (Her IV.166,2); but, then, he had no obligation to support his allegations and back his pretext, as he was the agent of Ahura-mazda (DB 52 & 56) and his word *was* by definition The Truth.

The new satrap must have been less co-operative and sterner; moreover, continuous demands for resources, in labour for the pharaonic undertakings, such as the canal between the Nile and the Red Sea and the palace at Susa, but mostly in wheat and gold for the continuous campaigns, were bankrupting the clergy and the populace (Mumford 2019). It is very doubtful whether Darius ever implicated Egyptian units in his campaigns. There are two exceptions: the Scythian campaign, when

Herodotus declares that Darius led representative contingents from all his subject nations (Her IV.87,1); and the campaign to quell the Ionian revolt (Her VI.6). Under such circumstances, the Egyptians revolted and a new Pharaoh, Psamtik IV was inaugurated (Klotz 2015; Mumford 2019; Wijnsma 2019).

Darius died before being able to deal with the situation (Her VII.4), and Egypt reemerged partially, with a new native Pharaoh and a problem with the Persian administrative staff located there (Wijnsma 2019). Xerxes swiftly dealt with the situation, probably by dispatching the army prepared by Darius and not by leading it (Klotz 2015). When the army conquered, his brother Achaemenes was appointed satrap and savage retribution was exacted (Her VII.7); its religious nature suggest the hand of the native clergy in the uprising, and/or the religious fanaticism and intolerance of Xerxes as described in the 'Daiva inscription'-XPh (Klotz 2015; Herzfeld 1932), and despite concerted efforts to interpret the latter in benign terms (Kuhrt 1997; Abdi 2007).

Most scholars agree that there were two rebellions in Babylon after Xerxes was enthroned and before his campaign in Greece (Ossendrijver 2018; Waerzeggers 2018). It is true that Xerxes ultimately struck the Babylonian titles from his royal etiquette (Waerzeggers 2018; Llewellyn-Jones 2017). This says little; it could be because he left them to the viceroy of Babylon, as he had been. But Herodotus mentions a satrap, not a viceroy, later in Babylon (Her VII.62,2), which means Xerxes abolished the Trinity introduced by Cyrus and confirmed by Darius; he had not appointed one of his sons as viceroy, the heir-apparent, but established a nobleman as satrap.

Moreover, in Xerxes' campaign Herodotus, and Diodorus, mention no Babylonian contributions. There were contributions from the area (Her VII.63), but not from Babylon, and Aeschylus' contrary testimony (Persai 52–4) in this case may well be due to poetic licence. This proves that before Xerxes invaded Greece there was at least one Babylonian uprising, and it was dealt with swiftly and savagely (Waerzeggers 2018; Llewellyn-Jones 2017). There is no need to assume a second one, and, even more important, we do not need to assume this first uprising taking place *after* his coronation in 486 BC, although some arguments do indeed corroborate it (Llewellyn-Jones 2017). It could have been during his years as a viceroy (Gertoux 2018), and one may dare to blame his religious zeal in a city most liberal, at least in terms of scruples. The second rebellion must have been during his sojourn in Greece (Mumford 2019; Waerzeggers 2018; Llewellyn-Jones 2017), most probably after the battle of Salamis, a perfect reason to expedite his return (Her VIII.103) and to stay for quite some time in Sardis instead of returning to Susa (Her VIII.117,2). As in Egypt, he dispatched someone to do the job and in this case, we have a name: Megabyzus (Burn 1962; Green 1970), one of his six marshals (Her VII.82). He was the son of Zopyrus, who had reconquered Babylon for Darius and he himself did it for Xerxes, probably to quell the second rebellion which had claimed the life of his father Zopyrus, established in Babylon as Satrap (Gertoux 2016) after Xerxes had advanced to kingship.

In any case, the safe conclusion is that once the army of the Egyptian expedition was back and disbanded and Achaemenes firmly established at the satrapal seat (an indication that he had commanded the task force sent to crush the rebellion), Xerxes dwelt upon the Greek expedition. With two major revolts in ten years, if not three, he might have been skeptical. The wisdom of straining the resources for a massive European campaign, not only against Greece, could cause further dissatisfaction. On the other hand, success could well bring in a hefty profit, not only from spoils, slaves and from hammering the imperial identity into dissatisfied subjects, but also from the increase of his own splendour, radiance and prestige as a warrior king. This was his prerogative: a warrior chosen by warriors (Fields 2007), as inscribed on Darius' grave (Dnb 9). Once his mind had been made up, Xerxes hated half-measures and novelties to the tune of the campaign of Datis. He liked grandiose things. After all, he was to take the field himself this time. But it must be noted that the spirit of Datis was living and his house suffered no dishonour due to the defeat: his two sons were the two out of three cavalry generals (Her VII.88,1) and, more importantly, the fleet would not move independently but would be augmented with a most powerful marine contingent (Her VII.184,2) which included masses of cavalry, with mounts loaded on horse transports (Her VII.97).

Bibliography

Ancient (re)sources
Homer The Iliad
Homer Odyssey
Hesiod Ehoiai
Alcaeus fr 357 (Armory)
Alcaeus fr 350
Herodotus *Mousae*
Thucydides *Histories*
Andocides Orations
Aristophanes Birds
Xenophon *Anabasis*
Xenophon *Hellenika*
Xenophon *Cyropaedeia*
Xenophon *Lacedaimonion Politeia*
Xenophon *Agesilaus*
Xenophon *Hipparchikos*
Xenophon On Horsemanship
Plato Laws
Plato Dialogues (*Menexenus* & *Laches*)
Demosthenes Orations
Aeschines Orations
Aristotle *Athinaion Politeia*
Aristotle *Politika*
Hellenica Oxyrhynchia
Diodorus Sicilus *Bibliotheke Historike*
Pausanias *Hellados Periegesis/Graecae descriptio*
Plutarch *Vitae*
Plutarch *De Gloria Atheniensium*
Plutarch *De Herodoti Malignitate*
Plutarch Moralia/*Apophthegmata Laconica*
Plutarch Moralia/ *Regum et Imperatorum Apophthegmata*
Pollux *Onomasticon*
Clement of Alexandria *Stromateis*
Justin *Epitome*
Nepos *De Viris Illustribus*
Frontinus *Strategemata*
Polyaenus *Strategemata*
Livy *Ab urbe condita libri*

Strabo *Geographica*
Dionysius of Halicarnassus *Antiquitates Romanae*
Polybius *Histories*
Tzetzes I *Chiliades*
Books of Ezra/ The Holy Bible/The Old Testament
Book of Esther/ The Holy Bible/The Old Testament

Modern Scholarship
Abdi K. 2007. The 'Daivā' Inscription Revisited. Nāme-ye Irān-e Bāstān 6(1&2): 45–74.
Adcock F.E. 1957. The Greek and Macedonian Art of War. University of California Press, Berkeley.
Anderson J.K. 1991. Hoplite weapons and offensive arms. In Hanson VD (Ed) Hoplites: The Classical Greek battle experience. Routledge NY 2003, pp 15–37.
Badian E. 1993. From Plataea to Potidaea. The Johns Hopkins University Press Charles Village.
Barkworth P.R. 1993. The organization of Xerxes' army. *Iranica antiqua* 27: 149–167.
Benaissa A. 2018. Donysius the epic Fragments, Cambridge University Press.
Berthold R.M. 1976. Which way to Marathon? *Revue des Etudes Anciennes* 78–79 (1–4): 84–95.
Blair C. 1996. Hitler's U-Boat War: The Hunters, 1939–1942. Modern Library, New York.
Bodzek J. 2014. Achaemenid Asia Minor: Coins of the Satraps and of the Great King", In: First International Congress of the Anatolian Monetary History and Numismatics 25–28 February 2013, Antalya, Proceedings, pp. 59–78.
Bonaparte N. 1830. Maximes de Guerre 104 Paris.
Bonner R.J. 1910. The Boeotian Federal Constitution. *Classical Philology* 5(4): 405–417.
Boteva D. 2011. Re-Reading Herodotus On The Persian Campaigns In Thrace. In: Rollinger R, Truschnegg B, Bichler R (Eds) Herodotus and the Persian Empire. Wiesbaden, 735–759.
Boyce M. 1983. "Aməša Spənta", Encyclopaedia Iranica, 1, Routledge New York.
Bradford E. 1980. Year Of Thermopylae. Macmillan New York.
Bradford A.S. 2001. With arrow, sword and spear. Greenwood PG CT
Brown D. 1977. *WWII Fact Files: Aircraft Carriers.* Arco Publishing New York.
Bryan E. 2013. The Turtle Ship. *Military History Monthly* 34. Accessed 8 Jul 2020 from https://www.military-history.org/articles/wmd-the-turtle-ship.
Buck R.J. 1972. The Formation of the Boeotian League. *Classical Philology*, 67(2): 94–101.
Bugh G.R. 1988. The Horsemen of Athens. Princeton University Press Princeton.
Burn A.R. 1962. Persia and The Greeks the Defense of the West, c.546–478 B.C. St Martin's Press New York.
Campbell D.B. 2012. Spartan warrior 735–331 BC. Osprey Warrior 163 Oxford.
Carmichael C.M. 2009. Managing munificence. *Historical Methods* 42(3): 83–96.
Cartledge P. 2006. Thermopylae: the battle that changed the world. Macmillan New York.
Charles M.B. 2011. Immortals And Apple Bearers: Towards A Better Understanding Of Achaemenid Infantry Units. *The Classical Quarterly* 61(1): 114–33.
Charles M.B. 2012. Herodotus, Body Armour And Achaemenid Infantry. *Histroria* 61(3):257–69.

Charles M.B. 2015. Achaemenid elite cavalry: from Xerxes to Darius III. *The Classical Quarterly* 65(1): 14–34.

Cilliers L. 1991. Menelaus' 'Unnecessary Baseness Of Character' In Euripides' "Orestes". *Acta Classica* 34: 21–31.

Cole M. 2019. The Sparta Fetish Is a Cultural Cancer. The New Republic.

Connolly P. 1981. Greece and Rome at War. Greenhill Books London.

de la Graviere J. 1885. La Marine des Anciens: La Bataille de Salamine Et l'Expédition de Sicile. Plon & cie Paris.

Delbrück H. 1920. History of the Art of War. University of Nebraska Press 1990.

Deligiannis P. 2014. The battle of Cumae, Italy (524 bc) https://periklisdeligiannis. wordpress.com/2014/06/04/the-battle-of-cumae-italy-524-bc/

DeRosa C.S. 2006. Political Indoctrination in the U.S. Army from World War II to the Vietnam War. University of Nebraska Press.

de Souza P. 2003. The Greek and Persian Wars 499–386 bc. *Osprey Essential Histories* 36 Oxford.

Dezső T. 2012. The Assyrian Army Eotvos University Press, Budapest.

Dickins G. 1912. The Growth of Spartan Policy. JHS 32: 1–42.

Elliott-Bateman M. 1968. Defeat in the East: The Mark of Mae Tse-Tung on War. Oxford UP.

Emanuel J.P. 2012. Race in Armor, Race with Shields: The Origin and Devolution of the Hoplitodromos. In University of Pennsylvania Center for Ancient Studies Conference "Crowned Victor: Competition and Games in the Ancient World". Philadelphia.

Encyclopaedia Britannica https://www.britannica.com/biography/Peisistratus

Encyclopaedia Britannica Vol 13 Herodotus.

Encyclopaedia Britannica https://www.britannica.com/biography/Akhenaten

Engels D. 1985. The Length of Eratosthenes' Stade. *American Journal of Philology* 106 (3): 298–311.

Epps P.H. 1933. Fear in Spartan Character. Classical. *Philology* 28(1): 12–29.

Evangelista M.A. 1983. Stalin's postwar army reappraised. *International Security* 7: 110–38.

Evans J.A.S. 1968. Father of History or Father of Lies; The Reputation of Herodotus. *The Classical Journal* 64(1): 11–17.

Farahmand A. 2015. Darius the Great Zoroastrian versus Cyrus the Emperor.. https:// authenticgathazoroastrianism.org/2015/04/06/darius-the-great-zoroastrian-and-cyrus-the-emperor/

Ferrill A. 1966. Herodotus and the Strategy and Tactics of the Invasion of Xerxes. *The American Historical Review* 72(1): 102–115.

Fields N. 1994. The anatomy of a mercenary. PhD Dissertation, University of Newcastle-upon-Tyne.

Fields N. 2007. Thermopylae 480 bc Osprey Campaign 188 Oxford.

Fields N. 2007. Ancient Greek warships 500–322 bc. *Osprey New Vanguard* 132 Oxford.

Fields N. 2013. The Spartan way. Pen & Sword Military Barnsley.

Flower M.A. 1998. Simonides, Ephorus, and Herodotus on the Battle of Thermopylae, *The Classical Quarterly*, New Series, 48(2): 365–379.

Forrest W.G. 1968. A History of Sparta. Bloomsbury Publishing Pl, London 1995.

Gaebel R.E. 2004. Cavalry Operations in the Ancient Greek World. University of Oklahoma Press.

García-Sánchez M. 2014. The Second after the King and Achaemenid Bactria on Classical Sources. In: Antela-Bernárdez B, Vidal-Palomino J (Eds) Central Asia in Antiquity. *Interdisciplinary Approaches*, BAR International Series 2665, Oxford, p. 53–63.

Garrison M.B. 2007. By the favor of Ahuramazda. In: Iossif PP, Chankowski AS, Lorber CC (Eds) More than men, less than Gods. Peeters Leuven.

Gertoux G. 2018. Dating the Reigns of Xerxes and Artaxerxes. Orbis Biblicus et Orientalis Series. *Archaeologica* 40:179–206.

Gertroux G. 2016. Queen Esther Wife Of Xerxes: Historical And Archaeological Evidence. lulu.com

Goldsworthy A.K. 1997. The "Othismos", Myths and Heresies: The Nature of Hoplite Battle. *War in History* 4(1):1–26.

Grant P. 2012. From Minnow to Leviathan: Transformation of the Athenian Navy (499–480 BC). Drumspeak: *International Journal of Research in the Humanities*. NS 4: 267–298.

Green P. 1970. The year of Salamis 480–479 BC. Weidenfeld & Nicolson London.

Haas C.J. 1985. Athenian naval power before Themistocles. Historia 34(1): 29–46.

Hale J.R. 2009. Lords of the Sea: The Epic Story of the Athenian Navy and the Birth of Democracy. Penguin New York.

Haubold J. 2012. The Achaemenid empire and the sea. *Mediterranean Historical Review* 27(1): 4–23.

Hammond N.G.L. 1996. Sparta at Thermopylae. JSTOR *Historia* 45(1): 1–20.

Hammond N.G.L. 1968. The Campaign and the Battle of Marathon. *JHS* 88: 13–57.

Hanson V.D. 1983. Warfare and Agriculture in Classical Greece. University of California Press.

Hanson V.D. 1989. The Western Way of War. AA Knopf NY

Hanson V.D. 1999. The Wars of the Ancient Greeks. Cassell London.

Hanson V.D. 1991. Hoplite technology in phalanx battle. In Hanson VD (Ed) Hoplites: The Classical Greek Battle Experience. Routledge NY 2003, pp 63–85.

Heliopoulos G.Z. 2020. The Chimerae of War. Bartzoulianos Athens [In Greek].

Henkelman W. 2011a. Herodotus and the Persian Empire. In: Rollinger R, Truschnegg B, Bichler R (Eds) Herodotus and the Persian Empire. Harrassowitz-Verlag Wiesbaden.

Henkelman W. 2011b. Herodotus and Babylon Reconsidered. In: Rollinger R, Truschnegg B, Bichler R (Eds) Herodotus and the Persian Empire. Harrassowitz-Verlag Wiesbaden.

Herzfeld E. 1932. A New Inscription of Xerxes from Persepolis (Studies in Ancient Oriental Civilization 5). The University of Chicago Press Chicago.

Hignett C. 1963. Xerxes invasion of Greece. Clarendon Press, Wotton-under-Edge

Hodkinson S. 2006. Was classical Sparta a military society? In: Hodkinson S, Powell A, Christien J (Eds) Sparta and War. Classical Press of Wales Swansea.

Holland T. 2005. Persian fire. Doubleday New York.

Holoka J.P. 1999. Marathon and the myth of the same-day march. GRBS 38:329–353

Humble R. 1980. Warfare in the Ancient World. Book Club Associates London

Hyland J. 2018. Hystaspes, Gobryas, and elite marriage politics in Teispid Persia. *DABJR* 5: 30–36.

Jameson M.H. 1960. A decree of Themistocles from Troezen. Hesperia 29: 198–223.

Kambouris M.E. and Bakas S 2017. Gaugamela 331 BC: the triumph of tactics. *Archaeology and Science* 13: 17–33.

Kambouris M.E. et al 2019. The Hypaspist Corps: Evolution and Status of the Elite Macedonian Infantry Unit. *Archaeology and Science* 15: 19–30.

Kambouris M.E. et al 2015a. Greco-Macedonian Influences in the Manipular Legion System. *Archaeology and Science* 11: 145–154.

Kambouris M.E. et al 2015b. Thermopylae Revisited. *Archaeology and Science* 11: 127–44.

Kambouris M.E. 2008. Warriors of Ancient Greece Vol I. Alkalio Athens [In Greek]

Kambouris M.E. 2000. Ancient Greek Warriors. Communications SA Athens [In Greek].

Karber P.A. and Combs J.A. 1998. The United States, NATO, and the Soviet Threat to Western Europe: Military Estimates and Policy Options, 1945–1963. *Diplomatic History* 22(3): 399–429.

Klotz D. 2015. Persian Period. In: Grajetzki W & Wendrich W (Eds) UCLA Encyclopedia of Egyptology, UCLA, Los Angeles.

Krentz P. 1985. The Nature of Hoplite Battle. *Classical Antiquity* 4(1): 50–61.

Krentz P. 2002. Fighting by the Rules: The Invention of the Hoplite Agôn. *Hesperia: The Journal of the American School of Classical Studies at Athens* 71(1): 23–39.

Kuhrt A. 1997. The Ancient Near East: c.3000–330 BC. Routledge New York.

Kuhrt A. 2001. The Achaemenid Persian empire (c. 550–330). In: *Alcock* SE, D' Altroy TN, *Morrison* KD and Sinopoli CM (Eds) *Empires*: Perspectives from Archaeology and History, Cambridge University Press.

Kuhrt A. 2007. The Problem of Achaemenid Religious Policy. In: Groneberg B & Spieckermann H (Eds) Die Welt der Götterbilder. De Gruyter Berlin.

Kuhrt A. 2014. State Communications in the Persian Empire. In: Radner K (Ed) State Correspondence in the Ancient World. Oxford University Press.

Kuhrt A. 2015. Can we understand how the Persians perceived 'other' gods / 'the gods of others? De Gruyter Berlin.

Lazaridis D. 1978. The interior of Aegean Thrace. *Ekistics* 45(271):279–282.

Lazenby J.F. 1987. The Diekplous. Greece & Rome 34(2): 169–77.

Lazenby J.F. 1989. Hoplite Warfare. In: Hackett J (Ed) Warfare in the ancient world. Sidgwick & Jackson Ltd London.

Lazendy J.F. 1993. The defense of Greece. Aris & Phillips Oxford.

Lazenby J.F. and Whitehead D 1996. The myth of the Hoplite's hoplon. *The Classical Quarterly* 46(1): 27–33.

Lewis D.M. 1980. Datis the Mede. *JHS* 100: 194–195.

Llewellyn-Jones L. 2012. King and court in ancient Persia 559–331 BCE. Edinburgh University Press.

Llewellyn-Jones L. 2017. The Achaemenid Empire. T Daryaee (Ed) King Of The Seven Climes. Samuel Jordan Center of Persian Studies, UCI, Irvine.

Llewellyn-Jones L. & Robson J. 2009. Ctesias' 'History of Persia': Tales of the Orient. Routledge London.

Luginbill R.D. 1994. Othismos: The Importance of the Mass-Shove in Hoplite Warfare. *Phoenix* 48(1): 51–61.

Malye J. 2007. La veritable histoire de Sparte et la bataille des Thermopyles. Les Belles Lettres Paris.

Matthew C.A. 2012. A Storm of spears. Pen & Sword Military Barnsley.

Matthew C.A. 2013a. Towards the Hot Gates. In: Matthew CA & Trundle M (Eds) After the gates of fire. Pen & Sword Military Barnsley.

Matthew C.A. 2013b Was the Greek Defence of Thermopylae in 480 BC a Suicide Mission? In: Matthew C.A .& Trundle M. (Eds) After the gates of fire. Pen & Sword Military Barnsley.

Maurice F. 1930. The Size of the Army of Xerxes in the Invasion of Greece 480 B.C. *JHS* 50(2): 210–235.

Meijer F. 1986. A History of Seafaring in the Classical World. Routledge Revivals New York 2014.

Miller M. 2004. Athens and Persia in the Fifth Century bc: A Study in Cultural Receptivity. Cambridge University Press, Cambridge.

Montagu J.D. 2000. Battles of the Greek and Roman worlds. Greenhill Books London.

Montagu J.D. 2006. Greek and Roman warfare. Greenhill Books London.

Morris D.R. 1965. The Washing of the Spears: A History of the Rise of the Zulu Nation Under Shaka and Its Fall in the Zulu War of 1879. Simon and Schuster New York.

Morrison J.S .& Coates J.F. 2000. The Athenian trireme: Reconstruction of an ancient Greek warship. 2nd Ed. CUP Cambridge.

Mumford G. 2019. Lecture 28: Dynasty 27 Persian Empire in Egypt Anth. 310: Imperial and Post Imperial Egypt, ca. 1550–332 bce, Department of Anthropology. Birmingham: The University of Alabama at Birmingham.

Munro J.A.R. 1902. Some observations on the Persian wars 2. The Campaign of Xerxes. *JHS* 22: 294–332.

Nefedkin A.K. 2014. Once More on the Origin of Scythed Chariot. *AHB* 28(3–4): 112–8.

Nelopoulos E.D. 1999. The Greek Trireme. Floros, Athens (In Greek).

Nilsson M.P. 1929. The Introduction of Hoplite Tactics at Rome: Its Date and Its Consequences. J *Roman Studies* 19, 1–11.

Ossendrijver M. 2018. Babylonian scholarship and the calendar during the reign of Xerxes. In: C. Waerzeggers, M. Seire (Eds) Xerxes and Babylonia. The Cuneiform Evidence. *Peeters* Leuven.

Pagliaro A. 1943. Fortuna di parole iraniche in occidente. *Asiatica* 9: 36–42.

Pagliaro A. 1954. Riflessi di etimologie iraniche nella tradizione storiografica greca. Rendiconti dell'Accademia Nazionale dei Lincei. Classe di Scienze morali, storiche e filologiche, 8th series, 9: 133–53.

Potts D.T. 2005. Cyrus the Great and the Kingdom of Anshan, in: Sarkhosh Curtis V and Stewart S. (Eds) Birth of the Persian Empire. I B Tauris London.

Potts S. 2008. The Athenian Navy. PhD Dissertation, Cardiff University ProQuest LLC.

Pritchett W.K. 1957. New Light on Plataia. *AJA* 61(1): 9–28.

Pritchett W.K. 1958. New Light on Thermopylae. *AJA* 62(2): 203–13.

Raaflaub K.A. 2013. Early Greek Infantry Fighting in a Mediterranean Context. In: Kagan D, Viggiano GF (Eds) Men of Bronze: Hoplite Warfare in Ancient Greece. Princeton University Press Princeton.

Rados C.N. 1915. La bataille de Salamine. Fontemoing Paris.

Rankov B. 2017. Ancient Naval Warfare, 700 bc–ad 600 In: Whitby M, Sidebottom H (Eds) The encyclopedia of Ancient battles. John Wiley & Sons Ltd Hoboken.

Ray F.E. 2009. Land battles in 5th century B.C. Greece. McFarland & Company Inc Jefferson.

Recaldin J. 2011. What Was The Main Purpose Of The Ephebeia? MA Dissertation School of Archaeology and Ancient History University of Leicester.

Rey F.E. 2011. Taktike Techne: the neglected element in classical Hoplite battles. *Ancient Society* 41, 45–82.

Ridley R.T. 2007. The Hoplite as Citizen : Athenian military Institutions in their social context. In: Wheeler EL (Ed) The Armies of Classical Greece. Ashgate Farnham.

Roisman J. 2017. The Classical Art of Command. Oxford University Press.

Rollinger & Ulf (Eds) 2004. Commerce and Monetary Systems in the Ancient World, Franz Steiner Verlag.

Rookhuijzen J.Z. 2019. Herodotus and the Topography of Xerxes' Invasion. De Gruyter Berlin.

Rupp G. 2013. The Topography of the Pass at Thermopylae Circa 480 BC. In: Matthew CA & Trundle M (Eds) After the gates of fire. Pen & Sword Military Barnsley.

Sage M.M. 1996. Warfare in ancient Greece: A sourcebook. Routledge London.

Samuels M. 1997. Alexander the Great and Manoeuvre War. Available at: https://www.academia.edu/15306853/Alexander_the_Great_and_Manoeuvre_War

Sarantis T.H. 1975. Alexander the Great. Alkyon Athens (in Greek).

Sealey R .1976. A History of the Greek City States, 700–338 B. C. University California Press, Berkeley.

Sears M.A. 2019. Understanding Greek Warfare. Routledge, London.

Sears M.A. & Willekes C 2016. Alexander's Cavalry Charge at Chaeronea, 338 BCE. *JMH* 80: 1017–1035.

Seevers B. 2013. Warfare in the Old Testament: The Organization, Weapons, and Tactics of Ancient Near Eastern Armies. Kregel Academic, Grand Rapids.

Sekunda N. & Chew S 1992. The Persian Army 560–330 BC. Osprey Elite 42 Oxford.

Sekunda N. & Northwood S 1995. Early Roman Armies. Osprey Men-at-Arms 283 Oxford.

Sekunda N. 1986. The Ancient Greeks. Osprey Elite 7 Oxford.

Sekunda N. 1989. The Persians. In: Hackett J (Ed) Warfare in the ancient world. Sidgwick & Jackson Ltd London.

Sekunda N. 1998. The Spartan Army. Osprey Elite 66 Oxford.

Sekunda N. 2000. The Greek Hoplite. Osprey Warrior 27 Oxford.

Sekunda N. 2002. Marathon, 490 BC: The first Persian invasion of Greece. Osprey Campaign 108 Oxford.

Shepherd W. 2010. Salamis 480 BC. Osprey Campaign 222 Oxford.

Shepherd W. 2012 Plataea 479 BC. Osprey Campaign 239 Oxford.

Shimpson R.H. 1972. Leonidas' decision. *Phoenix* 26(1): 1–11.

Sidebotham S. 1982. Herodotus on Artemisium. *The Classical World*. 75(3): 177–186.

Snodgrass A.A. 1965. The Hoplite revolution and History. JHS 85: 110–22.

Snodgrass A.M. 1967. Arms and Armour of the Greeks. Cornell University Press (Ithaca, NY).

Spence I.G. 1993. The Cavalry of Classical Greece. Clarendon Press, Wotton-under-Edge.

Stein G.J. 2014. Persians on the Euphrates? In: Kozuh M, Henkelman WFM, Jones CE and Woods C (Eds) Extraction and Control. The Oriental Institute of the University of Chicago.

Sternberg E. 2005. Classical Precariousness vs. Modern Risk: Lessons in Prudence from the Battle of Salamis. *Humanitas* 18(1&2): 141–63.

Strauss B. 2017. War and Battle in the Greek World, 800–168 BC. In: Whitby M, Sidebottom H (Eds) The encyclopedia of Ancient battles. John Wiley & Sons Ltd Hoboken.

Strauss B. 2008. Battle. In: Sabin P, van Wees H and Whirby M (Eds) The Cambridge History of Greek and Roman Warfare Vol I. Cambridge University Press, 2008, pp 223–47.

Soudavar A. 2012, Astyages, Cyrus And Zoroaster: solving a historical dilemma. *IRAN* 50:45–78.

Suda Lexicon, Letter X, 10th Century AD.

Sweet W.E. 1987. Sport and Recreation in Ancient Greece: A Sourcebook with Translations. Oxford University Press.

Tarn W.W. 1908. The Fleet of Xerxes. *JHS* 28: 202–233

Tarn W.W. 1948. Alexander the Great, vol. 2, Sources and Studies. Cambridge University Press.

Trundle M. 2013. Thermopylae. In: Matthew CA & Trundle M (Eds) After the gates of fire. Pen & Sword Military Barnsley.

Tuplin C. 2017. War and Peace in Achaemenid Imperial Ideology. *Electrum* 24: 31–54.

van der Spek R.J. 2014. Cyrus the Great exiles and foreign gods? In: Kozuh M, Henkelman W FM, Jones CE and Woods C (Eds) Extraction and Control. The Oriental Institute of the University of Chicago.

van Wees H. 2004. Greek Warfare: Myths and Realities. Gerald Duckworth, London.

van Wees H. 2013. Ships and silver, taxes and tribute. I.B. Tauris, London

Waerzeggers C. 2018. Debating Xerxes' Rule In Babylonia. In: Waerzeggers C, Seire M (Eds) Xerxes and Babylonia: The Cuneiform Evidence. *Peeters* Leuven.

Ward C. 2012. Building pharaoh's ships: Cedar, incense and sailing the Great Green. British Museum Studies in Ancient Egypt and Sudan 18: 217–32.

Warry J. 1980. Warfare in the classical world. Salamander London.

Waterfield R. 2006. Xenophon's Retreat: Greece, Persia, and the End of the Golden Age. Belknap Press of Harvard University Press Cambridge.

Waters M. 2011. Parsumas, Ansan and Cyris. In: Álvarez-Mon J and Garrison MB (Eds) Elam and Persia. Eisenbrauns Winona Lake.

Waters M. 2014a. Darius the first, the ninth king. In: Daryaee T, Mushavi A and Rehakhani K (Eds) Excavating an Empire. Mazda Publishers, Costa Mesa.

Waters M.W. 2014b. Earth, water and friendship with the king. In: Kozuh M, Henkelman W, Jones WC, Woods C (Eds) Extraction & Control. The Oriental Institute of the University of Chicago.

Waters M. 2004. Cyrus And The Achaemenids. *Journal Of Persian Studies* 42: 91–102.

Waugh R.L. Jr 1995. The Eye and Man in Ancient Egypt. Kugler Publications Amsterdam.

Whitehead I. 1987. The Periplous. *Greece & Rome* 34(2): 178–85.

Wijnsma U.Z .2019. "And in the fourth year Egypt rebelled ..." The Chronology of and Sources for Egypt's Second Revolt (ca. 487–484 BC). *Journal of Ancient History* 7(1): 32–61.

Wilson A .2005. An Analysis of the Possible Routes of Xerxes and the Persian Army from Cappadocia to Phrygia in Herodotus' Histories 7.26. EES 24, Furman University Greenville.

Wood A.K. 2013. Warships of the ancient world, Osprey New Vanguard 196 Oxford.

Index